Musical knights

Wood · Beecham · Boult
Barbirolli · Goodall · Sargent

Discographies compiled
by John Hunt

Sole distributors:
Travis & Emery,
17 Cecil Court,
London, WC2N 4EZ,
United Kingdom.
(+44) 20 7 459 2129.
sales@travis-and-emery.com

ACKNOWLEDGEMENT

This publication has been made possible by generous support from the following:

Richard Ames, New Barnet

Yoshihiro Asada, Osaka

Andrew Barker, Rochester

Edward Chibas, Caracas

F. De Vilder, Bussum

John Derry, Newcastle-upon-Tyne

Robert Donaldson, Edinburgh

Henry Fogel, Chicago

J.-P. Goossens, Luxembourg

Michael Harris, London

Tadashi Hasegawa, Nagoya

Martin Holland, Sale

John Hughes, Brisbane

Eugene Kaskey, New York

John Larsen, Mariager

James Pearson, Vienna

Donald Priddon, London

Vivienne Rendall, Great Ayton

Peter Russell, Calstock

Robin Scott, Bradford

Robert Simmons, Brentford

Göran Söderwall, Stockholm

Roger Smithson, London

Neville Sumpter, Northolt

Giovanna Visconti, Jackson Heights

David Woodhead, Ravenglass

CONTENTS

3	Acknowledgement
5	Introduction
7	Henry Wood
45	Thomas Beecham
155	Adrian Boult
265	John Barbirolli
379	Reginald Goodall
393	Malcolm Sargent
474	Credits

Musical Knights
Published by John Hunt.
Designed by Richard Chluparty
© 1995 John Hunt
reprinted 2009
ISBN 978-0-952582-70-0

MUSICAL KNIGHTS

One of the musicians featured in this set of discographies was once asked in a BBC interview what essential quality was needed to make a good conductor. The answer was "showmanship", by which he understood the indication, by means of gesture and technique, of what his feelings and requirements were.

Sargent and Beecham, to name the most obvious examples, possessed this quality in its most flamboyant aspect, thus winning the whole-hearted approval of their audiences. At the other extreme were men like Boult and Goodall, whose modest and inward techniques were directed at the orchestra alone. In between stand the pioneering figures of Wood and Barbirolli: the former having a permanent monument in the Promenade Concerts which he founded, the latter the creator of the Hallé Orchestra as it stands today. Wood was probably Britain's greatest promoter of new music (although his discography does not fully reflect it), Barbirolli our most cosmopolitan figure in his mastery of Italian and German idiom on the one hand and an instinctive feeling for the composers Elgar and Vaughan Williams on the other.

A word or two is needed about the special case of Reginald Goodall. Although his recorded legacy is modest in size, so modest that some might feel a discography to be unjustified, yet the quality of his work, devoted almost exclusively to Wagner, is inseparably linked to the most important traditions in performing that composer. He fully commanded Wagner's _melos_ and the large paragraph, with a very special skill at helping singers to breathe on that same scale, so essential in singing both Wagner and Strauss. To quote John Holmes in "Conductors on Record", "Goodall's interpretations have a broad, unhurried majesty and a conviction that goes far beyond the imitation of Furtwängler and Knappertsbusch".

And there at the centre stands Sir Thomas Beecham, that mercurial figure who never lets us forget that pleasure and enjoyment are central elements in the business of music-making. He alone seemed able to bring alive music which in lesser hands might be dismissed as trivial or insignificant. Beecham biographies abound, and indeed all our conductors can be studied in books which should be tracked down in public libraries if they are out of print. Alan Jefferson has written about Beecham, Charles Reid on Sargent and Barbirolli, Arthur Jacobs on Wood, Michael Kennedy on Boult and John Lucas on Goodall. That, of course, is only a selection of the available literature.

It should most certainly be possible to compile discographies for a second group of musical knights, extending to the present day with Sir Charles Mackerras and Sir Simon Rattle, let alone the many British conducting talents from the distant and recent pasts who have not been favoured with ennoblement........

John Hunt

Sir Henry Wood
1869-1944

Discography compiled by John Hunt

ALBENIZ

Catalonia

London ca. January 1918	Orchestra	78: Columbia L 1216 Coupled with Granados Danzas espanolas

ALLITSEN

Since we two parted

London June 1909	O.Wood Wood, piano	G & T GC 3833 Coupled with Rogers At parting

ARCADELT

Ave Maria, arranged by Wood

London July 1919	Orchestra	78: Columbia L 1379 Coupled with Gounod Funeral March of a Marionette

AUBER

Fra Diavolo, Overture

London December 1920	Orchestra	78: Columbia L 1402

BACH

Air (Suite No 3), arranged by Wilhelmj

London October 1932	British SO	78: Columbia DX 475 Coupled with Gavotte in E

Brandenburg Concerto No 3

London June 1932	British SO	78: Columbia LX 173 CD: Dutton 2CDAX 2002
London June 1942	BBCSO	CD: Symposium 1150 Rehearsal extract only

Brandenburg Concerto No 6

London June 1930	Symphony Orchestra	78: Columbia LX 41-42

Gavotte in E, arranged by Wood

London May 1923	New Queens Hall Orchestra	78: Columbia L 1515 Coupled with Beethoven Rondino
London October 1932	British SO	78: Columbia DX 475 Coupled with Air (Suite No 3)

Piano Concerto in D minor

London September 1924	New Queens Hall Orchestra Cohen	78: Columbia L 1624-1626

Prelude (Partita in E), arranged by Wood

London June 1929	New Queens Hall Orchestra	78: Columbia DX 10 Coupled with Liszt Hungarian Rhapsody No 2 (DX 9-10)

Suite No 6, arranged by Wood

London February 1925	New Queens Hall Orchestra	78: Columbia L 1684-1685

Toccata and Fugue in D minor, arranged by Klenovsky

London May 1935	Queens Hall Orchestra	78: Decca K 768

BANTOCK

Pierrot of the minute

London December 1922	Orchestra	78: Columbia L 1463

BAX

Symphony No 3

London June 1942	BBCSO	CD: Symposium 1150 Rehearsal extract only

Cello Concerto

London February 1938	BBCSO Harrison	CD: Symposium 1150 Some bars missing

Violin Concerto

London November 1943	BBCSO Kersey	Unpublished radio broadcast

BEETHOVEN

Symphony No 3 "Eroica"

London June 1922	Orchestra	78: Columbia L 1447-1449 Abridged version
London November and December 1926	New Queens Hall Orchestra	78: Columbia L 1868-1874

Symphony No 5

London April and May 1935	Queens Hall Orchestra	78: Decca K 757-760 CD: Dutton 2CDAX 2002 Wood's first recording for Decca

Coriolan, Overture

London ca. December 1915	Orchestra	78: Columbia L 1021 Coupled with Wagner Grand March (Tannhäuser)
London April 1927	New Queens Hall Orchestra	78: Columbia L 1021R Coupled with Wagner Grand March (Tannhäuser); both works newly recorded but published with same catalogue number as the 1915 versions

Leonore No 3, Overture

London August 1918	Orchestra	78: Columbia L 1319-1320 Coupled with Minuet (Septet)
London February 1927	New Queens Hall Orchestra	78: Columbia L 1978-1979 LP: Pearl GEMM 161

Minuet (Septet)

London August 1918	Orchestra	78: Columbia L 1320 Coupled with Leonore No 3 Overture (L 1319-1320)

Rondino for wind

London May 1923	New Queens Hall Orchestra	78: Columbia L 1515 Coupled with Bach Gavotte in E

BERLIOZ

Le carnaval romain, Overture

London March 1940	LPO	78: Columbia DX 982 CD: Dutton CDAX 8008

BIZET

Carmen Suite, including Ballet music

London ca. July 1917	Orchestra	78: Columbia L 1208-1209 Not published until 1920

BRAHMS

Haydn Variations

London April 1935	Queens Hall Orchestra	78: Decca K 763-764 CD: Pearl GEMMCDS 9373 CD: Dutton 2CDAX 2002 Pearl incorrectly published this as a recording by Toscanini and the New York Philharmonic

Hungarian Dances Nos 5 and 6

London ca. August 1918	Orchestra	78: Columbia L 1054

BRUCKNER

Overture in G minor

London April 1937	Queens Hall Orchestra	78: Decca X 192-193 CD: Beulah 1PD 3 CD: Dutton 2CDAX 2002 78 version coupled with Glinka Russlan and Ludmilla (X 193)

CAPEL

Star and Rose

London June 1909	O.Wood Wood, piano	G & T 03161 Coupled with Love is a dream

CARR

Lt. Warneford VC

London July 1919	Orchestra	78: Columbia L 1367

CHABRIER

Espana

London ca. January 1916	Orchestra	78: Columbia L 1024 Coupled with Grainger Londonderry Air

COATES

London Suite: Covent Garden; Westminster; Knightsbridge

London November 1935	Queens Hall Orchestra	78: Decca K 800-801 CD: Dutton CDAX 8008 78 version coupled with London Bridge March (K 801)

London Bridge March

London November 1935	Queens Hall Orchestra	78: Decca K 801 CD: Dutton CDAX 8008 78 version coupled with London Suite (K 800-801)

Orpheus with his lute; Under the greenwood tree

London June 1909	O.Wood Wood, piano	G & T GC 3835

Who is Sylvia?; It was a lover and his lass

London June 1909	O.Wood Wood, piano	G & T 03162

CORDER

Prospero, Overture

London ca. September 1916	Orchestra	78: Columbia L 1066 Coupled with Gounod Faust Music Nos 6 and 7

DELIUS

Dance Rhapsody

London May 1923	New Queens Hall Orchestra	78: Columbia L 1505-1506 CD: Beulah 1PD 3

DOHNANYI

Symphonische Minuten

London March 1937	Queens Hall Orchestra	78: Decca X 190-191 CD: Beulah 1PD 3

DONIZETTI

Lucrezia Borgia: Excerpt (Il segreto)

London ca. October 1916	Orchestra Butt	78: Columbia 74012 Versions of the aria sung by Butt and re-issued on LP appear to be later recordings not conducted by Wood

DELIUS

L'apprenti sorcier

London ca. April 1917	Orchestra	78: Columbia L 1172 Abridged version; coupled with Wagner Der fliegende Holländer Overture

DVORAK

Symphonic Variations

London April 1937	Queens Hall Orchestra	78: Decca X 182-184 CD: Beulah 1PD 3 CD: Dutton 2CDAX 2002 78 version coupled with Handel Dances from Rodrigo and Almira (X 184)

Symphonic Variations, rehearsal extract

London April 1937	Queens Hall Orchestra	CD: Dutton 2CDAX 2002

Humoresque

London May 1935	Queens Hall Orchestra	78: Decca K 762 Coupled with Rachmaninov Prelude in C sharp minor

Slavonic Dance No 1

London July 1919	Orchestra	78: Columbia L 1387 Coupled with Slavonic Dance No 2

Slavonic Dance No 2

London July 1919	Orchestra	78: Columbia L 1387 Coupled with Slavonic Dance No 1

Slavonic Dance No 8

London March 1929	New Queens Hall Orchestra	78: Columbia L 2313 Coupled with Weber Oberon Overture cond. Mengelberg (L 2312-2313)

ELGAR

Violin Concerto

London ca. August 1916	Orchestra Sammons	78: Columbia L 1071-1072 <u>Abridged version</u>
London March and April 1929	New Queens Hall Orchestra Sammons	78: Columbia L 2346-2351 CD: Novello NVLCD 901

Enigma Variations

London July 1924	New Queens Hall Orchestra	78: Columbia L 1629-1632
London November 1935	Queens Hall Orchestra	78: Decca K 837-840 <u>Coupled with Handel Solomon</u> <u>Overture (K 840)</u>

The Dream of Gerontius: Excerpts (My work is done; I see not those false spirits; We now have passed the gate; Softly and gently)

London ca. May 1915	Orchestra Chorus Butt, D'Oisly	78: Columbia 75005-75008 <u>Softly and gently</u> LP: EMI HLM 7025 LP: Arabesque 8027

Pomp and Circumstance, March No 1

London March 1940	LPO	78: Columbia DX 965 CD: Dutton CDAX 8008 <u>78 version coupled with March No 4</u>

Pomp and Circumstance, March No 4

London March 1940	LPO	78: Columbia DX 965 CD: Dutton CDAX 8008 <u>78 version coupled with March No 1</u>

FRANCK

Symphony in D minor

London July 1924	New Queens Hall Orchestra	78: Columbia L 1569-1572

Variations symphoniques for piano and orchestra

London
March and
November
1931

LPO
Gieseking

78: Columbia LX 192-193
78: Columbia (France) LFX 311-312
78: Columbia (USA) X 210
LP: EMI 3C 053 01609
LP: EMI 3C 153 52700-52705M
LP: Melodiya M10 43701-43702
CD: Classical Collector FDC 2008
According to Wood's biographer,
Arthur Jacobs, this recording
was made in October 1932

Le chasseur maudit

London
December 1921

Orchestra

78: Columbia L 1423

GLINKA

Russlan and Ludmilla, Overture

London
April 1937

Queens Hall
Orchestra

78: Decca X 193
CD: Beulah 1PD 3
78 version coupled with Bruckner
Overture in G minor (X 192-193)

GLUCK

Orfeo ed Euridice: Excerpt (Che farò)

London ca. August 1917	Orchestra Butt	78: Columbia 74038 LP: EMI HLM 7025 LP: Arabesque 8027

GOUNOD

Faust, Ballet music

London ca. September 1916	Orchestra	78: Columbia L 1063-1064 and L 1066 L 1066 coupled with Corder Prospero Overture
London December 1925	New Queens Hall Orchestra	78: Columbia L 1794-1795

Faust: Excerpt (Si le bonheur)

London ca. September 1915	Orchestra Butt Sung in English	78: Columbia 74003 Wood's first recording with orchestra Versions of the aria sung by Butt and re-issued on LP appear to be later recordings not conducted by Wood

Funeral March of a Marionette

London July 1919	Orchestra	78: Columbia L 1379 Coupled with Arcadelt Ave Maria
London March 1940	LPO	78: Columbia DX 969 CD: Dutton CDAX 8008

O divine redeemer

London ca. September 1916	Orchestra Butt	78: Columbia 7135

Judex (Mors et vita)

London June 1921	Orchestra	78: Columbia L 1427 Coupled with Wagner Entry of the Gods (Das Rheingold)

GRAINGER

Handel in the Strand, arranged by Wood

| London
ca. January
1917 | Orchestra | 78: Columbia L 1125
Coupled with Wagner Dance of the
Apprentices (Die Meistersinger) |

| London
April 1935 | Queens Hall
Orchestra | 78: Decca K 767
CD: Dutton CDAX 8008
78 version coupled with
Mock Morris |

Londonderry Air

| London
ca. January
1916 | Orchestra | 78: Columbia L 1024
Coupled with Chabrier Espana |

Mock Morris

| London
October 1932 | British SO | 78: Columbia LX 200
CD: Dutton CDAX 8008
78 version coupled with
Molly on the Shore |

| London
April 1935 | Queens Hall
Orchestra | 78: Decca K 767
Coupled with Handel in the Strand |

Molly on the Shore

| London
October 1932 | British SO | 78: Columbia LX 200
CD: Dutton CDAX 8008
78 version coupled with
Mock Morris |

Shepherd Fennel's Dance

| London
ca. March
1916 | Orchestra | 78: Columbia L 1033
Coupled with Wagner Träume |

Shepherd's Hey

| London
ca. September
1915 | Orchestra | 78: Columbia L 1006
Coupled with Tchaikovsky
Scherzo (Symphony No 4) |

GRANADOS

5 Danzas espanolas

London ca. January 1918	Orchestra	78: Columbia L 1214-1216 <u>Coupled with Albeniz</u> <u>Catalonia (L 1216)</u>

Danzas espanolas nos. 1, 4 and 5

London March 1937	Queens Hall Orchestra	78: Columbia X 180-181

HANDEL

Berenice, Overture

| London | Queens Hall | 78: Decca K 819 |
| November 1935 | Orchestra | |

Largo, arranged by Wood

| London | Orchestra | 78: Columbia L 1403 |
| December 1920 | | Coupled with Meyerbeer Coronation March (Le Prophète) |

Messiah: Excerpt (He shall feed his flock)

| London | Orchestra | 78: Columbia L 7139 |
| ca. November 1916 | Butt | LP: Cantilena 6214 |

Messiah: Excerpt (And the Glory of the Lord)

London	New Queens Hall	78: Columbia L 1768
June 1926	Orchestra	CD: Koch 3-7703-2
	Handel Festival	78 version coupled with
	Chorus	Behold the Lamb of God

Messiah: Excerpt (Behold the Lamb of God)

London	New Queens Hall	78: Columbia L 1768
June 1926	Orchestra	LP: Pearl GEMM 161
	Handel Festival	CD: Beulah 1PD 1
	Chorus	CD: Koch 3-7703-2
		78 version coupled with
		And the Glory of the Lord

Messiah: Excerpt (He trusted in God)

London June 1926	New Queens Hall Orchestra Handel Festival Chorus	Columbia unpublished
London September 1931	New Queens Hall Orchestra Handel Festival Chorus	78: Columbia L 1769 CD: Koch 3-7703-2 <u>78 version coupled with Let</u> <u>break their bonds</u>

Messiah: Excerpt (Let us break their bonds)

London June 1926	New Queens Hall Orchestra Handel Festival Chorus	Columbia unpublished
London September 1931	New Queens Hall Orchestra Handel Festival Chorus	78: Columbia L 1769 CD: Koch 3-7703-2 <u>78 version coupled with</u> <u>He trusted in God</u>

Messiah: Excerpt (Lift up your heads)

London June 1926	New Queens Hall Orchestra Handel Festival Chorus	78: Columbia D 1550 CD: Koch 3-7703-2

Sailors Dance (Rodrigo) and Rigaudon (Almira)

London April 1937	Queens Hall Orchestra	78: Decca X 184 CD: Beulah 1PD 3 <u>78 version coupled with Dvorak</u> <u>Symphonic Variations (X 182-184)</u>

Samson, Overture

London November 1935	Queens Hall Orchestra	78: Decca K 812 CD: Beulah 1PD 3

Serse: Excerpt (Ombra mai fù)

London ca. December 1915	Orchestra Butt	78: Columbia 7121 <u>Versions of the aria sung by Butt</u> <u>and re-issued on LP appear to be</u> <u>later recordings not conducted</u> <u>by Wood</u>

Solomon, Overture

London November 1935	Queens Hall Orchestra	78: Decca K 840 <u>Coupled with Elgar Enigma</u> <u>Variations (K 837-840)</u>

Sosarme: Excerpt (Rend' il sereno)

London ca. September 1916	Orchestra Butt	78: Columbia 74009

Water Music Suite, arranged by Harty

London May 1944	Massed Brass Bands	Unpublished radio broadcast

HAYDN

Symphony No 45 "Farewell"

London April 1934	LSO	78: Columbia LX 323-325 CD: Dutton 2CDAX 2002

Symphony No 94 "Surprise"

London February and March 1925	New Queens Hall Orchestra	78: Columbia L 1668-1670 <u>Coupled with Jaernefelt</u> <u>Praeludium (L 1670)</u>

HEROLD

Zampa, Overture

London August 1918	Orchestra	78: Columbia L 1247

HOLBROOKE

Three Blind Mice

London ca. January 1917	Orchestra	78: Columbia L 1134 CD: Beulah 1PD 3

IRELAND

Epic March

London June 1942	LPO	Unpublished radio broadcast

JAERNEFELT

Praeludium

London March 1925	New Queens Hall Orchestra	78: Columbia L 1670 Coupled with Haydn Symphony No 94 (L 1668-1670)
London March 1929	Symphony Orchestra	78: Columbia DX 194 CD: Dutton CDAX 8008
London May 1935	Queens Hall Orchestra	78: Decca K 766 Coupled with Wagner Song of the Rhine Maidens (Götterdämmerung) (K 765-766)

LALO

Symphonie espagnole

London July 1919	Orchestra Sammons	78: Columbia L 1365 Selection only

Aubade in D

London May 1924	New Queens Hall Orchestra	78: Columbia L 1531 Coupled with Aubade in G minor

Aubade in G minor

London May 1924	New Queens Hall Orchestra	78: Columbia L 1531 Coupled with Aubade in D

LISZT

Piano Concerto No 1

London March 1931	LPO Gieseking	78: Columbia LX 181-182 LP: EMI 3C 053 01609 LP: EMI 3C 153 52425-52431M CD: Classical Collector FDC 2008 <u>According to Wood's biographer, Arthur Jacobs, this recording was made in October 1932</u>

Hungarian Rhapsody No 1, arranged by Wood

London July 1919	Orchestra	78: Columbia L 1412

Hungarian Rhapsody No 2, arranged by Wood

London August 1919	Orchestra	78: Columbia L 1415
London April 1925	New Queens Hall Orchestra	78: Columbia L 1796-1797
London June 1929	New Queens Hall Orchestra	78: Columbia DX 9-10 <u>Coupled with Bach Prelude (Partita in E)</u>

LITOLFF

Scherzo (Concerto symphonique)

London October 1933	LSO Scharrer	78: Columbia DB 1267 CD: Dutton 2CDAX 2002

MASCAGNI

Cavalleria rusticana, Intermezzo

London June 1922	Orchestra	78: Columbia L 1436 <u>Coupled with Rossini William Tell Overture</u>
London June 1930	Symphony Orchestra	78: Columbia DX 194

Cavalleria rusticana, orchestral selection

London August 1918	Orchestra	78: Columbia L 1354

MASSENET

Le Cid, Ballet music

London August 1918	Orchestra	78: Columbia L 1327-1329

MENDELSSOHN

Elijah: Excerpt (O rest in the Lord)

London ca. July 1916	Orchestra Butt	78: Columbia 7127

The Hebrides, Overture

London April 1923	Orchestra	78: Columbia L 1478
London March 1929	New Queens Hall Orchestra	78: Columbia 9843-9844 Coupled with Spring Song and Bees Wedding (9844)

A Midsummer Night's Dream, Overture

London December 1922	Orchestra	78: Columbia L 1462
London July 1928	New Queens Hall Orchestra	78: Columbia 9559-9560 LP: Pearl GEMM 161 78 version coupled with Scherzo (A Midsummer Night's Dream) conducted by Mengelberg

Spring Song; The Bees Wedding (Songs without Words)

London March 1929	New Queens Hall Orchestra	78: Columbia 9844 Coupled with Hebrides Overture (9843-9844)

MEYERBEER

Le Prophète, Coronation March

London December 1920	Orchestra	78: Columbia L 1403 Coupled with Handel Largo
London May 1944	Massed Brass Bands	Unpublished radio broadcast

MOZART

Don Giovanni, Overture

London April 1934	LSO	78: Columbia DX 587 LP: Melodiya M10 43701-43702

Exsultate jubilate: Excerpt (Alleluia)

London September 1936	BBCSO Schumann	CD: Symposium 1150

Il re pastore: Excerpt (L'amerò saro costante)

London September 1936	BBCSO Schumann	CD: Symposium 1150

Sinfonia concertante K364

London September 1936	BBCSO Pougnet, Shore	CD: Symposium 1150

MUSSORGSKY

Pictures from an Exhibition, arranged by Wood

London June 1918	Orchestra	**78: Columbia L 1341-1342** Abridged version

Night on Bare Mountain

London November 1920	Orchestra	78: Columbia L 1417

NICOLAI

Die lustigen Weiber von Windsor, Overture

London New Queens Hall 78: Columbia L 1723
December 1925 Orchestra LP: Pearl GEMM 161
  Wood's first electrical recording

PITT

Love is a dream

London O.Wood G & T 03161
June 1909 Wood, piano Coupled with Capel Star and Rose

PROKOFIEV

Violin Concerto No 2

London LPO Unpublished radio broadcast
December 1936 Soetens

PURCELL

Suite, arranged by Wood

London Queens Hall 78: Decca K 975-976
April 1937 Orchestra

QUILTER

A Childrens' Overture

London LPO 78: Columbia DB 951-952
October 1932

RACHMANINOV

Prelude in C sharp minor, arranged by Wood

London ca. September 1915	Orchestra	78: Columbia L 1005 <u>Coupled with Wagner Lohengrin Act 3 Prelude</u>
London April 1926	New Queens Hall Orchestra	78: Columbia L 1005R <u>Coupled with Wagner Lohengrin Act 3 Prelude; both works newly recorded but published with the same catalogue number as the 1915 versions</u>
London June 1930	Symphony Orchestra	78: Columbia DX 87 CD: Dutton 2CDAX 2002 <u>78 version coupled with Volga Boat Song</u>
London May 1935	Queens Hall Orchestra	78: Decca K 762 <u>Coupled with Dvorak Humoresque</u>

RAFF

Cavatina, arranged by Wood

London ca. September 1916	Orchestra	78: Columbia L 1118 <u>Coupled with Saint-Saens Danse macabre; not published until 1920</u>

RAMEAU

Tambourin (Fêtes d'Hébé)

London May 1923	New Queens Hall Orchestra	78: Columbia L 1506 CD: Beulah 1PD 3

RIMSKY-KORSAKOV

Capriccio espagnol

London ca. February 1917	Orchestra	78: Columbia L 1148

ROGERS

At parting

London June 1909	O.Wood Wood, piano	G & T GC 3833 Coupled with Allitsen Since we two parted

ROSSINI

Semiramide, Overture

London July 1919	Orchestra	78: Columbia L 1395

William Tell, Overture

London June 1922	Orchestra	78: Columbia L 1435-1436 Coupled with Mascagni Intermezzo (Cavalleria rusticana) (L 1436)
London July 1928	New Queens Hall Orchestra	78: Columbia 5058-5059

SAINT-SAENS

Danse macabre

London ca. August 1916	Orchestra	78: Columbia L 1118 Coupled with Raff Cavatina; not published until 1920
London December 1926 and April 1927	New Queens Hall Orchestra	78: Columbia L 1987 LP: Pearl GEMM 161

Samson et Dalila: Excerpt (Mon coeur s'ouvre à ta voix)

London ca. December 1915	Orchestra Butt	78: Columbia 74004 Version by Butt re-issued on LP appears to be a later recording not conducted by Wood

SCHUBERT

Symphony No 8 "Unfinished"

London July 1919	Orchestra	78: Columbia L 1360-1361
London April 1926	New Queens Hall Orchestra	78: Columbia L 1791-1793
London October 1933	LSO	78: Columbia DX 551-553 LP: Melodiya M10 43701-43702 CD: Dutton 2CDAX 2002

Rosamunde, Entr'acte and Ballet music No 1

London September 1936	BBCSO	CD: Symposium 1150

Wanderer Fantasy, arranged by Liszt

London April 1937	Queens Hall Orchestra Curzon	78: Decca X 185-187

SHOSTAKOVICH

Symphony No 7 "Leningrad", extracts

London June 1942 (22 June)	LSO	Unpublished radio broadcast
London June 1942 (24 June)	LPO	Unpublished rehearsal extract

SIBELIUS

Finlandia

London March 1929	New Queens Hall Orchestra	78: Columbia 9655

Valse triste

London May 1935	Queens Hall Orchestra	78: Decca F 5582

SOMERVELL

Sleep, baby, sleep

London June 1909	O.Wood Wood, piano	G & T GC 3834

RICHARD STRAUSS

Till Eulenspiegels lustige Streiche

London ca. August 1916	Orchestra	78: Columbia L 1067 Abridged version

TCHAIKOVSKY

Symphony No 4, Scherzo

London　　　　　　　　Orchestra　　　　　　　　78: Columbia L 1006
ca. September　　　　　　　　　　　　　　　　　　Coupled with Grainger
1915　　　　　　　　　　　　　　　　　　　　　　Shepherd's Hey

Symphony No 6 "Pathétique"

London　　　　　　　　Orchestra　　　　　　　　78: Columbia L 1489-1492
April 1923　　　　　　　　　　　　　　　　　　　Abridged version

The Battle of Poltava

London　　　　　　　　Orchestra　　　　　　　　78: Columbia L 1378
July 1919　　　　　　　　　　　　　　　　　　　Coupled with Wagner Venusberg
　　　　　　　　　　　　　　　　　　　　　　　Music (Tannhäuser)

Capriccio italien

London　　　　　　　　Orchestra　　　　　　　　78: Columbia L 1230
ca. September
1918

Chant sans paroles

London　　　　　　　　New Queens Hall　　　　　78: Columbia L 1766
April 1926　　　　　　　Orchestra　　　　　　　　LP: Pearl GEMM 161
　　　　　　　　　　　　　　　　　　　　　　　78 version coupled with
　　　　　　　　　　　　　　　　　　　　　　　1812 Overture

The Maid of Orleans: Excerpt (Adieu forêts)

London　　　　　　　　O.Wood　　　　　　　　　G & T GC 3778
July 1908　　　　　　　Wood, piano
　　　　　　　　　　　Sung in English

1812 Overture

London　　　　　　　　New Queens Hall　　　　　78: Columbia L 1764-1766
January and　　　　　　Orchestra　　　　　　　　Coupled with Chant sans
April 1926　　　　　　　　　　　　　　　　　　　paroles (L 1766)

TURINA

Danzas fantasticas

London December 1922	Orchestra	78: Columbia L 1467-1468

VAUGHAN WILLIAMS

Symphony No 2 "A London Symphony"

London April 1936	Queens Hall Orchestra	78: Decca X 114-118 LP: Decca ACL 255 CD: Dutton CDAX 8004

Greensleeves Fantasia

London April 1936	Queens Hall Orchestra	78: Decca K 822 LP: Decca ACL 255 CD: Dutton CDAX 8004 78 version coupled with Wasps Overture (K 821-822)

Serenade to music

London October 1938	BBCSO BBC Chorus Desmond, Brunskill, Baillie, Jarred, Stiles-Allan, Suddaby, Turner, Balfour, Nash, Widdop, Jones, Titterton, Henderson, Easton, Williams, Allin	78: Columbia LX 757-758 45: Columbia SED 5533 CD: Pearl GEMMCD 9342 CD: Dutton CDAX 8004

The Wasps, Overture

London April 1936	Queens Hall Orchestra	78: Decca K 821-822 LP: Decca ACL 255 CD: Dutton CDAX 8004 78 version coupled with Greensleeves Fantasia (K 822)

WAGNER

Der fliegende Holländer, Overture

London ca. April 1917	Orchestra	78: Columbia L 1172 Abridged version; coupled with Dukas L'apprenti sorcier

Götterdämmerung: Excerpt (Gesang der Rheintöchter)

London ca. February 1916	Orchestra	78: Columbia L 1027 Coupled with Ride of the Valkyries
London April 1926	New Queens Hall Orchestra	78: Columbia L 1993-1994 Coupled with Ride of the Valkyries
London May 1935	Queens Hall Orchestra	78: Decca K 765-766 Coupled with Jaernefelt Praeludium

Lohengrin, Act 3 Prelude

London ca. September 1915	Orchestra	78: Columbia L 1005 Coupled with Rachmaninov Prelude in C sharp minor
London April 1926	New Queens Hall Orchestra	78: Columbia L 1005R Coupled with Rachmaninov Prelude in C sharp minor; both works newly recorded but published with the same catalogue number as the 1915 versions
London May 1944	Massed Brass Bands	Unpublished radio broadcast

Die Meistersinger von Nürnberg, Dance of the Apprentices

London ca. January 1917	Orchestra	78: Columbia L 1125 Coupled with Grainger Handel in the Strand

Das Rheingold, Entry of the Gods into Valhalla

London November 1921	Orchestra	78: Columbia L 1427 Coupled with Gounod Judex

Rienzi, Overture

London ca. July 1917	Orchestra	78: Columbia L 1182

Tannhäuser, Overture

London ca. July 1917	Orchestra	78: Columbia L 1196

Tannhäuser, Venusberg Music

London July 1919	Orchestra	78: Columbia L 1378 Coupled with Tchaikovsky Battle of Poltava

Tannhäuser, Grand March (Entry of the Guests)

London ca. December 1915	Orchestra	78: Columbia L 1021 <u>Coupled with Beethoven Coriolan Overture</u>
London April 1927	New Queens Hall Orchestra	78: Columbia L 1021R <u>Coupled with Beethoven Coriolan Overture; both works newly recorded but published with the same catalogue number as the 1915 versions</u>

Tristan und Isolde, Prelude and Liebestod

London ca. January 1916	Orchestra	78: Columbia L 1013 <u>Abridged version</u>

Die Walküre, Ride of the Valkyries

London ca. February 1916	Orchestra	78: Columbia L 1027 <u>Coupled with Gesang der Rhein- töchter (Götterdämmerung)</u>
London April 1927	New Queens Hall Orchestra	78: Columbia L 1994 LP: Pearl GEMM 161 <u>78 version coupled with Gesang der Rheintöchter (Götterdämmerung)</u>
London May 1935	Queens Hall Orchestra	78: Decca K 761 CD: Dutton CDAX 8008

Träume (Wesendonk-Lieder), arranged by Wood

London ca. March 1916	Orchestra	78: Columbia L 1033 <u>Coupled with Grainger Shepherd Fennel Dance</u>

WEBER

Oberon, Overture

London March 1925	New Queens Hall Orchestra	78: Columbia L 1677

WOOD

Fantasia on British Sea Songs

London ca. June 1916	Orchestra	78: Columbia L 1052
London November 1939	LSO	78: Columbia DX 954-955 CD: Dutton CDAX 8008

TRADITIONAL

Volga Boat Song, arranged by Wood

London June 1930	Symphony Orchestra	78: Columbia DX 87 Coupled with Rachmaninov Prelude in C sharp minor

WOOD ON FILM

For the 60th anniversary of Wood's death BBC TV showed a short feature film, in August 1994, which included film of him conducting Grainger's Shepherds Hey; reminiscences were contributed by Jessie Wood, Tania Cardew, Sidonie Goossens, Roy Henderson, Arthur Jacobs and Richard Baker

DE MONTFORD HALL - LEICESTER

Sunday, December 28th, 1941, at 2.45 p.m.

CARNEGIE TRUST CONCERT

MUSICAL CULTURE LIMITED

presents

THE LONDON PHILHARMONIC ORCHESTRA
(*Leader* - REGINALD MORLEY)

Conductor:

SIR HENRY J. WOOD

Sir Thomas Beecham
1879-1961

with valuable assistance
from Michael Gray

Discography compiled by John Hunt

13½p

Sir Thomas Beecham

ARNELL

Punch and the Child

London May 1950	RPO	78: Columbia LX 1391-1393 LP: Columbia (USA) ML 4593 LP: CBS 61431 CD: Sony SMK 46683

ATTERBERG

Symphony No 6

London August 1928	Orchestra of the Royal Philharmonic Society	78: Columbia L 2160-2163 78: Columbia (USA) 9068-9071/ 7166-7169 LP: Beecham Society WHS 105 LP: World Records SHB 100

BACH

Phoebus and Pan, Minuet and Gavotte (Cantata No 105)

London August and October 1918	Beecham SO	Columbia unpublished

Sinfonia (Christmas Oratorio)

London April and May 1947	RPO	78: Victor 12-0583 LP: Beecham Society WHS 106

BALAKIREV

Symphony No 1

London November and December 1955	RPO	LP: Columbia 33CX 1450 LP: Angel 35399/60062 LP: EMI XLP 30002/SXLP 30002 LP: EMI SXLP 30171/1C 047 01567 CD: EMI CDM 763 3752

Thamar

Walthamstow April 1954	RPO	LP: Philips ABL 3047/GL 5717 LP: Columbia (USA) ML 4974

BALFE

The Bohemian Girl, excerpts

London August 1951	Covent Garden Orchestra Peters, Marlowe, Glynne	LP: Voce 17 LP: HRE Records HRE 267

BANTOCK

Fifine at the Fair

London	RPO	78: HMV DB 21145-21148
June, July and		45: Victor WHMV 1026
October 1949		LP: HMV BLP 1016/HQM 1165
		LP: Victor LHMV 1026
		CD: EMI CDM 763 4052

BAX

The Garden of Fand

London	RPO	78: HMV DB 6654-6655
December 1947		LP: EMI HQM 1165
		CD: EMI CDM 763 4052

ADRIAN BEECHAM

O mistress mine

London	N.Evans	78: HMV C 3165
January 1940	Beecham, piano	LP: EMI HLM 7145

Outward bound

London	N.Evans	78: HMV C3165
January 1940	Beecham, piano	

Willow song

London	N.Evans	78: HMV C 3165
January 1940	Beecham, piano	LP: EMI HLM 7145

BEETHOVEN

Symphony No 2

London November 1926	LSO	78: Columbia L 1864-1867 78: Columbia (USA) M 45 LP: Beecham Society WHS 101
London October, November and December 1936	LPO	78: Columbia LX 586-589 78: Columbia (USA) M 302 LP: EMI RLS 734 CD: Beecham Trust BEECHAM 5
London May and September 1956 and March 1957	RPO	LP: HMV ALP 1596/ASD 287 LP: Angel 35509 LP: EMI HQS 1154 LP: Turnabout THS 65104 CD: EMI CDM 769 8112

Symphony No 3 "Eroica"

London December 1951 and August 1952	RPO	LP: Columbia 33CX 1086 LP: Columbia (USA) ML 4698 LP: Philips SBL 5223

Symphony No 4

London August and October 1945	LPO	78: HMV DB 6280-6283 78: Victor M 1081 45: Victor WDM 1081 LP: Victor LM 1026 <u>Test recording of side 1 made in</u> <u>December 1944 but unpublished</u>
New York January 1957	Symphony of the Air	LP: Beecham Society WSA 504-505

Symphony No 5, rehearsal extracts of 3rd and 4th movements

London July 1951	RPO	CD: EMI CDM 764 4652

Symphony No 6 "Pastoral"

London December 1951 and May 1952	RPO	LP: Columbia 33CX 1062 LP: Columbia (USA) ML 4828 LP: Philips GL 5745/EFL 2505

Symphony No 7

London October 1936	LPO	LP: Sirius 5023 CD: Symposium 1096-1097 Recording consists only of approx. first 8 minutes of 1st movement
Paris October 1957	RPO	LP: HMV ALP 1748 LP: Capitol G 7223
Ascona October 1957	RPO	CD: Eremitage ERM 132
London October 1958 and April and July 1959	RPO	LP: HMV ASD 311 LP: Capitol SG 7223 LP: EMI SXLP 30286/1C 053 03461 CD: EMI CDM 764 4462
London November 1959	RPO	LP: Beecham Society WSA 508/WSA 519 CD: Music and Arts CD 281

When the HMV LP editions of this symphony were first published, no indication was given that the mono and stereo versions were of two different performances

Symphony No 8

London May, October, November and December 1951	RPO	LP: Columbia 33CX 1039 LP: Columbia (USA) ML 4681 LP: Philips GL 5730/CFL 1004 LP: Philips EFL 2507/EFR 2020 CD: EMI CDM 763 3982

Symphony No 9 "Choral"

Edinburgh August 1956	RPO Edinburgh Choral Union Raisbeck, Merriman, Lewis, Borg	LP: Beecham Society WSA 504-505

Piano Concerto No 4

London September and December 1947	RPO Rubinstein	78: HMV DB 6732-6735/ DB 9405-9408 auto 78: Victor M 1345 45: Victor WDM 1345/WCT 48 LP: Victor LCT 1032 LP: World Records SHB 100 LP: EMI 1C 137 1544273

Fidelio

Buenos Aires September 1958	Teatro Colon Chorus & Orchestra Brouwenstijn, Chelavine, Hopf, Dickie, Schöffler, Van Mill	LP: Beecham Society WSA 524-525

Missa Solemnis

Leeds October 1937	LPO Leeds Festival Chorus Baillie, Jarred, Nash, Faulkner	CD: Beecham Trust BEECHAM 5

Mass in C

London May and November 1956	RPO Beecham Choral Society Fisher, Sinclair, Lewis, Stalman	HMV unpublished <u>Recording incomplete</u>
London April 1958	RPO Beecham Choral Society Vyvyan, Sinclair, Lewis, Nowakowski	LP: HMV ALP 1674/ASD 280 LP: Capitol G 7168/SG 7168 LP: EMI SXLP 30284/1C 053 03157 CD: NotaBlu 935 1123-1124

Coriolan, Overture

Walthamstow December 1953	RPO	LP: Philips ABL 3247 LP: Philips (USA) ML 5029/ML 5247 LP: Philips GL 5714/SBR 6218/SBR 6244

Die Ruinen von Athen, Incidental music

London March 1957 and Paris October 1957	RPO Beecham Choral Society	LP: HMV ALP 1956/ASD 287/HQS 1154 LP: Angel 35509 LP: Turnabout THS 65104 CD: EMI CDM 769 8712/CDM 764 3852 CD: NotaBlu 935 1112 Excerpts LP: EMI SXLP 30158/1C 047 01489 LP: EMI YKM 5005/CFP 40358 CD: EMI CDM 764 8982

BERKELEY

The First Gentleman, Incidental music

London 1948	RPO	Film soundtrack <u>Film also known as Affairs of a Rogue</u>

BERLIOZ

Symphonie fantastique

Paris November 1957 and March 1958	Orchestre National	LP: HMV ALP 1633 LP: Capitol G 7102 CD: EMI CDM 764 0322
Paris November and December 1959	Orchestre National	LP: HMV ASD 399 LP: Angel 60165 LP: EMI 1C 053 00150 CD: EMI CDC 747 8632

When the HMV editions were first published, no indication was given that the mono and stereo versions were of two different performances

Harold en Italie

London November 1951	RPO Primrose	LP: Columbia 33CX 1019 LP: Columbia (USA) ML 4542/Y 33286 LP: Philips GL 5715/KFR 4002 LP: CBS 77395 CD: Sony MPK 47679
Edinburgh August 1956	RPO J.Kennedy	LP: Beecham Society WSA 506-507

Requiem (Grande messe des morts)

London December 1959	RPO Beecham Choral Society Lewis	LP: Beecham Society WSA 502-503 LP: Cetra DOC 30 CD: Hunt CDLSMH 34012

Te Deum

Walthamstow December 1953	RPO LPO Choir Young	LP: Philips ABL 3006/GL 5637 LP: Columbia (USA) ML 4897 LP: Columbia (USA) 3216 0206 LP: CBS 77395

Les Troyens

London June and July 1947	RPO BBC Theatre Chorus Ferrer, Joachim, Gireaudeau, Vroons, Cambon, Dowling	LP: Beecham Society WSA 513-516 LP: Melodram MEL 303 La prise de Troie LP: Ed Smith EJS 377 Les Troyens à Carthage LP: Ed Smith EJS 378

Les Troyens, Marche troyenne

London January 1945	LPO	HMV unpublished
London August 1945	LPO	78: HMV DB 6238 78: Victor M 1141
Walthamstow December 1953	RPO	45: Philips ABE 10020 LP: Philips SBR 6215 LP: Columbia (USA) ML 5321/Y 33288 LP: CBS 61655
New York January 1957	Symphony of the Air	LP: Beecham Society WSA 505
London November 1959	RPO	45: HMV 7ER 5527/RES 4306 LP: HMV ALP 1862/ASD 432/SXLP 30260 LP: Angel 35865 LP: World Records T 744/ST 744 CD: EMI CDM 763 4122
Seattle February 1960	Seattle SO	LP: Beecham Society WSA 517-518

Les Troyens, Royal Hunt and Storm

London November 1938	LPO	Columbia unpublished
London August and October 1945	LPO	78: HMV DB 6241 78: Victor M 1141 78: HMV (Australia) ED 417
London March 1957	RPO Beecham Choral Society	LP: HMV ALP 1533/ASD 259 LP: Angel 35506 LP: EMI SXLP 30260/1C 053 03195 CD: EMI CDC 747 8632

Les Troyens à Carthage, Overture

Walthamstow December 1954	RPO	45: Philips ABE 10020 LP: Philips SBR 6215/GL 5714 LP: Columbia (USA) ML 5321/Y 33288

Le Carnaval romain, Overture

London ca. 1916	Beecham SO	78: Columbia L 1105 78: Columbia (USA) 65018D/7903M LP: Beecham Society WHS 102-104
London November 1936	LPO	78: Columbia LX 570 78: Columbia (USA) M 552 LP: World Records SHB 100 CD: EMI CDM 764 0322 CD: Dutton CDLX 7009
Walthamstow December 1954	RPO	LP: Philips ABL 3083/**SBR 6244** LP: Columbia (USA) ML 5064/Y 33287 LP: Philips GL 5633/GL 5714 LP: CBS 77395

Le Corsaire, Overture

Walthamstow April and May 1954	RPO	45: Philips ABE 10016 LP: Philips ABL 3083/GL 5633 LP: Columbia (USA) ML 5064/Y 33287 LP: CBS 77395
London November 1958	RPO	LP: HMV ALP 1846/ASD 420/HQS 1136 LP: Capitol G 7251/SG 7251 LP: HMV ALP 1870-1871/SXLP 30158 LP: Angel 3621 LP: Pickwick/Quintessence (USA) PC 4035/PMC 7004 LP: EMI CFP 40358 CD: EMI CDC 747 8632/CDM 763 4072
Seattle February 1960	Seattle SO	LP: Beecham Society WHS 517-518

La Damnation de Faust, Marche hongroise

London ca. 1916	Beecham SO	78: Columbia L 1105 LP: Beecham Society WHS 102-104
London March 1925	LSO	Columbia unpublished
London October and December 1937 and February 1938	LPO	78: Columbia LX 702 78: Columbia (USA) X 94 LP: World Records SHB 55 CD: Pearl GEMMCD 9065 CD: Dutton CDLX 7002

La Damnation de Faust, Menuet des follets

London December 1937	LPO	78: Columbia LX 703 78: Columbia (USA) X 94 LP: World Records SHB 55 CD: Pearl GEMMCD 9065 CD: Dutton CDLX 7002
London March 1957	RPO	LP: HMV ALP 1862/ASD 432/HQS 1136 LP: Angel 35865 CD: EMI CDM 763 4122

La Damnation de Faust, Danse des sylphes

London December 1937	LPO	78: Columbia LX 702 78: Columbia (USA) X 94 LP: HMV ALP 1870-1871 LP: Angel 3621 LP: World Records SHB 55 CD: Pearl GEMMCD 9065 CD: Dutton CDLX 7002 German Columbia 78 issue (LWX 236) was incorrectly labelled as conducted by Weingartner
London March 1957	RPO	45: HMV 7ER 5170/RES 4271 LP: HMV ALP 1533/ASD 259 LP: Angel 35506 CD: EMI CDM 763 4122

Les francs juges, Overture

Walthamstow December 1954	RPO	45: Philips ABE 10190 LP: Philips ABL 3083/SBR 6243/GL 5633 LP: Columbia (USA) ML 5064/Y 33287 LP: CBS 77395

Le roi Lear, Overture

London September and November 1947	RPO	78: HMV DB 6581-6582/ DB 9614-9615 auto CD: EMI CDM 764 0322
Walthamstow April and May 1954	RPO	LP: Philips ABL 3083/SBR 6243/GL 5633 LP: Columbia (USA) ML 5064/Y 33287 LP: CBS 77395 CD: Sony MPK 47679

Waverley, Overture

Walthamstow April and May 1954	RPO	45: Philips ABE 10040 LP: Philips ABL 3083/GL 5633 LP: Columbia (USA) ML 5064/Y 33287 LP: CBS 77395

BERNERS

The Triumph of Neptune, Ballet suite

London December 1937	LPO	78: Columbia LX 697-698 78: Columbia (USA) X 92 CD: EMI CDM 763 4052
Philadelphia February 1952	Philadelphia Orchestra	LP: Columbia (USA) ML 4593 LP: CBS 61431 CD: Sony SMK 46683

BIZET

Carmen

New York March 1943	Metropolitan Opera Orchestra & Chorus Djanel, Albanese, Jobin, Warren	LP: Ed Smith EJS 212 LP: Melodram MEL 057 Excerpts LP: Ed Smith UORC 289 Some issues described this as a performance from Chicago
Paris June 1958 and September 1959	Orchestre National French Radio Chorus De los Angeles, Micheau, Gedda, Blanc	LP: HMV ALP 1762-1764/ASD 331-333 LP: Angel 3613 LP: EMI SLS 755/SLS 5021 CD: EMI CDS 749 2402 Excerpts 45: HMV 7ER 5200/5214/5218/5300 45: HMV RES 4287/4292/4297/4301 LP: HMV ALP 2041/ASD 590/ESD 7047 LP: EMI SLS 5012/ALP 1870-1871 CD: EMI CDZB 769 1282 CD: NotaBlu 935 1112 The 4 orchestral preludes for this recording of the opera were recorded separately, and also published in the usual form of a suite (see over)
Buenos Aires July 1958	Teatro Colon Orchestra & Chorus Madeira, Broggini, Ferraro, Taddei	LP: Melodram MEL 451

Carmen, Suite

London April 1939	LPO	78: Columbia LX 823-824 78: Columbia (USA) X 144 LP: World Records SHB 55 CD: Dutton CDLX 7003 <u>German Columbia 78 issue (LWX 305-306) was incorrectly labelled as conducted by Weingartner</u>
New York December 1949	Columbia SO	78: Columbia (USA) MX 333/A 333 45: Philips CFE 15019 LP: Columbia 33CX 1037 LP: Columbia (USA) ML 4287/3216 0117 LP: Philips GL 5270 LP: CBS 54035
Paris January 1958	Orchestre National	LP: HMV ALP 1843/HQM 1108 LP: Angel 60734 LP: EMI SXLP 30276/1C 053 01330 CD: EMI CDC 747 7942 CD: EMI CDM 763 3792 (Suite 1 only) <u>The versions of the 4 Preludes contained in these suites were also used in the complete recording of the opera (see opposite page)</u>

<u>The contents of the various versions of the Carmen Suites differ slightly in
each recorded edition</u>

La jolie fille de Perth

London September and October 1956	RPO Dobbs, Pollack, Young, Ward, Brannigan	LP: Ed Smith EJS 269/EJS 438 LP: Patheon XLNC 107

La jolie fille de Perth, Suite

London June 1934	LPO	78: Columbia LX 317-318 78: Columbia (USA) X 28 LP: World Records SHB 55 CD: Dutton CDLX 7002
London February 1950	RPO	78: Columbia LX 8790-8791 78: Columbia (USA) MX 345 45: Philips CFE 15059 LP: Columbia (USA) ML 2133 LP: Philips GL 5693/CFL 1033

La jolie fille de Perth, Minuet only

London ca. 1918	Beecham SO	78: Columbia L 1227 LP: Beecham Society WHS 102-104

L'Arlésienne, Suite No 1

London February 1936	LPO	78: Columbia LX 541-542 78: Columbia (USA) X 69 LP: World Records SHB 55
London September 1956	RPO	LP: HMV ALP 1487/ASD 252/HQM 1108 LP: Angel 35460 LP: EMI SXLP 30276/1C 053 01330 CD: EMI CDC 747 7942

L'Arlésienne, Suite No 2

London February and June 1936	LPO	78: Columbia LX 614 78: Columbia (USA) 68882D LP: World Records SHB 55
London September 1956	RPO	LP: HMV ALP 1487/ASD 252/HQM 1108 LP: Angel 35460 LP: EMI SXLP 30276/1C 053 01330 CD: EMI CDC 747 7942

Symphony in C

Paris January 1958	Orchestre National	LP: HMV ALP 1761 LP: Capitol G 7237
Paris October and November 1959	Orchestre National	LP: HMV ASD 388/SXLP 30260 LP: Capitol SG 7237 LP: Angel 60192 LP: EMI 1C 053 00175 CD: EMI CDC 747 7942

When the HMV LP editions of this symphony were first published, no indication was given that the mono and stereo versions were of two different performances

Patrie, Overture

London October 1956	RPO	LP: HMV ALP 1497/HQM 1162 LP: Angel 35460 CD: EMI CDM 763 4012

Carnaval à Rome (Roma)

Paris October 1957	RPO	LP: HMV ALP 1656/HQM 1162 CD: EMI CDM 763 4012

BLOCH

Violin Concerto

London March 1939	LPO Szigeti	LP: Beecham Society WSA 5 Gaps in original acetates filled in with a commercial recording by Szigeti conducted by Münch

BOCCHERINI

Symphony in C op 12 no 3

New York June 1941	Columbia SO	LP: Beecham Society WSA 520

Overture in D

Walthamstow December 1953	RPO	LP: Philips ABL 3247/GL 5029 LP: Columbia (USA) ML 5029 LP: Philips SBR 6218/SBR 6244
Edinburgh August 1956	RPO	LP: Beecham Society WSA 521-522

BORODIN

Prince Igor, Overture

London ca. 1918	Beecham SO	Columbia unpublished
London August 1945	LPO	78: HMV DB 6237-6238 78: Victor M 1141

Prince Igor, Polovtsian March

London ca. 1915	Beecham SO	78: Columbia L 1011 LP: Beecham Society WHS 102-104 CD: Symposium 1096-1097
London December 1927	LSO	78: Columbia L 2058 78: Columbia (USA) 7193M/50130D LP: Beecham Society WHS 105
London October 1938	LPO	78: Columbia LX 769 78: Columbia (USA) X 123 CD: Dutton CDLX 7003

Prince Igor, Polovtsian Dances

London ca. 1915	Beecham SO	78: Columbia L 1002 78: Columbia (USA) A 5808 LP: Beecham Society WHS 102-104
London March 1925	LSO	Columbia unpublished
London June 1926	LSO	78: Columbia L 1811-1812 78: Columbia (USA) 7138-7139M LP: Beecham Society WHS 101
Leeds October 1934	LPO Leeds Festival Chorus	78: Columbia LX 369-370 78: Columbia (USA) X 54/M 238 LP: World Records SHB 100 CD: Dutton CDLX 7003 Excerpt LP: HMV ALP 1870-1871 LP: Angel 3621
London November 1956	RPO Beecham Choral Society	LP: EMI SXLP 30171/1C 047 01567 CD: EMI CDC 747 7172/WHS 568 4102

BRAHMS

Symphony No 2

London March 1936	LPO	78: Columbia LX 515-519 78: Columbia (USA) M 265 LP: EMI RLS 733 CD: Dutton 2CDAX 2003
London December 1939	LPO	Unpublished test pressings of excerpts only
London May and September 1956	RPO	HMV unpublished
London April, November and December 1958 & May, July and November 1959	RPO	LP: HMV ALP 1770/ASD 348/HQS 1143 LP: Capitol G 7228/SG 7228 LP: Angel 60083 LP: EMI 1C 053 00649 CD: EMI CDM 763 2212
London November 1959	RPO	LP: Beecham Society WSA 523

Symphony No 3

New York January 1957	Symphony of the Air	LP: Beecham Society WSA 508

Violin Concerto

London November 1951	RPO Stern	LP: Philips ABL 3023/GBL 5638 LP: Columbia (USA) ML 4530 CD: NotaBlu 935 1112 CD: Sony SM3K 45952

Academic Festival Overture

London November 1956	RPO	LP: Columbia 33CX 1429 LP: Angel 35400/60083 LP: EMI HQS 1143/SXLP 30158 LP: EMI 1C 047 01489/1C 053 00649 CD: EMI CDM 763 2212/CDM 764 4462

Tragic Overture

London March 1937	LPO	78: Columbia LX 638-639 78: Columbia (USA) X 85 LP: EMI RLS 733 CD: Dutton CDLX 7009
Walthamstow December 1953	RPO	LP: Philips ABL 3247/SBR 6218/GL 5714 LP: Columbia (USA) ML 5029/ML 5247

Haydn Variations

London March 1949	RPO	LP: Beecham Society WSA 508

Hungarian Dances Nos 5 and 6

London March 1939	LPO	LP: Beecham Society WSA 526 CD: Symposium 1096-1097 Recorded for a Radio Luxemburg broadcast

Alto Rhapsody

New York September 1941	Columbia SO Scola cantorum J.Busch	LP: Beecham Society WSA 523

Song of Destiny

London May and November 1956	RPO Beecham Choral Society Sung in English	LP: Columbia 33CX 1429 LP: Angel 35400 CD: EMI CDM 763 2212

DEBUSSY

Prélude à l'après-midi d'un faune

London	LPO
November 1938	
and January	
and February 1939	

78: Columbia LX 805
78: Columbia (USA) 69600D
LP: World Records SHB 55
CD: Pearl GEMMCD 9065
CD: Dutton CDLX 7002

London	RPO
March 1957	

LP: HMV ALP 1533/ASD 259
LP: Angel 35506
LP: EMI EMX 41 20771
CD: EMI CDM 763 3792
CD: NotaBlu 935 11234

Printemps

London	RPO
November 1946	
and April 1947	

78: HMV DB 6549-6550
78: Victor M 1293
45: Victor WDM 1293
LP: Victor LM 9001
LP: World Records SHB 100

L'enfant prodigue, Cortège et air de danse

London	RPO
October and	
November 1959	

45: HMV 7P 291
LP: HMV ALP 1862/ASD 432
LP: Angel 35865/60084
LP: World Records T 558/ST 558
LP: EMI EMX 41 20771
CD: EMI CDM 763 4122

London	RPO
November 1959	

LP: Beecham Society WSA 508/WSA 519
CD: Music and Arts CD 218

Ballet (Petite Suite)

London	Beecham SO
August and	
October 1918	

78: Columbia L 1248
LP: Beecham Society WHS 102-104
CD: Symposium 1096-1097

En bateau (Petite Suite)

London	Beecham SO
August and	
October 1918	

78: Columbia L 1248
LP: Beecham Society WHS 102-105
CD: Symposium 1096-1097

Detroit	Detroit SO
June 1942	

LP: Beecham Society WSA 526

DELIBES

Le roi s'amuse, Ballet suite

Paris May 1958	RPO	45: HMV 7ER 5159 LP: HMV ALP 1656/HQS 1136 LP: Angel 60084 LP: EMI SXLP 30260/1C 053 03195 CD: EMI CDM 763 3792
Seattle February 1960	Seattle SO	LP: Beecham Society WSA 517-518

DELIUS

A Village Romeo and Juliet

London May and July 1948	RPO RPO Chorus Bond, Ritchie, Dyer, Soames, Dowling, Sharp, Clinton	78: HMV DB 6751-6762/ DB 9306-9317 auto CD: EMI CMS 764 3862

A Village Romeo and Juliet, Walk to the Paradise Garden

London December 1927	Orchestra of the Royal Philharmonic Society	78: Columbia L 2087 78: Columbia (USA) X 31 LP: World Records SHB 32 CD: Beecham Trust BEECHAM 3
New York April 1945	ABC Orchestra	LP: Beecham Society WHS 107
Ascona October 1957	RPO	CD: Eremitage ERM 132

A Mass of Life

London November and December 1952 and January, April and May 1953	RPO LPO Chorus Fisher, Raisbeck, Sinclair, Craig, Boyce	LP: Columbia 33CX 1078-1079 LP: Columbia (USA) SL 197 LP: Philips CFL 1005-1006 LP: CBS 61182-61183

CHABRIER

España

London November and December 1939	LPO	78: Columbia LX 880 78: Columbia (USA) 71250D LP: World Records SHB 55 CD: EMI CDM 763 4012 CD: Beulah 2PD 4
London April 1950	RPO	78: Columbia LX 1592 45: Columbia SEL 1509 45: Philips CFE 15000/EFF 521 LP: Columbia (USA) ML 5171 LP: Philips GL 5692/EFR 2029/CFL 1021

Gwendoline, Overture

Paris November 1957	Orchestre National	LP: HMV ALP 1843/HQM 1162 CD: EMI CDM 763 4012

Joyeuse marche

London November 1946	RPO	78: HMV DB 6422/DB 9109 78: Victor M 1295 LP: HMV ALP 1870-1871 LP: Angel 3621
London March 1957	RPO	45: HMV 7ER 5170/RES 4271 LP: HMV ALP 1533/ASD 259 LP: Angel 35506 LP: EMI EMX 41 20771 CD: EMI CDM 763 4122

CHARPENTIER

Louise

New York February 1943	Metropolitan Opera Chorus & Orchestra Moore, Doe, Jobin, Pinza	LP: Ed Smith EJS 164 CD: Walhall WHL 9

CHERUBINI

Les deux journées

London December 1947	RPO BBC Theatre Chorus Micheau, Gianolli, Paul, Régnier	LP: Ed Smith UORC 174 LP: Voce 73 LP: Cetra LO 49 CD: Intaglio INCD 7432 Excerpts LP: Ed Smith EJS 385

D'ALBERT

Tiefland, orchestral selection I

London August 1910	Beecham SO	G & T 0629/040635/65054/ES 79 LP: Beecham Society WHS 102-104 LP: World Records SHB 100

Tiefland, orchestral selection II

London August 1910	Beecham SO	G & T 0630/040636/65054/ES 79 LP: Beecham Society WHS 102-104 LP: World Records SHB 100

A Mass of Life, Prelude to Part 2

London   RPO   LP: World Records SHB 54
November 1946   CD: EMI CDM 764 0542

London   RPO   LP: World Records SHB 32
May 1948

A Mass of Life, Prelude to Part 2 No 3

London   LPO   LP: World Records SHB 32
February 1938

Piano Concerto

London   LPO   HMV unpublished
October and   Humby-Beecham
December 1945

London   RPO   78: HMV DB 6428-6430/
October and   Humby-Beecham   DB 9273-9275 auto
December 1946   78: Victor M 1185
                                        LP: Victor LVT 1045
                                        LP: World Records SHB 54
                                        LP: HMV ALP 1890

Violin Concerto

London   RPO   78: HMV DB 6369-6371/
October and   Pougnet   DB 9092-9094 auto
November 1946   78: HMV (Australia) ED 536-538
                                        LP: World Records SHB 54
                                        LP: HMV ALP 1890
                                        CD: EMI CDM 764 0542

Appalachia

London   LPO   Unpublished and incomplete
November 1935   test pressings

London   LPO   78: Columbia SDX 15-19
January 1938   BBC Chorus   78: Columbia (USA) M 355
                                        LP: World Records SHB 32
                                        CD: Dutton CDLX 7011

London   RPO   LP: Columbia 33CX 1112
October,   RPO Chorus   LP: Columbia (USA) ML 4915/Y 33283
November and   LP: Philips GL 5690/CFL 1009
December 1952   LP: CBS 61354

An Arabesque

Leeds October 1934	LPO London Select Choir Henderson	Columbia unpublished Recording may be incomplete
Walthamstow October and November 1955	RPO BBC Chorus Norby	LP: Columbia (USA) ML 5268 LP: Philips GL 5690/CFL 1009 CD: Sony MPK 47680

Brigg Fair

London July 1928	LSO	Columbia unpublished
London November and December 1928 and July 1929	Orchestra	78: Columbia L 2294-2295 78: Columbia (USA) X 30 LP: World Records SHB 32 CD: Beecham Trust BEECHAM 3
London November 1946 and April 1947	RPO	78: HMV DB 6452-6453 78: Victor M 1206 45: Victor WDM 1206 LP: World Records SHB 54
London October 1956 and April 1957	RPO	LP: HMV ALP 1586/ASD 357 LP: Capitol G 7116/SG 7116 LP: Angel 60185 CD: EMI CDS 747 5098

Dance Rhapsody No 1

London November 1946	RPO	HMV unpublished
London May 1948 and February 1949	RPO	HMV unpublished
London October 1952	RPO	78: HMV DB 9785-9786 LP: HMV ALP 1889/HQM 1165 LP: Victor LHMV 1050/LVT 1020

Dance Rhapsody No 2

London October 1945	LPO	HMV unpublished
London October 1946	RPO	78: HMV DB 6451 LP: World Records SHB 54 DB 6451 not published
London November 1956	RPO	LP: HMV ALP 1697/ASD 329/HQS 1126 LP: Capitol G 7193/SG 7193 LP: Angel 60212 CD: EMI CDS 747 5098

Eventyr

London November 1934	LPO	78: Columbia SDX 4-5 78: Columbia (USA) M 305 LP: World Records SHB 32 CD: Beecham Trust BEECHAM 2
London January and April 1951	RPO	78: Columbia LX 8931-8932 45: Philips CFE 15022 LP: Columbia (USA) ML 4637/Y 33284 LP: Philips CFL 1042 LP: CBS 61271 CD: Sony SMK 58934

Fennimore and Gerda, Intermezzo

London September 1936	LPO	78: Columbia SDX 11 78: Columbia (USA) M 290 LP: World Records SHB 32 CD: Beecham Trust BEECHAM 2
London November 1956	RPO	LP: HMV ALP 1586/ASD 357 LP: Capitol G 7116/SG 7116 LP: Angel 60183 CD: EMI CDS 747 5098

Florida Suite

London November and December 1956	RPO	LP: HMV ALP 1697/ASD 329/HQS 1126 LP: Capitol G 7193/SG 7193 LP: Angel 60212 CD: EMI CDS 747 5098

Florida Suite, La calinda (Dance)

London January 1938	LPO	LP: World Records SHB 32

Hassan, Incidental music

Walthamstow October 1955 and London May and October 1956	RPO BBC Chorus Fry, Riley	LP: Columbia (USA) ML 5268 LP: Philips GL 5691/CFL 1020 LP: CBS 61224 CD: Sony MPK 47680 Excerpts LP: Philips GL 5673/CFL 1033 LP: CBS 30056

Hassan, Intermezzo and Serenade

London December 1934	LPO	78: Columbia SDX 7 78: Columbia (USA) M 305 LP: World Records SHB 32 CD: Dutton CDLX 7011
London October 1952	RPO	78: HMV DB 9786 LP: Victor LHMV 1050/LVT 1020 LP: HMV ALP 1870-1871/ALP 1889 LP: Angel 3621
Seattle February 1960	Seattle SO	LP: Beecham Society WSA 517-518

Hassan, Closing scene

London June 1938	LPO Covent Garden Chorus Van der Gucht	78: Columbia SDX 20 78: Columbia (USA) M 355 45: Columbia SEL 1700 LP: World Records SHB 32 CD: Dutton CDLX 7011

Hassan, Unaccompanied wordless chorus

London October 1934	London Select Choir	LP: World Records SHB 32

Heimkehr

London April 1949	RPO M.Thomas	LP: World Records SHB 54

In a Summer Garden

London October 1936	LPO	78: Columbia DSX 13-14 78: Columbia (USA) M 290 LP: World Records SHB 32 CD: Beecham Trust BEECHAM 3
London October 1951	RPO	LP: Columbia 33C 1017 LP: Philips SBR 6242/GL 5713 LP: CBS 30056

Irmelin, Excerpts from Acts 2 and 3

London
September and
December 1954
	RPO
	Chorus
	Stewart, Round
		LP: Beecham Society WSA 501
		   (Act 2 scenes)
		LP: Beecham Society WSA 521-522
		   (Acts 2 and 3 scenes)
		<u>December 1954 performance was for
		a BBC TV programme</u>

Irmelin, Prelude

London January and July 1938	LPO	78: Columbia SDX 21 78: Columbia (USA) M 355 LP: World Records SHB 32 CD: Beecham Trust BEECHAM 2
London December 1946	RPO	78: HMV DB 6371/DB 9092 78: HMV (Australia) ED 536 LP: HMV ALP 1889/HLM 7093 LP: EMI 1C 047 06168M LP: World Records SHB 54
London October and November 1956	RPO	LP: HMV ALP 1968/ASD 518 LP: Angel 60000 LP: World Records T 774/ST 774 CD: EMI CDS 747 5098

Koanga, Closing scene

London December 1934	LPO London Select Choir	78: Columbia SDX 6 78: Columbia (USA) M 305 45: Columbia SEL 1700 LP: World Records SHB 32 CD: Dutton CDLX 7011
London January 1951	RPO RPO Choir	78: Columbia LX 1502 LP: Columbia 33CX 1112 LP: Columbia (USA) ML 4915/Y 33284 LP: Philips CFL 1003/GL 5693 LP: CBS 61271 CD: Sony SMK 58934

Koanga, La Calinda

London February 1938	LPO	78: Columbia SDX 21 78: Columbia (USA) M 355 45: Columbia SEL 1700 LP: World Records SHB 32 CD: Beecham Trust BEECHAM 3 CD: Dutton CDLX 7003
Detroit June 1942	Detroit SO	LP: Beecham Society WSA 526

Marche caprice

London December 1946	RPO	78: HMV DB 6430/DB 9273 78: Victor M 1185 LP: World Records SHB 54
London October 1956	RPO	LP: HMV ALP 1586/ASD 357 LP: Capitol G 7116/SG 7116 LP: Angel 60185 CD: EMI CDS 747 5098

North Country Sketches

London October 1945	LPO	HMV unpublished
London February 1949	RPO	78: Columbia LX 1399-1401 LP: Columbia (USA) ML 4637/Y 33283 LP: Philips CFL 1020/GL 5691 LP: CBS 61354 CD: Sony SMK 58934
London November 1959	RPO	CD: Music and Arts CD 281

On hearing the First Cuckoo in Spring

London December 1927	Orchestra of the Royal Philharmonic Society	78: Columbia L 2096 78: Columbia (USA) X 31 LP: World Records SHB 32 CD: Beecham Trust BEECHAM 3 CD: Dutton CDLX 7011
Ludwigshafen November 1936	LPO	Experimental tape recording issued on Chandos cassette DBTD 2007
London October and December 1946 and May 1948	RPO	78: HMV DB 6293 78: Victor 12-1093 45: HMV 7P 231 45: Victor WDM 1206 LP: Victor LHMV 1050/LVT 1020 LP: World Records SHB 54
London October 1956	RPO	45: HMV 7ER 5198/RES 4286 LP: HMV ALP 1586/ASD 357 LP: Capitol G 7116/SG 7116 LP: Angel 60134 LP: World Records SHB 100 CD: EMI CDS 747 5098

Over the Hills and Far Away

London September 1936	LPO	78: Columbia SDX 12-13 78: Columbia (USA) M 290 LP: World Records SHB 32 CD: Beecham Trust BEECHAM 2
London April 1957 and Paris October 1957	RPO	LP: HMV ALP 1697/ASD 329/HQS 1126 LP: Capitol G 7193/SG 7193 LP: Angel 60212 CD: EMI CDS 747 5098
London February 1950	RPO	LP: Columbia 33C 1017 LP: Columbia (USA) ML 2133/ML 5268 LP: Philips SBR 6242/GL 5713 CD: Sony SMK 58934

Paris

London April 1934	LPO	78: Columbia SDX 1-3 78: Columbia (USA) M 305 LP: World Records SHB 32 CD: Beecham Trust BEECHAM 2 CD: NotaBlu 935 11234
London November 1952	RPO	Columbia unpublished <u>Recording incomplete</u>
Walthamstow November and December 1955	RPO	LP: Philips ABL 3088 LP: Columbia (USA) ML 5079/Y 33284 LP: CBS 61271 CD: Sony SMK 46683

Sea Drift

London November 1928	LSO Manchester Beecham Opera Chorus Noble	LP: Beecham Society WHS 107
London April and November 1936	LPO London Select Choir Brownlee	78: Columbia SDX 8-11 78: Columbia (USA) M 305 LP: World Records SHB 32 CD: Beecham Trust BEECHAM 3
London January 1951	RPO RPO Chorus Clinton	CD: EMI CMS 764 3862
Walthamstow April and December 1954	RPO BBC Chorus Boyce	LP: Philips ABL 3088 LP: Columbia (USA) ML 5079 LP: CBS 61224 CD: Sony MPK 47680 CD: NotaBlu 935 11234

Sleigh Ride (Winternacht)

London November 1956	RPO	45: HMV 7ER 5198/RES 4286 LP: HMV ALP 1586/ASD 357 LP: Capitol G 7116/SG 7116 CD: EMI CDS 747 5098

A Song before sunrise

London October 1945	LPO	HMV unpublished
London December 1946	RPO	HMV unpublished
London February and April 1949	RPO	78: HMV DB 9757-9758 LP: Victor LHMV 1050/LVT 1020 LP: HMV ALP 1889 LP: World Records SHB 54
London November 1956	RPO	45: HMV 7ER 5198/RES 4286 LP: HMV ALP 1586/ASD 357 LP: Capitol G 7116/SG 7116 LP: Angel 60185 CD: EMI CDS 747 5098

Song of the high hills

London November 1946	RPO Luton Choral Society Hart, L.Jones	78: HMV DB 6470-6472/ DB 9151-9153 auto 78: Victor M 1185 LP: Victor LVT 1045 LP: HMV ALP 1889 LP: World Records SHB 54 CD: EMI CDM 764 0542

Songs of sunset

Leeds October 1934	LPO London Select Choir Haley, Henderson	Columbia unpublished <u>Recording may be incomplete</u>
London November 1946	RPO BBC Chorus N.Evans, Llewellyn	LP: World Records SHB 54
London April 1957	RPO BBC Chorus Forrester, Cameron	LP: HMV ALP 1983/SXLP 30440 LP: Arabesque 8026 CD: EMI CDS 747 5098

Summer Evening

London February 1949	RPO	78: HMV DB 9758 LP: Victor LHMV 1050/LVT 1020 LP: HMV ALP 1889 LP: World Records SHB 54
London October 1956	RPO	LP: HMV ALP 1968/ASD 518 LP: Angel 60000 CD: EMI CDS 747 5098/CDM 763 4122

Summer Night on the river

London July 1928	Orchestra of the Royal Philharmonic Society	78: Columbia D 1638 78: Columbia (USA) 17017D
London October 1935	LPO	78: Columbia LB 44 78: Columbia (USA) 17087D LP: World Records SHB 32 CD: Beecham Trust BEECHAM 3 CD: Dutton CDLX 7011
London February 1949	RPO	78: HMV DB 9757-9758 45: Victor EHA 12 LP: Victor LHMV 1050/LVT 1020 LP: World Records SHB 54
London March 1957	RPO	45: HMV 7ER 5198/RES 4286 LP: HMV ALP 1586/ASD 357 LP: Capitol G 7116/SG 7116 LP: Angel 60185 CD: EMI CDS 747 5098

Le ciel est par-dessus le toit

London July 1930	Labette Beecham, piano	LP: World Records SHB 32 LP: EMI EX 29 09113

Cradle song

London June 1929	Labette Beecham, piano	78: Columbia L 2344 78: Columbia (USA) 9092M LP: EMI HLM 7033 LP: World Records SHB 32

Evening voices

London July 1930	Labette Beecham, piano	LP: Columbia L 2344 LP: Columbia (USA) 9092M LP: EMI HLM 7033/ALP 1870-1871 LP: World Records SHB 32 LP: Angel 3621 CD: Dutton CDLX 7011
London February 1938	LPO Labette	Columbia unpublished
London April 1951	RPO Suddaby	LP: Victor LHMV 1050/LVT 1020 LP: World Records SHB 54

I Brasil

London February 1938	LPO Labette	LP: World Records SHB 32

Irmelin Rose

London June 1929	Labette Beecham, piano	LP: World Records SHB 32 LP: EMI EX 29 01693

Klein Venevil

London February 1938	LPO Labette	LP: World Records SHB 32

The nightingale

London June 1929	Labette Beecham, piano	78: Columbia L 2344 78: Columbia (USA) 9092M LP: EMI HLM 7033 LP: World Records SHB 32

So white, so soft, so sweet is she

London   Labette   Columbia unpublished
December 1934   Beecham, piano

To daffodils

London   Labette   Columbia unpublished
December 1934   Beecham, piano

The Violet

London   Labette   LP: EMI EX 29 09113
July 1930   Beecham, piano   LP: World Records SHB 32

London   LPO   LP: World Records SHB 32
February 1938   Labette

London   RPO   LP: World Records SHB 54
October 1949   Suddaby

Whither?

London   LPO   LP: World Records SHB 32
February 1938   Labette

London   RPO   LP: World Records SHB 54
October 1949   Suddaby

DUPARC

Chanson triste

Detroit   Detroit SO   LP: Beecham Society WSA 526
June 1942   Pons

DVORAK

Symphony No 5

London October 1936	LPO	LP: Sirius 5023 CD: Symposium 1096-1097

Symphony No 8

London October 1959	RPO	LP: EMI ALP 2003 CD: EMI CDM 763 3992

Symphony No 9 "From the New World"

London August and October 1918	Beecham SO	Columbia unpublished Excerpts only recorded

Symphonic Variations

Walthamstow December 1953	RPO	LP: Philips ABL 3047/GL 5714 LP: Columbia (USA) ML 4974

The Golden Spinning Wheel

London February, September and November 1947	RPO	78: HMV DB 6656-6658/ DB 9284-9286 auto 78: Victor M 1291 LP: World Records SHB 100

Legend No 2

London April 1935	LPO	Columbia unpublished

Legend No 3

London April 1935	LPO	78: Columbia LX 403 78: Columbia (USA) X55/M 239 CD: Pearl GEMMCD 9094 CD: Dutton CDLX 7003
London November 1959	RPO	LP: HMV ALP 1968/ASD 518/EMX 2103 LP: Angel 60000 LP: World Records T 774/ST 774 CD: EMI CDM 763 4122

Slavonic Rhapsody No 3

London March, April and July 1935	LPO	78: Columbia LX 402-403 78: Columbia (USA) X55/M 239 CD: Pearl GEMMCD 9094 CD: Dutton CDLX 7002

EASDALE

The Red Shoes, Ballet music

Denham July 1947	RPO	78: Victor (Japan) JAS 93 LP: Sirius 5032 Film soundtrack recording

ELGAR

Enigma Variations

Walthamstow November and December 1954	RPO	LP: Philips ABL 3053 LP: Columbia (USA) ML 5031 LP: Philips SBR 6224/GBL 5646 LP: CBS 61660

Cockaigne Overture

Walthamstow November and December 1954	RPO	45: Philips ABE 10041 LP: Philips ABL 3053 LP: Columbia (USA) ML 5031/ML 5247 LP: Philips SBR 6224/GBL 5646 LP: CBS 61660

Serenade for strings

Walthamstow November 1954	RPO	45: Philips ABE 10188 LP: Philips ABL 3053/BGL 5646 LP: Columbia (USA) ML 5031 LP: CBS 61660

FALLA

El amor brujo, extracts

Rome 1958	Orchestra	LP: Sirius 5022 Soundtrack recording for the film Honeymoon (Luna de miel)

FAURÉ

Pavane

London March 1925	LSO	Columbia unpublished
Paris December 1959	Orchestre National	LP: HMV ALP 1968/ASD 518 LP: Angel 60000/60134 LP: EMI HQS 1136/EMX 41 20771 CD: EMI CDM 763 3792 Beecham's last official recording

Dolly Suite

Paris December 1959	Orchestre National	LP: HMV ALP 1843 LP: Angel 60084 LP: EMI HQS 1136/EMX 41 20771 CD: EMI CDM 763 3792 Excerpt CD: EMI CDM 764 8982

FRANCK

Symphony in D minor

London January 1940	LPO	78: Columbia LX 904-908 78: Columbia (USA) M 479 LP: EMI RLS 733 CD: Pearl GEMMCD 9065 CD: Dutton 2CDAX 2003 CD: EMI CDM 764 0532
Paris November 1957	Orchestre National	LP: HMV ALP 1686 LP: Capitol G 7157
Paris December 1959	Orchestre National	LP: HMV ASD 458/SXLP 30256 LP: Angel 60012 LP: World Records T 596/ST 596 CD: EMI CDM 763 3962

When the HMV editions were first published, no indication was given that the mono and stereo versions were of two different performances

Le chasseur maudit

London March 1951	RPO	78: Columbia LX 8813-8814 LP: Columbia 33CX 1087 LP: Columbia)USA) ML 4474 LP: Philips CFL 1042/KFR 4000

GERMAN

Have you news of my boy Jack?

London February- March 1917	Beecham SO Butt	78: Columbia 7145 LP: Beecham Society WHS 102-104 LP: World Records SHB 100

Other vocal items, including "Back from the front" with Butt and/or other artists, were probably recorded at the same time but remained unpublished

Gipsy Suite

London October 1956	RPO	LP: HMV ALP 1983 LP: World Records T 558/ST 558

GODARD

Concerto romantique

London December 1955	RPO Campoli	LP: Beecham Society WSA 501

GOLDMARK

Rustic Wedding Symphony

London May 1952	RPO	LP: Columbia 33CX 1067 LP: Columbia (USA) ML 4626 LP: Philips GL 5719/NBL 5041

GOUNOD

Faust

London April 1929 and January 1930	Orchestra BBC Choir Licette, Vane, Brunskill, Nash, Easton, Williams Sung in English	78: Columbia DX 88-103/ DX 8025-8040 auto CD: Dutton 2CDAX 2001 Excerpts LP: EMI HLM 7052 LP: Turnabout THS 65065 CD: Pearl GEMMCD 9473 Additional recording session in January 1930 was conducted by Raybould
New York January 1943	Metropolitan Opera Orchestra & Chorus Albanese, Votipka, Browning, Jobin, Pinza	LP: Magnificent Editions ME 104 CD: AS-Disc AS 1104-1105 Excerpts LP: Ed Smith EJS 265/EJS 531
London November and December 1947 and January and June 1948	RPO RPO Chorus Géori-Boué, St. Arnaud, Bannermann, Noré, Bourdin	78: HMV DB 9422-9437 78: Victor M 1300 and M 1303 LP: Victor LCT 6100 Excerpts 78: HMV DB 6964-6967 45: Victor WCT 1100 LP: Victor LCT 1100/LM 1162

Faust, unspecified extracts

London November 1934	LPO Chorus and soloists unspecified	HMV unpublished Private recordings for V.Shavitch

Faust, Ballet music

London March 1939	LPO	LP: Beecham Society WSA 526 CD: Symposium 1096-1097 CD: Dutton CDAX 2001 <u>Recorded for a Radio Luxemburg broadcast</u>
Paris October and November 1957	RPO	LP: HMV ALP 1656/HQM 1162 CD: EMI CDM 763 4012
London October 1958	RPO	VHS Video: Teldec 4509 950383 Laserdisc: Teldec 4509 950386 <u>Excerpt only</u>
Seattle February 1960	Seattle SO	LP: Beecham Society WSA 517-518

Roméo et Juliette, March

London ca. 1917	Beecham SO	78: Columbia L 1162 LP: Beecham Society WHS 102-104 CD: Symposium 1096-1097

Roméo et Juliette, Le sommeil de Juliette

London October and November 1959	RPO	45: HMV 7ER 5527/RES 4306 LP: HMV ALP 1862/ASD 432 LP: Angel 35865/60084 LP: World Records T 558/ST 558 LP: EMI EMX 41 20771 CD: EMI CDM 763 4122
London November 1959	RPO	LP: Beecham Society WSA 508/WSA 519 CD: Music and Arts CD 218
Seattle February 1960	Seattle SO	LP: Beecham Society WSA 517-518

GRETRY

Zémire et Azor

Bath May 1955	Bournemouth SO Mandikian, Boulangot, Sénéchal, Lefort	Unpublished radio broadcast or private recording

Zémire et Azor: Excerpt (Ariette)

London December 1927	Orchestra Labette	Columbia unpublished

Zémire et Azor, Ballet music

London October 1956	RPO	45: HMV 7ER 5169 LP: HMV ALP 1656/HQM 1162 CD: EMI CDM 763 4012 Excerpt LP: HMV ALP 1870-1871 LP: Angel 3621

Zémire et Azor, Air de ballet

London January 1940	LPO	78: Columbia LX 885 78: Ciolumbia (USA) X 215 LP: World Records SHB 55
Walthamstow April 1954	RPO	LP: Philips SBR 6215/SBR 6245/GL 5713 LP: Columbia (USA) ML 5029

GRIEG

Peer Gynt, Incidental music

London	RPO	LP: HMV ALP 1530/ASD 258/SXLP 30423
November 1956	Beecham Choral	LP: Angel 35445
and March and	Society	CD: EMI CDM 764 7512/CDM 769 0392
April 1957	Hollweg	Excerpts
		45: HMV 7P 253/266/366
		45: HMV 7ER 5124/RES 4251
		45: HMV 7ER 5133/RES 4263
		LP: HMV ALP 1870-1871
		LP: Angel 3621
		CD: EMI CDM 652 0325/WHS 568 4102
		Morison replaced Hollweg in the March 1957 session, but is not heard in the published recording

Peer Gynt, Orchestral suite

London	LPO	78: Columbia LX 838-839
April and		78: Columbia (USA) X 180
July 1939		CD: Pearl GEMMCD 9094

The Last Spring

New York	Symphony	LP: Beecham Society WSA 505
January 1957	of the Air	

In Autumn, Overture

London   RPO
November 1955

LP: Columbia 33CX 1363
LP: EMI ENC 108/XLP 30028
LP: EMI SXLP 30530/EMX 2103
CD: EMI CDM 764 7512/CDM 769 0392

Old Norwegian Romance with Variations

London   RPO
November and
December 1955

LP: Columbia 33CX 1363
LP: EMI ENC 108/XLP 30028
CD: EMI CDM 764 7512

Symphonic Dances

London   RPO
December 1955

LP: Sirius 5023

Symphonic Dance No 2

London   Beecham SO
1916-1917

78: Columbia L 1132
LP: Beecham Society WHS 102-104

London   RPO
November 1959

LP: HMV ALP 1968/ASD 518/EMX 2103
LP: Angel 60000
LP: World Records T 744/ST 744
CD: EMI CDM 763 4122/CDM 769 0392

The discreet nightingale; The emigrant

London   Orchestra
December 1927   Labette

78: Columbia 9423

HANDEL

Messiah

London
June, July and
October 1927
	Orchestra
	BBC Choir
	Brunskill, Walker,
	Eisdell, Williams
		78: Columbia L 2018-2035/
		    9320-9337 auto
		78: Columbia (USA) M 271
		CD: Pearl GEMMCDS 9456
		Excerpts
		78: Columbia DX 630-637/L 2345
		78: Columbia (USA) 7189/7190/7191M/
		    50092/50093/50094D/71606D
		LP: EMI HLM 7053
		CD: VAI Audio VAIA 1045
		CD: Koch 3-7703-2
		Pearl issue incorrectly dated
		November and December 1927

London February- October 1947	RPO Luton and Special Choirs Suddaby, M.Thomas, Nash, Antony	78: Victor M 1194 and M 1195 LP: Victor LCT 6401 LP: HMV ALP 1077-1080 Excerpts 78: HMV DB 6879 78: Victor 12-0584 45: HMV 7RF 280 45: Victor ERBT 1/49-0819 LP: Victor LCT 1130 Introductory talk by Beecham (1 78 rpm side) not published
Walthamstow June, July and August 1959	RPO RPO Chorus Vyvyan, Sinclair, Vickers, Tozzi	LP: RCA RE 25002-4/SER 4501-4504 LP: RCA SER 5631-5634/AGL3-2444 LP: RCA LD 4069/LDS 4069/LSC 9892 CD: RCA/BMG 09026 612662 Excerpts LP: RCA LD 2447/LDS 2447/CRL2-0192 CD: RCA/BMG 74321 178852 Complete recording contains additional numbers, rarely performed at the time, added as an appendix

Solomon

London
November and
December 1955
and January
and May 1956
	RPO
	Beecham Choral
	Society
	Morison, Marshall,
	Young, Cameron
		LP: Columbia 33CX 1397-1398/
		    SAX 2499-2500
		LP: Angel 3546/6039
		LP: World Records T 82-83/ST 82-83
		LP: EMI SLS 5163
		Excerpts
		45: HMV 7P 324
		LP: HMV ALP 1912/ASD 480/EMX 2103
		LP: Angel 60134
		LP: World Records T 837/ST 837
		CD: CDC Enterprises (Canada)
		    PSCD 2001

Solomon, Entrance of the Queen of Sheba

London May 1933	LPO	78: Columbia LX 255 78: Columbia (USA) 9077M LP: HMV ALP 1870-1971/MRS 5185 LP: Angel 3621 LP: World Records SHB 100 CD: Dutton CDLX 7003 CD: VAI Audio VAIA 1045

Israel in Egypt: Excerpt (The Lord is a man of war)

Leeds October 1934	LPO Leeds Festival Chorus	78: Columbia LB 20 78: Columbia (USA) 17044D LP: World Records SHB 100 CD: VAI Audio VAIA 1045

Israel in Egypt: Excerpts (Moses and the children of Israel; But as for his people

Leeds October 1934	LPO Leeds Festival Chorus	78: Columbia LX 378 78: Columbia (USA) 68412D LP: World Records SHB 100 CD: VAI Audio VAIA 1045

Piano Concerto, arranged by Beecham

London January 1945	LPO Humby-Beecham	HMV unpublished
New York April 1945	ABC Orchestra Humby-Beecham	LP: Beecham Society WSA 520

Amaryllis, Suite arranged by Beecham

Seattle February 1960	Seattle SO	LP: Beecham Society WSA 517-518

Gavotte (Amaryllis Suite)

London April and May 1947	RPO	78: Victor 12-0583 LP: Beecham Society WHS 106
London October 1958	RPO	LP: HMV ALP 1912/ASD 480 LP: World Records T 837/ST 837

Sarabande (Amaryllis Suite)

London June 1949	RPO	HMV unpublished

Scherzo (Amaryllis Suite)

London February and May 1947	RPO	78: HMV DB 6821 78: Victor M 1264
London October 1958	RPO	LP: HMV ALP 1912/ASD 480 LP: World Records T 837/ST 837 CD: EMI CDM 763 3742

The Faithful Shepherd, Suite arranged by Beecham

London March and April 1940	LPO	78: Columbia LX 915-917 78: Columbia (USA) M 458 LP: Beecham Society WHS 107 CD: VAI Audio VAIA 1045
London April and September 1950	RPO	78: Columbia (USA) MM 990 LP: Columbia 33CX 1105 LP: Columbia (USA) ML 4374/Y 33285 LP: Philips CFL 1008 <u>Excerpts</u> 78: Columbia LX 1600 LP: Columbia (USA) ML 5226

The Gods go a' Begging, Suite arranged by Beecham

London July 1928	Orchestra of the Royal Philharmonic Society	Columbia unpublished
London October 1928 and February 1929	Orchestra of the Royal Philharmonic Society	Columbia unpublished
London January 1933	LPO	78: Columbia LX 285 78: Columbia (USA) M 194 LP: Beecham Society WHS 107 CD: VAI Audio VAIA 1045
London July and November 1934	LPO	78: Columbia LX 340 78: Columbia (USA) X 60/68881D LP: Beecham Society WHS 107 CD: VAI Audio VAIA 1045
London October 1937	LPO	78: Columbia LX 756 78: Columbia (USA) M 360 LP: Beecham Society WHS 107 CD: VAI Audio VAIA 1045
London November 1938	LPO	Columbia unpublished
London June 1949	RPO	HMV unpublished
London April 1958	RPO	LP: HMV ALP 1912/ASD 480 LP: World Records T 837/ST 837 CD: EMI CDM 763 3742 Excerpts 45: HMV 7P 324 Rehearsal extract CD: EMI CDM 764 4652

The various recorded versions of the suite vary considerably in length and content, the 78rpm versions of 1933, 1934 and 1937 obviously being intended as a complementary set

The Great Elopement, Suite arranged by Beecham

New York April 1945	ABC Orchestra	LP: Beecham Society WSA 520
London August, October and December 1945	LPO	78: HMV DB 6295-6297 78: Victor M 1093 78: HMV (Australia) ED 477-479
London June 1949	RPO	78: HMV DB 21055 Not published
London March and April 1951	RPO	78: HMV DB 21396-21397/ DB 9672-9673 auto 45: Victor WHMV 1030 LP: Victor LHMV 1030

The recorded versions of the suite vary in length and content

Love in Bath, Suite arranged by Beecham

London November and December 1956, March and April 1957 and August, November and December 1959	RPO Hollweg	LP: HMV ALP 1729/ASD 298 LP: Angel 35504/60039 LP: World Records T 632/ST 632 LP: EMI SXLP 30156/1C 047 01482 CD: EMI CDM 763 3742 Excerpts LP: EMI SLS 5073
Ascona October 1957	RPO	CD: Eremitage ERM 132

The Origin of Design, Suite arranged by Beecham

London December 1932	LPO	Columbia unpublished
London January 1933	LPO	78: Columbia LX 224 78: Columbia (USA) 68156D LP: World Records SHB 100 LP: London Philharmonic LPJ 501 CD: VAI Audio VAIA 1045
London July and November 1934	LPO	78: Columbia LX 340 78: Columbia (USA) X 60/68881D LP: Beecham Society WHS 107 CD: VAI Audio VAIA 1045

The recorded suites vary in content, the 1933 and 1934 versions obviously being intended as a complementary set

Suite, arranged by Beecham

London April 1925	LSO	Columbia unpublished

Suite from Concerto no 3, arranged by Beecham

London July 1929	Orchestra	78: Columbia L 2345 CD: VAI Audio VAIA 1045

ROYAL FESTIVAL HALL
(General Manager — T. E. BEAN)

Saturday, November 3rd, 1956

COMUS ART SOCIETY LTD.

presents

SIR THOMAS BEECHAM, BART.

ROYAL PHILHARMONIC ORCHESTRA
(Led by Arthur Leavins)

MISCHA ELMAN

PROGRAMME

PETER ILJITCH TCHAIKOVSKY (1840-1893)

Fantasy Overture, Romeo and Juliet
Violin Concerto in D, Op. 35

Allegro moderato
Canzonetta: Andante
Allegro vivacissimo

INTERVAL

Symphony No. 6 in B minor, Op. 74 (Pathetique)

Adagio—Allegro non troppo
Allegro con grazia
Allegro molto vivace
Adagio lamentoso

ROYAL FESTIVAL HALL
(General Manager: T. E. Bean, C.B.E.)

SUNDAY, 6th DECEMBER, 1959

THOMAS BEECHAM CONCERTS SOCIETY LTD.

present

Sir Thomas Beecham Bart., C.H.

conducting the

ROYAL PHILHARMONIC ORCHESTRA
(Leader: Raymond Cohen)

Symphony No. 35 in D (*Haffner*) - Mozart
Symphony No. 100 in G (*Military*) - Haydn
Symphony No. 4 in B Flat - Beethoven
Overture, "The Flying Dutchman" - Wagner

Royal Opera Covent Garden

SEASON OF LONDON PHILHARMONIC CONCERT SOCIETY, LTD.
Under the direction of
SIR THOMAS BEECHAM, BART.

OPENING NIGHT OF THE SEASON

Before the Opera
God Save the King

Monday, May 1st, 1939, at 8.15

SMETANA'S OPERA

DIE VERKAUFTE BRAUT
In German

Kruschina	MARKO ROTHMÜLLER
Kathinka	SABINE KALTER
Marie	HILDE KONETZNI
Micha	ARNOLD MATTERS
Agnes	MARY JARRED
Wenzel	HEINRICH TESSMER
Hans	RICHARD TAUBER
Kezal	FRITZ KRENN
Springer	GERHARDT HINZE
Esmeralda	STELLA ANDREVA
Muff	GRAHAME CLIFFORD

Conductor . SIR THOMAS BEECHAM, Bart.

Producer - CHARLES MOOR
Dances arranged by ANTONY TUDOR

HAYDN

Symphony No 40

London   RPO   78: HMV DB 6823-6824
April 1948   45: HMV 7ER 5093
                               LP: World Records SHB 100

Symphony No 93

London   LPO   78: Columbia LX 771-773
December 1936   78: Columbia (USA) M 336
                               LP: EMI RLS 734
                               CD: Pearl GEMMCD 9064
                               CD: Dutton 2CDAX 2003

London   RPO   78: Columbia LX 1361-1363
April and   LP: Columbia (USA) MM 991
June 1950   LP: Columbia 33CX 1038
                               LP: Columbia (USA) ML 4374/Y 33285
                               LP: Philips NBL 5037/GL 5632
                               2nd movement
                               LP: Columbia (USA) ML 5227

Paris   RPO   LP: HMV ALP 1624/SLS 846
October 1957   LP: Capitol GCR 7127/SGCR 7127
                               LP: Angel 36242
                               LP: EMI SXLP 30285/1C 053 01425
                               LP: EMI 1C 137 50238-50243
                               CD: EMI CMS 764 3892

Symphony No 94 "Surprise"

London   RPO   78: Columbia LX 1499-1501
July and   LP: Columbia 33CX 1104
October 1951   LP: Columbia (USA) ML 4453
                               LP: Philips NBL 5037/GL 5632

Paris   RPO   LP: HMV ALP 1624/SLS 846/HQM 1148
October 1957   LP: Capitol GCR 7127/SGCR 7127
and London   LP: Angel 36242
April 1958   LP: EMI SXLP 30285/1C 053 01425
                               LP: EMI 1C 137 50238-50243
                               CD: EMI CDCFP 4559/CMS 764 3892

Symphony No 95

Paris	RPO	LP: HMV ALP 1625/SLS 846
October 1957		LP: Capitol GCR 7127/SGCR 7127
		LP: Angel 36243
		LP: EMI 1C 137 50238-50243
		CD: EMI CMS 764 3892

Symphony No 96 "Miracle"

Paris	RPO	LP: HMV ALP 1625/SLS 846/HQM 1148
October and		LP: Capitol GCR 7127/SGCR 7127
November 1957		LP: Angel 36243
		LP: EMI 1C 137 50238-50243
		CD: EMI CDCFP 4559/CMS 764 3892

Symphony No 97

London	LPO	78: HMV DB 9001-9003
December 1944		78: Victor M 1059
		78: HMV (Australia) ED 533-535

London	RPO	LP: HMV ALP 1626/SLS 846
March 1957		LP: Capitol GCR 7127/SGCR 7127
and April		LP: Angel 36244
1958		LP: EMI 1C 137 50238-50243
		CD: EMI CMS 764 3892

Symphony No 98

Paris	RPO	LP: HMV ALP 1626/SLS 846
October and		LP: Capitol GCR 7127/SGCR 7127
November 1957		LP: Angel 36244
and London		LP: EMI 1C 137 50238-50243
April 1958		CD: EMI CMS 764 3892

Symphony No 99

London	LPO	78: Columbia LX 505-507
October 1935		78: Columbia (USA) M 264
and February		LP: EMI RLS 734
1936		CD: Pearl GEMMCD 9064
		CD: Dutton 2CDAX 2003

Paris	RPO	LP: HMV ALP 1693/ASD 339/SLS 846
May 1958		LP: Capitol GCR 7198/SGCR 7198
and London		LP: Angel 36254
December 1958		LP: EMI 1C 137 50238-50243
and April 1959		CD: EMI CMS 764 0662

Symphony No 100 "Military"

Paris	RPO	LP: HMV ALP 1693/ASD 339/SLS 846
May 1958		LP: Capitol GCR 7198/SGCR 7198
and London		LP: Angel 35254
November 1958		LP: EMI 1C 137 50238-50243
and May 1959		CD: EMI CDCFP 4530/CMS 764 0662

Last movement
LP: HMV ALP 1870-1871
LP: Angel 3621
Rehearsal extracts
LP: HMV ALP 1874/SLS 846
LP: World Records SH 147
CD: EMI CDM 764 4652

Symphony No 101 "Clock"

Paris	RPO	LP: HMV ALP 1694/ASD 340/SLS 846
May 1958		LP: Capitol GCR 7198/SGCR 7198
and London		LP: Angel 36255
November and		LP: EMI SXLP 30265/1C 037 03178
December 1958		LP: EMI 1C 137 50238-50243
and May 1959		CD: EMI CMS 764 0662

Rehearsal extracts
LP: HMV ALP 1874/SLS 846
LP: World Records SH 147
CD: EMI CDM 764 4652

Symphony No 102

London	RPO	78: HMV DB 21042-21044/
June 1949		DB 9449-9451 auto

London	RPO	HMV unpublished
December 1955,		
May 1956 and		
March 1957		

Paris	RPO	LP: HMV ALP 1694/ASD 340/SLS 846
May 1958		LP: Capitol GCR 7198/SGCR 7198
and London		LP: Angel 36255
December 1958		LP: EMI 1C 137 50238-50243
		CD: EMI CDCFP 4559/CMS 764 0662

Symphony No 103 "Drum Roll"

London	RPO	LP: Columbia 33CX 1104
January and		LP: Columbia (USA) ML 4453
February 1951		LP: Philips SBR 6253

Paris   RPO   LP: HMV ALP 1695/ASD 341/SLS 846
May 1958   LP: Capitol GCR 7198/SGCR 7198
and London   LP: Angel 36256
December 1958   LP: EMI SXLP 30257/1C 037 03068
and May 1959   LP: EMI 1C 137 50238-50243
                                CD: EMI CDCFP 4530/CMS 764 0662

Symphony No 104 "London"

London   LPO   78: Columbia LX 856-858
January,   78: Columbia (USA) M 409
February and   LP: Columbia (USA) ML 4771
July 1939   CD: Pearl GEMMCD 9064
                                CD: Dutton 2CDAX 2003

Paris   RPO   LP: HMV ALP 1695/ASD 341/SLS 846
May 1958   LP: Capitol GCR 7198/SGCR 7198
and London   LP: Angel 36256
December 1958   LP: EMI SXLP 30257/1C 037 03178
                                LP: EMI 1C 137 50238-50243
                                CD: EMI CMS 764 0662
                                Rehearsal extracts
                                LP: HMV ALP 1874/SLS 846
                                LP: World Records SH 147
                                CD: EMI CDM 764 4652

Die Jahreszeiten

London   RPO   LP: HMV ALP 1606-1608/ASD 282-284
November 1956,   Beecham Choral LP: Capitol GCR 7184/SGCR 7184
March 1957   Society   LP: World Records T 786-788/
and April   Morison, Young,   ST 786-788
1958   Langdon   LP: EMI SLS 5158
                 Sung in English

LALO

Symphony in G

Paris   Orchestre National   LP: HMV ALP 1761
June 1958   LP: Capitol G 7237

Paris   Orchestre National   LP: HMV ASD 388/SXDW 3022
December 1959   LP: Capitol SG 7237
                                      LP: EMI 2C 053 00175
                                      CD: EMI CDM 763 3962

When the HMV editions of this symphony were first published, no indication was given that the mono and stereo versions were of two different performances

LISZT

A Faust Symphony

London
April, May and
October 1958
	RPO
	Beecham Choral
	Society
	Young
		LP: HMV ALP 1737-1738/ASD 317-318
		LP: Capitol GBR 7197/SGBR 7197
		LP: Angel 6017
		LP: World Records CM 78-79/
		     SCM 78-79
		LP: EMI 1C 187 01784-01785/
		     2C 181 01459-01460
		LP: EMI SXDW 3022
		CD: EMI CDC 749 2602/CDM 763 3712
		Rehearsal extract
		CD: EMI CDM 764 4652

Orpheus

London September and October 1947	RPO	78: HMV DB 6644-6645 78: Victor M 1295
London April 1958	RPO	LP: HMV ALP 1737-1738/ASD 317-318 LP: Capitol GBR 7197-SGBR 7197 LP: Angel 6017 LP: World Records CM 78-79/ SCM 78-79 LP: EMI 1C 181 01459-01460 CD: EMI CDM 763 2992 Rehearsal extract CD: EMI CDM 764 4652

Psalm XIII

London December 1955	RPO Beecham Choral Society Midgely	LP: Columbia 33CX 1429 LP: Angel 35400 LP: World Records T 909/ST 909 CD: EMI CDM 763 2992

Die Loreley

London November 1954	RPO Raisbeck	LP: Beecham Society WSA 501

LULLY

Les amants magnifiques, Minuet

London ca. 1918	Beecham SO	78: Columbia L 1227 LP: Beecham Society WHS 102-104 CD: Symposium 1096-1097

MASCAGNI

Cavalleria rusticana, Intermezzo

London ca. 1912	Beecham SO	78: Odeon 0772 LP: Beecham Society WHS 102-104 CD: Symposium 1096-1097

Cavalleria rusticana: Excerpt (Voi lo sapete)

London July 1928	Orchestra Turner	78: Columbia L 2118 78: Columbia (USA) 50109D LP: Columbia COLC 114 LP: HMV ALP 1870-1871/HQM 1209 LP: Angel 3621 CD: EMI CDH 769 7912

MASSENET

Manon

New York January 1943	Metropolitan Opera Orchestra & Chorus Sayao, Kullmann, Brownlee, Moscona	LP: Opera Archives OPA 1005 LP: Magnificent Editions ME 103 CD: Walhall WHL 11

Manon, Minuet

London 1915-1916	Beecham SO	78: Columbia L 1020 LP: Beecham Society WHS 102-104 CD: Symposium 1096-1097

Le dernier sommeil de la vierge

London February and April 1947	RPO	45: HMV DB 6645 78: Victor 12-0688 LP: World Records SHB 100 CD: EMI CDM 763 4012
Walthamstow December 1953	RPO	LP: Philips SBR 6215/GL 5713 LP: Columbia (USA) ML 5321/Y 33288 LP: CBS 61655

Cendrillon, Valse

Paris October 1957	RPO	LP: HMV ALP 1656/HQM 1162 CD: EMI CDM 763 4012

Thaïs, Méditation

London March 1939	LPO	LP: Beecham Society WSA 526 CD: Symposium 1096-1097 <u>Recorded for a Radio Luxemburg</u> <u>broadcast</u>

MEHUL

Symphony No 2

London December 1956	RPO	LP: Beecham Society WSA 521-522

Les deux aveugles de Tolède, Overture

London February, March, July and November 1947	RPO	78: HMV DB 21084 78: Victor M 1264

La chasse du jeune Henri, Overture

Walthamstow December 1953	RPO	LP: Philips ABR 4056 LP: Columbia (USA) ML 5029

Timoléon, Overture

Walthamstow December 1953	RPO	LP: Philips ABR 4056/SBR 6263 LP: Columbia (USA) ML 5029

Le tresor supposé, Overture

Walthamstow December 1953	RPO	LP: Philips ABR 4056 LP: Columbia (USA) ML 5029

MENDELSSOHN

Symphony No 4 "Italian"

New York June 1942	NYPO	78: Columbia (USA) M 538
London December 1951 and May and June 1952	RPO	LP: Columbia 33C 1006 LP: Columbia (USA) ML 4681 LP: Philips CFL 1008/EFL 2507 LP: Philips EFR 2021/GL 5745 CD: EMI CDM 763 3982

Symphony No 5 "Reformation"

London August, October and December 1945	LPO	78: HMV DB 6316-6319 78: Victor M 1104

Scherzo (Symphony No 1)

London September and December 1947	RPO	78: HMV DB 6653/DB 9711 78: Victor 12-0688

Violin Concerto

London September 1933	LPO Szigeti	78: Columbia LX 262-265 78: Columbia (USA) M 190 LP: Columbia (USA) ML 2217/ M6X 31513 LP: EMI HLM 7016 CD: EMI CDH 764 5622 CD: Pearl GEMMCD 9377 CD: Musica Memoria CD 30272 Also issued on LP by Franklin Mint

London
June 1949
	RPO
	Heifetz
		78: HMV DB 6956-6958/
		    DB 9413-9415 auto
		78: Victor DM 1356
		45: Victor WDM 1356
		LP: Victor LM 18/LM 9016
		LP: Angel 60162
		LP: EMI 1C 053 01365
		LP: World Records SHB 100
		CD: EMI CDH 565 1912
		CD: RCA/BMG 09026 617492/
		    09026 617782

Songs without words No 34 (The Bees' Wedding)

London ca. 1912	Beecham SO	78: Odeon 0772 LP: Beecham Society WHS 102-104 CD: Symposium 1096-1097

Sings without words Nos 44 and 45, arranged by Del Mar

London   RPO   HMV unpublished
November 1947

The Hebrides, Overture

London   LPO   78: Columbia LX 747
February and   78: Columbia (USA) M 552
October 1938   CD: Dutton CDLX 7001

London   RPO   45: Philips CFE 15004/EFF 513
February and   LP: Philips CFL 1021/EFR 2029/GL 5692
June 1950

A Midsummer Night's Dream, Overture

London   RPO   78: HMV DB 6820-6821
November and
December 1946

London   RPO   LP: HMV ALP 1846/ASD 420
November 1958   LP: Capitol G 7251/SG 7251
                                    LP: World Records T 558/ST 558
                                    LP: EMI SXLP 30158/CFP 40358
                                    LP: Pickwick/Quintessence (USA)
                                        PC 4035/PMC 7004
                                    CD: EMI CDM 763 4072

A Midsummer Night's Dream, Scherzo

London   Beecham SO   78: Columbia L 1075
May 1916   LP: Beecham Society WHS 102-104

London   LSO   Columbia unpublished
March 1925

London   LSO   78: Columbia L 1075R/L 1812
March 1926   78: Columbia (USA) 7139M
                                    LP: Beecham Society WHS 101

London   LPO   LP: Beecham Society WSA 526
March 1939   CD: Symposium 1096-1097
                                    CD: Dutton CDLX 7003
                                    Recording for a Radio Luxemburg
                                    broadcast

A Midsummer Night's Dream, Nocturne and Wedding March

London   LPO   78: Columbia LX 574
October 1936   78: Columbia (USA) 68888D
                                    CD: Pearl GEMMCD 9084
                                    CD: Dutton CDLX 7003

Ruy Blas, Overture

London November 1939	LPO	78: Columbia LX 879 78: Columbia (USA) 70352D CD: Pearl GEMMCD 9084 CD: Dutton CDLX 7001
London May 1949	RPO	HMV unpublished
London March 1951	RPO	78: Columbia LX 1584 45: Columbia SEL 1501 45: Philips CFE 15004/EFF 534 LP: Philips CFL 1021/GL 5692

Die schöne Melusine, Overture

London September and November 1947	RPO	78: HMV DB 6652-6653/ DB 9711-9712 auto
London November 1958	RPO	LP: HMV ALP 1846/ASD 420/EMX 2103 LP: Capitol G 7251/SG 7251 LP: Pickwick/Quintessence (USA) PC 4035/PMC 7004 CD: EMI CDM 763 4072
London November 1959	RPO	LP: Beecham Society WSA 508 CD: Music and Arts CD 281

MEYERBEER

Dinorah: Excerpt (Ombre legère)

Detroit June 1942	Detroit SO Pons	LP: Beecham Society WSA 526

MISSA

Muguette, Entr'acte

London ca. 1912	Beecham SO	78: Odeon 0795 LP: Beecham Society WHS 102-104 LP: World Records SHB 100 CD: Symposium 1096-1097

MOZART

Symphony No 27

London November and December 1947 and January 1948	RPO	78: Victor M 1264 LP: Beecham Society WHS 105

Symphony No 29

London November 1937	LPO	78: Columbia LX 687-689 78: Columbia (USA) M 333 LP: World Records SHB 20 LP: Turnabout THS 65022-65026 CD: EMI CHS 763 6982

Symphony No 31 "Paris"

London October and November 1938	LPO	78: Columbia LX 754-756 78: Columbia (USA) M 360 LP: World Records SHB 20 LP: Turnabout THS 65022-65026 CD: EMI CHS 763 6982
London March and May 1951	RPO	LP: Columbia 33CX 1038 LP: Columbia (USA) ML 4474 LP: Philips SBL 5226/GBR 6525 LP: Philips EFL 2503/GL 5742
Geneva March 1958	Suisse Romande Orchestra	CD: Cascavelle VEL 2002

Symphony No 34

| London
July 1928 | Orchestra | Columbia unpublished |

| London
October 1928 | Orchestra of the
Royal Philharmonic
Society | 78: Columbia L 2220-2222
78: Columbia (USA) M 123
LP: Beecham Society WHS 105 |

| London
March and
April 1940 | LPO | 78: Columbia LX 920-922
78: Columbia (USA) M 548
LP: Columbia (USA) ML 4781
LP: Turnabout THS 65022 -65026
LP: World Records SHB 20
CD: EMI CHS 763 6982 |

Symphony No 35 "Haffner"

| London
November 1938
and July 1939 | LPO | 78: Columbia LX 851-853
78: Columbia (USA) M 309
LP: Columbia (USA) ML 4770
LP: Turnabout THS 65022-65026
LP: World Records SHB 20
CD: EMI CHS 763 6982 |

| Walthamstow
December 1953 | RPO | Philips unpublished |

| Walthamstow
April and
May 1954 | RPO | LP: Philips A01216L/GBR 6265
LP: Philips EFL 2503/GL 5742
LP: Columbia (USA) M 5001/3236 0009 |

| Geneva
March 1958 | Suisse Romande
Orchestra | CD: Cascavelle VEL 2002 |

| London
December 1958 | RPO | CD: Music and Arts CD 631 |

Symphony No 36 "Linz"

| London
November and
December 1938 | LPO | 78: Columbia LX 797-800
78: Columbia (USA) M 387
LP: Columbia (USA) ML 4770
LP: Turnabout THS 65022 -65026
LP: World Records SHB 20
CD: EMI CHS 763 6982 |

| Walthamstow
November and
December 1955 | RPO | LP: Philips ABL 3067
LP: Columbia (USA) ML 5001/3236 0009
LP: CBS 54001 |

Symphony No 38 "Prague"

London March 1940	LPO	78: Columbia LX 911-913 78: Columbia (USA) M 509 LP: Turnabout THS 65022-65026 LP: World Records SHB 20 CD: EMI CHS 763 6982
London April 1950	RPO	78: Columbia LX 1517-1519 78: Columbia (USA) MM 934 LP: Columbia 33CX 1105 LP: Columbia (USA) ML 4313/ 3216 0023/3236 0009 LP: Philips SBL 5226/EFL 2503/GL 5742

Symphony No 39

Ludwigshafen November 1936	LPO	LP: World Records SHB 100 LP: London Philharmonic LPJ 50 <u>Experimental tape recording of</u> <u>2nd and 3rd movements; the above</u> <u>issues contain only 3rd movement</u> <u>but both selections were published</u> <u>on Chandos cassette DBTD 2007</u>
London March and April 1940	LPO	78: Columbia LX 927-929 78: Columbia (USA) M 456 LP: Columbia (USA) ML 4674 LP: Turnabout THS 65022-65026 LP: World Records SHB 20 CD: EMI CHS 763 6982
Walthamstow November and December 1955	RPO	LP: Philips ABL 3094/EFL 2503/GL 5742 LP: Columbia (USA) ML 5194/3236 0009 LP: CBS 54048
Geneva March 1958	Suisse Romande Orchestra	CD: Cascavelle VEL 2002

Symphony No 40

London February and September 1937	LPO	78: Columbia LX 656-658 78: Columbia (USA) M 316 LP: Columbia (USA) ML 4674 LP: Turnabout THS 65022-65026 LP: World Records SHB 20 CD: EMI CHS 763 6982
Walthamstow April 1954	RPO	LP: Philips ABL 3094/EFL 2518/GL 5747 LP: Columbia (USA) ML 5194/3236 0009 LP: CBS 54048

Symphony No 41 "Jupiter"

London June 1931	Orchestra	Columbia unpublished
London January 1934	LPO	78: Columbia LX 282-285 78: Columbia (USA) M 194 LP: World Records SHB 20 LP: Turnabout THS 65022-65026 CD: EMI CHS 763 6982 <u>Portions of this work were recorded</u> <u>stereophonically as a technical</u> <u>test; issued on Symposium 78</u> <u>1027-1028 and World Records LP</u> <u>SHB 100</u>
London February 1950	RPO	78: Columbia LX 1337-1340 78: Columbia (USA) MM 933 LP: Columbia (USA) ML 4313 LP: Philips GBR 6506/EFL 2518 LP: Philips GL 5747 LP: Columbia (USA) 3216 0023/3236 0009
London March 1957	RPO	LP: HMV ALP 1536/HQM 1117 LP: Angel 35459 CD: EMI CDM 769 8112

Piano Concerto No 12

London January and March 1940	LPO Kentner	78: Columbia LX 894-896 78: Columbia (USA) M 544 LP: World Records SHB 20 CD: EMI CDH 763 8202 CD: Pearl GEMMCD 9081

Piano Concerto No 16

London June 1949	RPO Humby-Beecham	HMV unpublished <u>Recording incomplete</u>

Bassoon Concerto

London December 1958	RPO Brooke	LP: HMV ALP 1768/ASD 344/SXLP 30246 LP: Capitol G 7201/SG 7201 LP: EMI 1C 053 00176/1C 037 00176 CD: EMI CDM 763 4082

Clarinet Concerto

Paris	RPO	LP: HMV ALP 1768/ASD 344/SXLP 30246
May 1958 and	Brymer	LP: Capitol G 7201/SG 7201
London		LP: Angel 60193
May 1958 and		LP: EMI 1C 037 00176/2C 061 00176
May 1959		CD: EMI CDC 747 8642/CDM 763 4082

Flute and Harp Concerto

London	RPO	78: HMV DB 6485-6487/
July 1947	Laskine, Le Roy	DB 9159-9161 auto
		78: Victor M 1292
		LP: World Records SH 316
		CD: EMI CDH 763 8202

Violin Concerto No 3

London	RPO	78: HMV DB 21177-21179/
May 1949	de Vito	DB 9570-9572 auto
		CD: EMI CDM 763 4082
		Issued on LP by Toshiba

Violin Concerto No 4

London	LPO	78: Columbia LX 386-388
October 1934	Szigeti	78: Columbia (USA) M 224
		LP: Columbia (USA) ML 4533/M6X 31513
		LP: EMI 1C 053 01364M
		CD: EMI CDH 764 5622
		CD: Pearl GEMMCD 9377
London	RPO	78: HMV DB 6678-6680/
November 1947	Heifetz	DB 9336-9338 auto
		78: Victor M 1267
		LP: Victor LCT 1051
		45: Victor WDM 1267
		LP: Angel 60162
		LP: EMI 1C 053 01365M
		CD: EMI CDH 763 8202
		CD: RCA/BMG 09026 617492/
		90926 617782

German Dance No 3 "Sleigh Ride" (3 German Dances K605)

London	RPO	78: Columbia LX 1587
May 1951		45: Columbia SCB 106
		45: Philips CFE 15005/EFF 518
		LP: Philips CFL 1021/GL 5692

Divertimento in D K131

London November 1947 and January 1948	RPO	78: HMV DB 6649-6651/ DB 9354-9356 auto 45: Victor WHMV 1030 LP: Victor LHMV 1030 LP: World Records SH 316 Omits first movement but includes Minuet from Divertimento K247
London December 1955 and May 1956	RPO	LP: HMV ALP 1536/HQM 1117 LP: Angel 35459 Minuet only CD: EMI CDM 763 4122

Adagio (Divertimento in D K131)

London April 1925	LSO	Columbia unpublished
London July 1939	LPO	78: Columbia LX 853 Not published

Minuet (Divertimento in D K131)

London 1916-1917	Beecham SO	78: Columbia L 1132 LP: Beecham Society WHS 102-104
London April 1925	LSO	Columbia unpublished

Minuet II (Divertimento in D K131)

London February 1929	Orchestra of Royal Philharmonic Society	78: Columbia 68646 78: Columbia (USA) X 42 LP: Beecham Society WHS 105

Divertimento in B flat K 247, Minuet, Theme and Variations

London April 1925	LSO	Columbia unpublished
London July 1947	RPO	HMV unpublished

Serenade No 13 "Eine kleine Nachtmusik"

London January 1945	LPO	78: HMV DB 6204-6205 78: Victor M 1163 78: HMV (Australia) ED 419-420 Rondo only 78: Victor M 1014/M 542

March in D K249

London February 1950	RPO	78: Columbia LX 1340/LX 1587 78: Columbia (USA) M 933 45: Columbia SCB 106 45: Philips CFE 15005/EFF 518 LP: Philips CFL 1021/CFL 1042 LP: Philips GL 5672
London March 1957	RPO	LP: HMV ALP 1533/ASD 259/SXLP 30246 LP: Angel 35506 LP: EMI 1C 053 52619 CD: EMI CDC 747 8642/CDM 763 4122 CD: EMI CDE 568 1252

Requiem

Walthamstow December 1954 and London May 1956	RPO BBC Chorus Morison, Sinclair, Young, Nowakowski	LP: Philips CFL 1000 LP: Columbia (USA) ML 5160 CD: Theorema TH 121.151

Mass in C minor: Excerpt (Kyrie)

Leeds October 1934	LPO Leeds Festival Chorus Labette	78: Columbia LB 19 78: Columbia (USA) 17050D CD: Pearl GEMMCD 9081

Mass in C minor: Excerpt (Qui tollis)

Leeds October 1934	LPO Leeds Festival Chorus	78: Columbia LX 370 78: Columbia (USA) X 54 CD: Pearl GEMMCD 9081

Mass in C minor: Excerpt (Sanctus)

Leeds October 1934	LPO Leeds Festival Chorus	Columbia unpublished

Ein deutsches Kriegslied K539

London July 1947	RPO	HMV unpublished

Concert arias: Vorrei spiegarvi o Dio!; Voi avete un cor fedele

Montreal March 1956	Montreal SO Stader	LP: Beecham Society WSA 521-522 Also unpublished video recording

La Clemenza di Tito. Overture

London December 1945	LPO	78: Victor M 1104

La Clemenza di Tito: Excerpts (Se al volto; S'altro che lagrime)

London June 1948	RPO Bond, Giancola, Anthony	LP: Ed Smith EJS 385 LP: Beecham Society WSA 521

Così fan tutte, Overture

London December 1945	LPO	HMV unpublished

Don Giovanni

London June 1939	LPO Covent Garden Chorus Rethberg, H.Konetzni, Tauber, Pinza, Lazzari, Biracci, Walker	Unpublished recording

Don Giovanni, Overture

London November 1939 and January 1940	LPO	78: Columbia LX 893 78: Columbia (USA) M 552/70365D LP: World Records SHB 20 LP: Turnabout THS 65022-65026 CD: Dutton CDLX 7009 CD: Pearl GEMMCD 9081

Die Entführung aus dem Serail

London May 1956	RPO Beecham Choral Society Marshall, Hollweg, Simoneau, Unger, Frick, Laubenthal	LP: Columbia 33CX 1402-1403/ SAX 2427-2429 LP: Angel 3555 LP: EMI HQM 1050-1051/HQS 1050-1051 LP: EMI SLS 5153 CD: EMI CHS 763 7152 Excerpts LP: HMV ALP 1912/ASD 480/SEOM 2 LP: World Records T 837/ST 837 LP: EMI 1C 147 30636-30637M Rehearsal extracts LP: HMV ALP 1874 LP: World Records SH 147 CD: EMI CDM 764 4652

Die Entführung aus dem Serail, Overture

London October 1945	LPO	78: HMV DB 6351 78: Victor 11-9191 78: HMV (Australia) ED 442

Le Nozze di Figaro, Overture

London ca. 1912	Beecham SO	78: Odeon X 84 LP: Beecham Society WHS 102-104 CD: Symposium 1096-1097
London 1916-1917	Beecham SO	78: Columbia L 1115 78: Columia (USA) 65018D/ 68016D/7093M
London March 1925	LSO	Columbia unpublished
London March 1926	LSO	Columbia unpublished
London March 1937	LPO	78: Columbia LX 639 78: Columbia (USA) X 85/71606D LP: HMV ALP 1870-1871 LP: Angel 3621 LP: World Records SHB 20 LP: Turnabout THS 65022-65026 CD: Dutton CDLX 7009 CD: Pearl GEMMCD 9094
London September 1937	LPO	Columbia unpublished

Le Nozze di Figaro, Fandango

London ca. 1918	Beecham SO	78: Columbia L 1227 LP: Beecham Society WHS 102-104 CD: Symposium 1096-1097

Der Schauspieldirektor, Overture

London   LPO   HMV unpublished
December 1945

Thamos König in Aegypten, Entr'acte No 2

London   RPO   LP: Ed Smith EJS 385
July 1948   LP: Beecham Society WSA 521

London   RPO   LP: HMV ALP 1682/ASD 432
March and   LP: Angel 35865
April 1957   LP: World Records T 558/ST 558
                                                LP: EMI SXLP 30246/1C 053 52619
                                                CD: EMI CDC 747 8642/CDM 763 4122

Thamos König in Aegypten: Excerpts (Schon weichet dir, Sonne; Ihr Kinder des Staubes)

London   RPO   LP: Ed Smith EJS 385
July 1948   BBC Theatre Chorus   LP: Beecham Society WSA 521
                   Rico

Die Zauberflöte

Berlin November 1937 and February and March 1938	BPO Favres Solisten Vereinigung Lemnitz, Berger, Beilke, Rosvaenge, Hüsch, Strienz, Grossmann	78: HMV DB 3465-3483/ DB 8475-8493 auto 78: Victor M 541 and M 542 78: Electrola C 6371-6389 45: Victor WCT 56 LP: Victor LCT 6101 LP: HMV ALP 1273-1275/143 4653 LP: World Records SH 158-160 LP: Turnabout THS 65078-65080 CD: EMI CHS 761 0342 CD: Nimbus 7827-7828 CD: Pearl GEMMCD 9371 CD: Calig 30845-30846 CD: Melodram CDM 27056 Excerpts 78: HMV DB 4637/4645/4656/4682 LP: HMV ALP 1870-1871 LP: Angel 3621 LP: World Records SHB 47/SHB 100 LP: EMI 1C 047 28556 LP: EMI 1C 147 28989-28990M LP: EMI 1C 187 29275-29276M LP: Preiser LV 101/LV 190 CD: Preiser 89092/89025 CD: Dutton CDLX 7009 Zum Leiden bin ich auserkoren conducted by Seidler-Winkler
Buenos Aires September 1958	Teatro Colon Orchestra & Chorus Lorengar, Streich, Chelavine, Dermota, Berry, Van Mill, Schöffler	LP: Melodram MEL 462

Die Zauberflöte, Overture

London ca. 1915	Beecham SO	78: Columbia L 1001/65019D LP: Beecham Society WHS 102-104 LP: HMV ALP 1870-1871 LP: Angel 3621
London March 1925	LSO	Columbia unpublished
London March 1926	LSO	78: Columbia L 1001R 78: Columbia (USA) 7123M LP: Beecham Society WHS 101
London June 1949	RPO	78: HMV DB 21023 78: Victor 149-0037

MUSSORGSKY

Dance of the Persian Slaves (Khovanschina)

London February and March 1947	RPO	78: HMV DB 6450 78: Victor 12-0239

NICOLAI

Die lustigen Weiber von Windsor, Overture

London October 1936	LPO	78: Columbia LX 596 78: Columbia (USA) M 552/68938D CD: Dutton CDLX 7001
New York December 1949	Columbia SO	78: Columbia (USA) 73052D 45: Philips CFE 15001/EFF 515 LP: Columbia (USA) ML 2134/ML 5171 LP: Columbia (USA) 3216 0117 LP: Philips CFL 1021/GL 5692

OFFENBACH

Les contes d'Hoffmann

New York February 1944	Metropolitan Opera Orchestra & Chorus Munsel, Novotna, Djanel, Glatz, Jobin, Pinza, Harrell	LP: Discocorp IGI 324-326 LP: Melodram MEL 312 CD: Myto MCD 94194
Shepperton August 1950	RPO Chorus Bond, Grandi, Ayars, Sinclair, Rounseville, Dickie, Brannigan, Clifford, Dargavel <u>Sung in English</u>	<u>Film soundtrack</u> 78: Decca AX 497-511 LP: Decca LXT 2582-2584 LP: London (USA) LLPA 4 LP: Decca ACL 177-178 LP: Turnabout THS 65012-65014 VHS Video: Home (USA) TAL 03 Laserdisc: Home (USA) TAL 060 Laserdisc: Criterion (USA) 1300

Les contes d'Hoffmann, Orchestral suite

London June 1936	LPO	78: Columbia LX 530 78: Columbia (USA) 68692D LP: World Records SHB 55 CD: Pearl GEMMCD 9065 CD: Dutton CDLX 7003
London January 1951	RPO	Columbia unpublished

Les contes d'Hoffmann: Excerpt (Les oiseaux dans la charmille)

London	Orchestra	G & T 03193
July 1910	Chorus	LP: Beecham Society WHS 102-104
	Hatchard	LP: World Records SHB 100
	Sung in English	

Les contes d'Hoffmann: Excerpt (Il était une fois à la cour D'Eisenach)

London	Orchestra	G & T 02256/D 106
July 1910	Hyde	LP: Beecham Society WHS 102-104
	Sung in English	

Les contes d'Hoffmann: Excerpt (Elle a fui, la tourterelle)

London	Orchestra	G & T 03194
July 1910	E.Evans	Not published
	Sung in English	

Les contes d'Hoffmann: Excerpt (Cher enfant)

London	Orchestra	G & T 04068
July 1910	E.Evans, Hatchard,	Not published
	Ranalow	
	Sung in English	

Les contes d'Hoffmann: Excerpt (Drig! drig! drig!)

London	Orchestra	G & T 04505
July 1910	Chorus	LP: Beecham Society WHS 102-104
	Sung in English	

Les contes d'Hoffmann: Excerpt (C'est une chanson d'amour qui s'envole)

London	Orchestra	G & T 02257/D 106
July 1910	Chorus	LP: Beecham Society WHS 102-104
	Hyde	
	Sung in English	

PAISIELLO

Nina, Overture

London February and July 1947	RPO	78: HMV DB 6499 78: Victor M 1264

PONCHIELLI

La Gioconda: Excerpt (Suicidio!)

London July 1928	Orchestra Turner	78: Columbia 50100D LP: EMI HQM 1209

La Gioconda, Dance of the hours

New York December 1949	Columbia SO	78: Columbia (USA) 73052D 45: Philips CFE 15001/EFF 515 LP: Columbia (USA) ML 2134/ML 5171 LP: Columbia (USA) 3216 0117 LP: Philips CFL 1021/GL 5692 ML 5171 incorrectly labelled RPO

PROKOFIEV

Violin Concerto No 1

London August 1935	LPO Szigeti	78: Columbia LX 433-435 78: Columbia (USA) M 244 LP: Columbia (USA) ML 4533/M6X 31513 LP: EMI HLM 7016 CD: EMI CDH 764 4562 CD: Pearl GEMMCD 9377

PUCCINI

La Bohème

New York March and April 1956	RCA Victor Orchestra New York City Opera Chorus De los Angeles, Amara, Björling, Merrill, Reardon, Tozzi, Corena	LP: HMV ALP 1409-1410 LP: Victor LM 6042 LP: Angel 6000/6099 LP: EMI SLS 896 CD: EMI CDS 747 2358 Excerpts 45: HMV 7ER 5179/5186/5190 LP: Victor LM 2045/LM 2574 LP: Victor LM 6001/RB 16268

La Bohème, Act Four

London November and December 1935	LPO Labette, Andreva, Nash, Brownlee, Easton	78: Columbia LX 523-526 78: Columbia (USA) M 274 LP: EMI HQM 1234 CD: Dutton CDLX 7012 Excerpt CD: Pearl GEMMCDS 9926 Labette named as "Perli" on original labels

La Bohème: Excerpt (Donde lieta uscì)

London March and April 1936	LPO Labette	78: Columbia LX 526 78: Columbia (USA) M 274 LP: EMI HQM 1234 CD: Pearl GEMMCD 9473 Labette named as "Perli" on original labels

Manon Lescaut, Intermezzo

London December 1945	BBCSO	HMV unpublished

Tosca: Excerpt (Vissi d'arte)

London July 1928	Orchestra Turner	78: Columbia L 2118/50100D LP: Columbia COLC 114 LP: EMI HQM 1209

RESPIGHI

Rossiniana

London October 1934 and March and April 1935	LPO	78: Columbia LX 391-392 78: Columbia (USA) X 56 LP: World Records SH 313 CD: Dutton CDLX 7002 CD: Pearl GEMMCD 9084

Tarantella (Rossiniana)

Detroit June 1942	Detroit SO	LP: Beecham Society WSA 526

REZNICEK

Donna Diana, Overture

London December 1945	LPO	HMV unpublished

RIMSKY-KORSAKOV

Scheherazade

London March 1957 and Paris October 1957	RPO	LP: HMV ALP 1564/ASD 251/SXLP 30253 LP: Angel 35505 LP: EMI 1C 053 00142/2C 063 00142 CD: EMI CDC 747 7172

Symphony No 2 "Antar", 3rd movement

London ca. 1915	Beecham SO	78: Columbia L 1011 LP: Beecham Society WHS 102-104 CD: Symposium 1096-1097
London March 1925	LSO	Columbia unpublished
London December 1927	Orchestra of Royal Philharmonic Society	78: Columbia L 2058 78: Columbia (USA) 7193M/50130D LP: Beecham Society WHS 105

Symphony No 2 "Antar", 4th movement

London March 1925	LSO	Columbia unpublished

Le coq d'or, Suite

New York June 1942	NYPO	Columbia unpublished
London January 1951	RPO	LP: Columbia 33CX 1087 LP: Columbia (USA) ML 4454 LP: Philips KFR 4000/GL 5692 Excerpts 45: Philips CFE 15030 LP: Columbia (USA) ML 5321/Y 33288 LP: Philips CFL 1021 LP: CBS 61655

Le coq d'or, Act 3 Introduction and Bridal Procession

Ludwigshafen November 1936	LPO	Experimental tape recording issued on Chandos cassette DBTD 2007

May Night, Overture

London October and December 1945	LPO	78: HMV DB 6308 78: HMV (Australia) ED 483

ROSSINI

Il Barbiere di Siviglia, Overture

London	Beecham SO
ca. 1916	

78: Columbia L 1075
LP: Beecham Society WHS 102-104
CD: Symposium 1096-1097

La cambiale di matrimonio, Overture

London	RPO
September 1950	

78: Columbia LX 1458
45: Columbia SEL 1509
45: Philips CFE 15005/EFF 535
LP: Philips CFL 1033/GL 5693

London	RPO
November 1958	
and November	
1959	

LP: HMV ALP 1846/ASD 420/EMX 2103
LP: Capitol G 7251/SG 7251
LP: World Records T 558/ST 558
LP: Pickwick/Quintessence (USA)
    PC 4035/PMC 7004
CD: EMI CDM 763 4072/CDZ 767 2552

La gazza ladra, Overture

London	LPO
September and	
October 1934	

78: Columbia LX 353
78: Columbia (USA) 68301D
LP: World Records SH 313
CD: Dutton CDLX 7001
CD: Pearl GEMMCD 9084

London	RPO
November 1958	

LP: HMV ALP 1846/ASD 420/SXLP 30158
LP: Capitol G 7251/SG 7251
LP: Angel 60134
LP: World Records T 744/ST 744
LP: Pickwick/Quintessence (USA)
    PC 4035/PMC 7004
CD: EMI CDM 763 4072/CDZ 767 2552

La scala di seta, Overture

London May 1933	LPO	78: Columbia LX 255 78: Columbia (USA) 9077M LP: World Records SH 313 LP: London Philharmonic LPJ 501 CD: Pearl GEMMCD 9084 CD: Dutton CDLX 7001/CDLX 7009

Semiramide, Overture

London November 1939	LPO	78: Columbia LX 884-885 78: Columbia (USA) X 215 LP: World Records SH 313 CD: Dutton CDLX 7001 CD: Pearl GEMMCD 9084
Philadelphia February 1952	Philadelphia Orchestra	45: Philips CFE 15058 LP: Philips CFL 1033/GL 5693
London November 1958	RPO	LP: HMV ALP 1912/ASD 480 LP: World Records T 837/ST 837 CD: EMI CDM 763 4072

William Tell, Overture

London ca. 1912	Beecham SO	78: Odeon 0795 LP: Beecham Society WHS 102-104 CD: Symposium 1096-1097 <u>March section only recorded</u>
London July, September and October 1934	LPO	78: Columbia LX 339-340 78: Columbia (USA) X 60 LP: World Records SH 313 CD: Dutton CDLX 7001 CD: Pearl GEMMCD 9084

SARASATE

Zapateado

Rome 1958	Orchestra	LP: Sirius 5022 <u>Soundtrack to the film Honeymoon</u> <u>(Luna de miel)</u>

SAINT-SAENS

Samson et Dalila

Buenos Aires August 1958	Teatro Colon Orchestra & Chorus Thebom, Vinay, Taddei, Corena	LP: Melodram MEL 449 <u>Melodram incorrectly describes</u> <u>this as a performance from</u> <u>Mexico</u>

Samson et Dalila, Bacchanale

London November 1959	RPO	45: HMV 7ER 5222/RES 4304 LP: HMV ALP 1862/ASD 432/HQS 1136 LP: Angel 35865/60084 CD: EMI CDM 763 4122
Seattle February 1960	Seattle SO	LP: Beecham Society WSA 517-518

Samson et Dalila, Dance of the Priestesses

London October 1958	RPO	LP: HMV ALP 1862/ASD 432/HQS 1136 LP: Angel 35865/60084 CD: EMI CDM 763 4122
London November 1959	RPO	LP: Beecham Society WSA 508/WSA 519
Seattle February 1960	Seattle SO	LP: Beecham Society WSA 517-518

Le rouet d'Omphale

London December 1946 and April 1947	RPO	78: HMV DB 6498 78: Victor 12-0152
London March 1957	RPO	LP: HMV ALP 1533/ASD 259/EMX 41 20771 LP: Angel 35506 CD: EMI CDM 763 3792 CD: NotaBlu 935.11234

SCHUBERT

Symphony No 1

Walthamstow December 1953	RPO	LP: Philips ABL 3001/GL 5634 LP: Columbia (USA) ML 4903

Symphony No 2

Walthamstow April 1954	RPO	LP: Philips ABL 3001/GL 5634 LP: Columbia (USA) ML 4903

Symphony No 3

Paris May 1958 and London May 1958 and May 1959	RPO	LP: HMV ALP 1743/ASD 345 LP: Capitol G 7212/SG 7212 LP: EMI SXLP 30204/1C 053 00171 CD: EMI CDM 769 7502 3rd movement LP: HMV ALP 1870-1871 LP: Angel 3621

Symphony No 5

London December 1939 and January 1939	LPO	78: Columbia LX 785-788 78: Columbia (USA) M 366 LP: Columbia (USA) ML 4771 LP: EMI RLS 733 CD: Pearl GEMMCD 9081 CD: Dutton CDLX 7014
Paris May 1958 and London December 1958 and May 1959	RPO	LP: HMV ALP 1743/ASD 345 LP: Capitol G 7212/SG 7212 LP: EMI SXLP 30204/1C 053 00171 CD: EMI CDM 769 7502

Symphony No 6

London November and December 1944	LPO	78: HMV DB 8977-8980 78: Victor M 1014 78: Pathé DB 11153-11156 78: HMV (Australia) ED 1169-1172 CD: Dutton CDLX 7014
London November and December 1955	RPO	LP: Columbia 33CX 1363 LP: Angel 35339 LP: World Records T 909/ST 909 LP: EMI ENC 104/XLP 30028 CD: EMI CDM 763 7502

Symphony No 8 "Unfinished"

London	LPO	78: Columbia LX 666-668
October and		78: Columbia (USA) M 330
November 1937		LP: EMI RLS 733
		CD: Dutton CDLX 7014

London	RPO	78: Columbia LX 8942-8944
January, May		LP: Columbia 33CX 1039
and July 1951		LP: Columbia (USA) ML 4474
		LP: Philips CFL 1004/EFL 2505
		LP: Philips EFR 2002/GL 5730
		CD: EMI CDM 763 3982

Marche militaire

London	LPO	LP: Beecham Society WSA 526
March 1939		CD: Symposium 1096-1097
		Recorded for a Radio Luxemburg broadcast

SCHUMANN

Manfred, complete incidental music

Walthamstow	RPO	LP: Philips CFL 1026-1027
December 1954	BBC Chorus	LP: Columbia (USA) M2L 245
and London	Various soloists	CD: Beecham Trust BEECHAM 4
May and	and speakers	Overture
October 1956		LP: Philips CFL 1042

Manfred, 3 excerpts from the incidental music

| London | Beecham SO | Columbia unpublished |
| August 1918 | | |

SIBELIUS

Symphony No 1

London May, November and December 1951 and May 1952	RPO	LP: Columbia 33CX 1085 LP: Columbia (USA) ML 4653 LP: Philips SBR 6245/GL 5716

Symphony No 2

London December 1946 and February and April 1947	RPO	78: HMV DB 6588-6592/ DB 9242-9246 auto 78: Victor DM 1334 45: Victor WDM 1335
London December 1954	BBCSO	LP: HMV ALP 1947 LP: World Records ST 1085/SHB 100 LP: Arabesque 8023 CD: EMI CDM 763 3992

Symphony No 4

London October, November and December 1937	LPO	78: HMV DB 3351-3355 78: Victor M 446 LP: World Records SH 133 LP: Turnabout THS 65059 CD: Koch 3-7061-2 CD: EMI CDM 764 0272

Symphony No 6

London May, July, September and November 1947	RPO	78: HMV DB 6640-6642/ DB 9466-9468 auto 78: Victor M 1271 LP: Beecham Society WHS 106 CD: EMI CDM 764 0272 M 1271 not published

Symphony No 7

New York June 1942	NYPO	78: Columbia (USA) M 524 78: Columbia (USA) ML 4086 CD: Dutton CDAX 8013
Boston January 1952	Boston SO	LP: Sirius 5023
Helsinki June 1954	Helsinki PO	CD: Ondine ODE 8092
London November 1955	RPO	LP: HMV ALP 1480/ASD 468/SXLP 30290 LP: Angel 35458 CD: EMI CDM 763 4002

Violin Concerto

London November and December 1935	LPO Heifetz	78: HMV DB 2791-1794 78: Victor M 309 45: Victor WCT 1113 LP: Victor LCT 1113 LP: World Records SH 207 LP: Angel 60221 LP: EMI 1C 053 01619/2C 053 01619 LP: EMI 143 3511M CD: EMI CDH 764 0302 CD: Biddulph LAB 018 CD: RCA/BMG 09026 617492/ 09026 617782 CD: Musica memoria MMA 30442 CD: Pearl GEMMCDS 9157
London November 1951	RPO Stern	78: Columbia LX 8947-8950 LP: Columbia 33C 1008 LP: Columbia (USA) ML 4550/Y 35200 LP: Philips NBL 5030/GL 5718 CD: Sony SMK 45956 CD: NotaBlu 935.1112

The Bard

London November 1938	LPO	78: HMV DB 3891 78: Victor M 658 LP: World Records SH 133 LP: Turnabout THS 65059 CD: Koch 3-7061-2 CD: EMI CDM 764 0272

En Saga

London November 1938 and June and July 1939	LPO	78: HMV DB 3888-3889 78: Victor M 658 LP: World Records SH 207 LP: EMI 1C 053 01619/2C 053 01619 CD: Koch 3-7061-2

Finlandia

London February 1938	LPO	78: Columbia LX 704 78: Columbia (USA) 69180D CD: EMI CDM 763 3972

In Memoriam, Funeral March

London November 1938	LPO	78: HMV DB 3890 78: Victor M 658 LP: World Records SH 133 LP: Turnabout THS 65059 CD: Koch 3-7061-2 CD: Dutton CDAX 8013

Karelia, Alla marcia

London December 1945	BBCSO	78: HMV DB 6248 78: Victor 11-9568 78: HMV (Australia) ED 515
Walthamstow December 1953	RPO	LP: Philips SBR 6215/GL 5716 LP: Columbia (USA) ML 5321/Y 33288 LP: CBS 61655 CD: EMI CDM 763 3972
Ascona October 1957	RPO	CD: Eremitage ERM 132

Karelia, Intermezzo

London December 1945	BBCSO	78: HMV DB 6248 78: Victor 11-9568 78: HMV (Australia) ED 515 CD: EMI CDM 763 3972

The Oceanides

London December 1955	RPO	LP: HMV ALP 1480/ASD 468 LP: Angel 35458 LP: EMI SXLP 30197/1C 053 01789 CD: EMI CDM 763 4002

Pelleas and Melisande, incidental music

London November and December 1955	RPO	LP: HMV ALP 1480/ASD 468 LP: Angel 35458 LP: EMI SXLP 30197/1C 053 01789 CD: EMI CDM 763 4002 Excerpts 45: HMV 7ER 5154/RES 4261

Pelleas and Melisande, excerpts from the incidental music

London June and July 1939	LPO	78: HMV DB 3892-3893 78: Victor M 658 CD: Dutton CDAX 8013 Further excerpts from the suite recorded but not published

Pelleas and Melisande, Melisande

New York June 1942	NYPO	78: Victor M 524 CD: Dutton CDAX 8013

The Return of Lemminkainen

London LPO
October 1937

78: HMV DB 3355-3356
78: Victor M 446
LP: World Records SH 133
LP: Turnabout THS 65059
CD: Koch 3-7061-2
CD: EMI CDM 764 0272
CD: Dutton CDAX 8013

Scènes historiques I and II, Excerpts

London RPO
September 1950
and June and
August 1952

LP: Columbia 33C 1018
LP: Columbia (USA) ML 4550/Y 35200
LP: Philips NBL 5030/GL 5718
CD: EMI CDM 763 3972
Excerpts
45: Columbia SEB 3504

Scènes historiques I, Excerpt (Festivo)

London LPO
December 1935

78: Columbia LX 501
78: Columbia (USA) 68590D
CD: Dutton CDAX 8013

Scènes historiques I, Excerpt (All' Overtura)

London RPO
September 1950
and June and
August 1952

Columbia unpublished

Swan White, Suite from the incidental music

London RPO
December 1955

LP: Sirius 5023

Tapiola

London RPO
November 1946

78: HMV DB 6412-6413
78: Victor M 1311
45: Victor M 1311
LP: Victor LM 9001

Helsinki Helsinki PO
June 1954

CD: Ondine ODE 8092

London RPO
December 1955

LP: HMV ALP 1968/ASD 518
LP: Angel 60000
LP: World Records T 744/ST 744
LP: EMI SXLP 30197/1C 053 01789
CD: EMI CDM 763 4002

The Tempest, Suite from the incidental music

London November and December 1937 and November 1938	LPO	78: HMV DB 3356-3357 and DB 3894 78: Victor M 446 and M 658 CD: Dutton CDAX 8013 CD: EMI CDM 764 0272 (Prelude only) DB 3894 and M 658 contained Prelude only
Walthamstow November and December 1955	RPO	LP: Philips ABR 4045 CD: EMI CDM 763 3972 Excerpts LP: Philips SBR 6215 LP: Columbia (USA) ML 5321/Y 33288 LP: CBS 61655
Helsinki June 1954	Helsinki PO	LP: Sirius 5023

The Tempest, Excerpts from the incidental music

Leeds October 1934	LPO	78: Columbia (USA) 68409D LP: Beecham Society WHS 106 These excerpts were issued by Columbia but later withdrawn, not having been approved for issue

Valse triste

London 1916-1917	Beecham SO	78: Columbia L 1162 LP: Beecham Society WHS 102-104
London November 1938	LPO	78: HMV DB 3893 78: Victor M 658 CD: Koch 3-7061-2
London March 1957	RPO	45: HMV 7ER 5170/RES 4271 LP: HMV ALP 1533/ASD 259 LP: Angel 35506/60134 CD: EMI CDM 763 4122

SMETANA

The Bartered Bride

London May 1939	LPO Covent Garden Chorus H.Konetzni, Kalter, Tauber, Krenn, Tessmer, Rothmüller <u>Sung in German</u>	CD: Legato SRO 830

The Bartered Bride, Overture

London 1916-1917	Beecham SO	78: Columbia L 1115 LP: Beecham Society WHS 102-104
London March 1925	LSO	Columbia unpublished
London March 1926	LSO	78: Columbia L 1810 <u>Not published</u>
London February and March 1947	RPO	78: Victor M 1294 LP: Beecham Society WHS 106

The Bartered Bride, Dance of the Comedians

London February 1947	RPO	78: HMV DB 6454 45: Victor M 1294 45: HMV 7R 102

The Bartered Bride, Polka

London February and November 1947	RPO	78: HMV DB 6454 78: Victor M 1294 45: HMV 7R 102

JOHANN STRAUSS

Die Fledermaus, Overture

London July 1910	Orchestra	G & T 0627/C 431 LP: Beecham Society WHS 102-104 LP: World Records SHB 100 CD: Symposium 1096-1097 Abridged version

Die Fledermaus: Excerpt (Mein Herr Marquis)

London July 1910	Orchestra & Chorus Hatchard Sung in English	G & T 03192 Not published

Die Fledermaus: Excerpt (Trinke, Liebchen, trinke schnell)

London July 1910	Orchestra E.Evans, Hyde Sung in English	G & T 04066 Not published

Die Fledermaus: Excerpt (Komm mit mir zum Souper)

London July 1910	Orchestra Hyde, Ranolow Sung in English	G & T 04065 Not published

Frühlingsstimmen, Waltz

London November 1939	LPO	78: Columbia LX 867 78: Columbia (USA) 70338D LP: EMI 1C 147 30226-30227M CD: Dutton CDLX 7003

Morgenblätter, Waltz

London February 1950	RPO	78: Columbia LX 1322 78: Columbia (USA) 73053D 45: Columbia SEL 1501 45: Philips CFE 15000/EFF 516 LP: Philips CFL 1021/GL 5692

RICHARD STRAUSS

Ariadne auf Naxos, complete opera without the prologue

Edinburgh August 1950	RPO Zadek, Hollweg, Springer, Cantelo, M.Thomas, Anders, Young, Dargavel	LP: Beecham Society WSA 511-512 Closing scene LP: Acanta DE 23.316-23.317

Ariadne auf Naxos, Prelude to the opera

London October 1947	RPO	LP: RCA RL 42821

Ariadne auf Naxos, Closing scene

London October 1947	RPO Cebotari, Furmedge, Field-Hyde, Garside, Friedrich	LP: Ed Smith EJS 536 LP: Beecham Society WSA 510 LP: RCA RL 42821

Le bourgeois gentilhomme, Incidental music excluding Minuet de Lully

London February and March 1947 and March 1948	RPO	78: HMV DB 6646-6648/ DB 9416-9418 auto LP: World Records SH 378 CD: EMI CDM 763 1062 DB 6646-6648 may not have been published

Le bourgeois gentilhomme, Minuet de Lully

London October 1947	RPO	78: HMV DB 6643 78: Victor 12-0735 45: HMV 7ER 5014 LP: World Records SH 378 CD: EMI CDM 763 1062

Don Quixote

New York April 1932	NYPO Wallenstein	78: Columbia LX 186-190 78: Victor M 144 LP: Victor LM 144 LP: EMI HLM 7154 CD: Pearl GEMMCD 9922 CD: RCA/BMG 09026 609292
London October 1947 and March 1948	RPO Tortelier	78: HMV DB 6796-6800/ DB 9357-9361 auto CD: EMI CDM 763 1062/CDH 565 5022 Finale only LP: HMV ALP 1870-1871 LP: Angel 3621

Elektra

London October 1947	RPO BBC Theatre Chorus Schlüter, Welitsch, Höngen, Widdop, Schöffler	LP: Ed Smith UORC 171 LP: Beecham Society WSA 509-512 LP: Rococo 1005 LP: Cetra ARK 9 LP: Melodram MEL 041 CD: Myto MCD 946 117 Rococo 1005 substitutes the HMV recording (see below) for the final scene

Elektra: Excerpt (Was willst du, fremder Mensch?...to end)

London October 1947	RPO Schlüter, Welitsch, Widdop, Schöffler	78: HMV DB 9393-9396 78: Victor M 1247 LP: Victor LCT 1135 LP: RCA RL 42821

Feuersnot, Love scene

London April 1947	RPO	78: HMV DB 21301 78: Victor 12-0289 45: HMV 7ER 5014 LP: World Records SH 378

Ein Heldenleben

London October, November and December 1947	RPO	78: HMV DB 6620-6624/ 　　DB 9204-9208 auto 78: Victor M 1321 45: Victor WDM 1321 LP: Victor LM 1059 LP: World Records SHB 100
London April and May 1958	RPO	LP: HMV ALP 1847/ASD 421/SXLP 30293 LP: Capitol G 7250/SG 7250 LP: World Records T 664/ST 664 LP: Angel 60041 CD: EMI CDM 763 2992

Intermezzo, Entr'acte in A flat

London October 1947	RPO	78: HMV DB 6643 78: Victor 12-0735 45: HMV 7ER 5014 LP: World Records SH 378

Der Rosenkavalier, Act II Waltz sequence

London 1915-1916	Beecham SO	78: Columbia L 1020 LP: Beecham Society WHS 102-104 CD: Symposium 1096-1097

Salome, Dance of the 7 veils

London October 1945	LPO	HMV unpublished
London September 1947	RPO	78: HMV DB 21149 78: Victor 12-0344 45: HMV 7R 103
New York January 1957	Symphony of the Air	LP: Beecham Society WSA 5

STRAVINSKY

L'oiseau de feu, Danse de l'oiseau de feu & Danse infernale

London May 1916	Beecham SO	78: Columbia L 1040 LP: Beecham Society WHS 102-104 LP: World Records SHB 100 CD: Symposium 1096-1097

L'oiseau de feu, Scherzo

London May 1916	Beecham SO	Columbia unpublished

SUPPE

Morning, Noon and Night in Vienna, Overture

London November 1939	LPO	78: Columbia LX 865 78: Columbia (USA) 71439D CD: Pearl GEMMCD 9094 CD: Dutton CDLX 7001
London April 1950	RPO	78: Columbia LX 1438 45: Philips CFE 15001/EFF 514 LP: Columbia (USA) ML 2134/ML 5171 LP: Philips CFL 1021/GL 5692

Poet and Peasant, Overture

London March 1957	RPO	LP: HMV ALP 1533/ASD 259 LP: Angel 35506 LP: EMI SXLP 30158/1C 047 01489 CD: EMI CDM 763 4072

TCHAIKOVSKY

Symphony No 2 "Little Russian"

Walthamstow   RPO
December 1953

LP: Philips ABL 3015/GL 5636
LP: Columbia (USA) ML 4872

Symphony No 3 "Polish"

London   RPO
February,
April and
May 1947

78: HMV DB 6583-6587/
     DB 9237-9241 auto
78: Victor M 1279
45: Victor WDM 1279
CD: Beecham Trust BEECHAM 1

Symphony No 4

Paris   RPO
October and
November 1957
and London
April 1958

LP: HMV ALP 1667/HQM 1162
LP: Capitol 21001
LP: Pickwick (USA) PC 4033
CD: EMI CDM 763 3802
Scherzo only
LP: HMV ALP 1870-1871
LP: Angel 3621

Symphony No 5

London   LPO
January 1939
and December
1940

78: Columbia LX 869-873
78: Columbia (USA) M 470
LP: EMI RLS 733
CD: EMI CDM 764 0532

Symphony No 6 "Pathétique", 2nd and 3rd movements (abridged)

London   Beecham SO   78: Columbia L 1016
ca. 1915   78: Columbia (USA) 7095M/65020D
                                     LP: Beecham Society WHS 102-104
                                     CD: Symposium 1096-1097

Symphony No 6 "Pathétique", 1st and 4th movements (abridged)

London   Beecham SO   Columbia unpublished
August and
October 1918

Capriccio italien

New York   NYPO   78: Columbia (USA) X 229
June 1942

New York   Columbia SO   78: Columbia LX 8924-8925
December 1949   78: Columbia (USA) MX 334
                                     45: Philips CFE 15028/KFR 4001
                                     LP: Columbia 33CX 1037
                                     LP: Columbia (USA) ML 4287/3216 0117
                                     LP: Philips GL 5270
                                     LP: CBS 54035

Casse noisette, Suite

Walthamstow   RPO   LP: Philips ABL 3247/SBR 6213
December 1953   LP: Columbia (USA) ML 5171
and December   CD: EMI CDM 763 3802
1954   Valse des fleurs
                                     LP: Columbia (USA) ML 4872

London   RPO   CD: Music and Arts CD 631
December 1958

Casse noisette, Valse des fleurs

London   LPO   LP: Beecham Society WSA 526
March 1939   CD: Symposium 1096-1097
                                     Recorded for a Radio Luxemburg
                                     broadcast

Eugene Onegin, Waltz

London October and December 1945	LPO	78: HMV DB 6266 78: Victor 11-9421
London October and November 1959	RPO	45: HMV 7ER 5222/RES 4304 LP: HMV ALP 1862/ASD 432/HQM 1167 LP: Angel 35865/60134 CD: EMI CDC 754 7782/CDM 763 4122 CD: EMI CDB 762 6462

Eugene Onegin, Polonaise

London October and December 1945	LPO	78: HMV DB 6266 78: Victor 11-9421

Francesca da Rimini

London December 1939	LPO	78: Columbia LX 887-889 78: Columbia (USA) M 447 CD: EMI CDM 764 0532

Romeo and Juliet

London December 1946 February 1947	RPO	78: HMV DB 6420-6422/ DB 9109-9111 auto CD: Beecham Trust BEECHAM 1

THEODORAKIS

The Lovers of Ternel

Rome 1958	Orchestra	LP: Sirius 5022 Soundtrack to the film Honeymoon (Luna de miel)

THOMAS

Mignon: Excerpt (Je suis Tytania)

Detroit June 1942	Detroit SO Pons	LP: Beecham Society WSA 526

VAUGHAN WILLIAMS

Flourish for a Coronation

London May 1937	LPO	LP: Beecham Society WSA 521 <u>Recorded at the opening of the</u> <u>Covent Garden Coronation season</u>

VERDI

Aida

London May 1939	LPO Covent Garden Chorus Caniglia, Stignani, Gigli, Zambelli, A.Borgioli	LP: Ed Smith UORC 300 LP: HRE Records HRE 260 CD: Eklipse EKRCD 03 <u>Final 10 minutes of the opera</u> <u>taken from 1946 commercial recording</u> <u>conducted by Serafin</u>

Aida: Excerpt (Ritorna vincitor)

London July 1928	Orchestra Turner	78: Columbia L 2150 LP: Columbia COLC 114 LP: EMI HQM 1209 CD: Nimbus NI 7802

Macbeth: Excerpt (La luce langue)

London September 1947	RPO Grandi	78: HMV DB 6740 LP: Australian Opera AO 1 LP: Bongiovanni GB 1037

Macbeth: Excerpt (Una macchia è qui tuttora)

London September 1947 and January 1948	RPO Grandi, Terry, Frank	78: HMV DB 6739-6740 LP: World Records SHB 100 LP: EMI EX 29 10753 LP: Bongiovanni GB 1037 <u>Bongiovanni incorrectly names</u> <u>conductor as Stanford Robinson</u>

Nabucco, orchestral selections

London	Beecham SO	ES 117
August 1910		LP: Beecham Society WHS 102-104

Otello

Buenos Aires	Teatro Colon	LP: Stradivarius STR 1014-1016
July 1958	Orchestra & Chorus	
	Stella, Vinay,	
	Taddei	

Il Trovatore: Excerpt (D'amor sull' ali rosee)

London	Orchestra	78: Columbia L 2156
July 1928	Turner	78: Columbia (USA) 50099D/5132M
		LP: Columbia COLC 114
		LP: EMI HQM 1209
		CD: EMI CDH 769 7912

VIDAL

Zino-Zina, Gavotte

Paris	RPO	LP: HMV ALP 1983
October 1957		LP: World Records T 558/ST 558
		CD: EMI CDM 763 4122

WAGNER

A Faust Overture

London April and July 1935 and February 1936	LPO	78: Columbia LX 481-482 78: Columbia (USA) X 63 LP: EMI HLM 7154 CD: Dutton CDLX 7009

Der fliegende Holländer, Overture

London November 1937	LPO	78: Columbia LX 732-733 78: Columbia (USA) X 167 CD: Dutton CDLX 7007 CD: Pearl GEMMCD 9094
Walthamstow April 1954	RPO	LP: Philips ABL 3039/GL 5635 LP: Columbia (USA) ML 4962

Götterdämmerung, Siegfried's Rhine Journey

Walthamstow April 1954	RPO	45: Philips ABE 10016 LP: Philips ABL 3039/GL 5635 LP: Columbia (USA) ML 4962

Götterdämmerung, Siegfried's Funeral March

Walthamstow December 1953	RPO	45: Philips ABE 10016 LP: Philips ABL 3039/GL 5635 LP: Columbia (USA) ML 4962

Götterdämmerung: Excerpt Act I (Wär' wider mich Wotans Sinn erweicht?/Höre mit Sinn/Ein Freier kam)

London May 1936 (14 May)	LPO Leider, Thorborg, Melchior	LP: Ed Smith EJS 167/UORC 234 CD: Legato LCD 146

Götterdämmerung: Excerpt Act I (Hier sitz' ich zur Wacht)

London May 1936 (29 May)	LPO Weber	78: Columbia LX 637 78: Columbia (USA) X 83 LP: EMI 1C 177 00933-00934M LP: EMI RLS 742 CD: Dutton CDLX 7007

Götterdämmerung: Excerpt Act 2 (Hoiho, Ihr Gibichsmannen!)

London	LPO	78: Columbia LX 636-637
May 1936	Covent Garden	78: Columbia (USA) X 83
(29 May)	Chorus	LP: EMI 1C 177 00933-00934M
	Weber, Janssen	LP: World Records SHB 100
		CD: EMI CMS 764 0082
		CD: Dutton CDLX 7007

Götterdämmerung: Excerpts Act 2 scenes 1-3

London	LPO	CD: Legato LCD 146
May 1936	Covent Garden	Incorrectly described by
(29 May)	Chorus	Legato as 14 May performance
	Szantho, Melchior,	
	Weber, Janssen	

Götterdämmerung: Excerpts Act 2 scene 4

London	LPO	LP: Ed Smith EJS 167/UORC 234
May 1936	Covent Garden	LP: Acanta 22.863/98.221776
(14 May)	Chorus	CD: Legato LCD 146
	Leider, Nezadal,	CD: Acanta 44.1055
	Melchior, List,	Ed Smith and Acanta incorrectly
	Janssen	name conductor as Furtwängler;
		Legato incorrectly names bass
		singer as Weber

Lohengrin, Act I Prelude

London	RPO	78: Columbia LX 1557
December 1951		

Lohengrin, Act 3 Prelude

London	LPO	78: Columbia LX 482
July 1935		78: Columbia (USA) X 63
		CD: Pearl GEMMCD 9094
		CD: Dutton CDLX 7007

Beecham

Die Meistersinger von Nürnberg

London May 1936	LPO Covent Garden Chorus Lemnitz, Booth, Ralf, Nash, Bockelmann, Janssen, Weber		Unpublished test pressings Da zu dir der Heiland kam 78: Columbia LX 645 78: Columbia (USA) X 87 LP: HMV ALP 1870-1871/RLS 742 LP: Angel 3621 LP: Ed Smith EJS 444 CD: Dutton CDLX 7007 Wach auf! 78: Columbia LX 645 78: Columbia (USA) X 87 LP: Ed Smith EJS 444 LP: EMI RLS 742 CD: Dutton CDLX 7007 Morgenlich leuchtend 78: Columbia LX 646 78: Columbia (USA) X 87 LP: Ed Smith EJS 444 LP: Rococo 5233 LP: HMV (Sweden) SCLP 1022 CD: Dutton CDLX 7007
London July 1951	Covent Garden Orchestra & Chorus Grümmer, Shacklock, Anders, Dickie, Hotter, Weber, Kusche, G.Evans		Unpublished radio broadcast Fanget an!/Am stillen Herd LP: Acanta DE 23.316-23.317

Die Meistersinger von Nürnberg, Act 1 Prelude

London June 1936	LPO	78: Columbia LX 557 78: Columbia (USA) 68854D CD: Pearl GEMMCD 9094 CD: Dutton CDLX 7007
London November 1959	RPO	LP: HMV ALP 2003 CD: EMI CDM 763 4072 CD: Music and Arts CD 631

Die Meistersinger von Nürnberg, Suite (Act 3 Prelude, Dance of the Apprentices and Entry of the Masters)

Walthamstow April 1954	RPO	LP: Philips ABL 3039/GL 5635 LP: Columbia (USA) ML 4962 Act 3 Prelude only 45: Philips ABE 10097

Parsifal, Good Friday Music

Walthamstow December 1953	RPO	45: Philips ABE 10184 LP: Philips ABL 3039/GL 5635 LP: Columbia (USA) ML 4962

Das Rheingold, unspecified extracts

London May 1936	LPO Wray, Furmedge, Szantho, Kremer, Bockelmann, Habich, Weber, Fleischer	HMV/Columbia unpublished test pressings

Das Rheingold, Entry of the Gods into Valhalla

London October 1945	LPO Barry, N.Evans, Ripley, P.Jones, Hancock	HMV unpublished
London September 1947	RPO Field-Hyde, Furmedge, N.Evans, Garside, P.Jones, Chitty, Schöffler	HMV unpublished
London October 1947	RPO Field-Hyde, Furmedge, Garside, Patriss, Widdop, T.Hermann	HMV unpublished

Tannhäuser, Overture

London October 1937 and October and November 1938	LPO	78: Columbia LX 768-769 78: Columbia (USA) X 123 CD: Dutton CDLX 7007

Tannhäuser, Overture and Venusberg Music

London September 1954	RPO	LP: Beecham Society WSA 506-507 CD: Music and Arts CD 631

Tannhäuser, Entry of the Guests (Grand March)

London June and July 1938	LPO	78: Columbia LX 733 78: Columbia (USA) X 107 CD: Dutton CDLX 7007
London March 1939	LPO	LP: Beecham Society WSA 526 CD: Symposium 1096-1097 Recorded for a Radio Luxemburg broadcast

Tannhäuser, Act 3 Prelude

London February 1947	RPO	HMV unpublished

Tristan und Isolde

London June 1937 (18 June)	LPO Covent Garden Chorus Flagstad, Klose, Melchior, Janssen, S.Nilssen	LP: Anna ANNA 1059 Act 1 LP: Ed Smith UORC 302 LP: Discocorp RR 223 Act 2 LP: Discocorp RR 223 CD: EMI CHS 764 0372 First third of Act 3 CD: EMI CHS 764 0372 Other excerpts LP: Ed Smith EJS 258 LP: Rococo 5382 Initial release of CHS 764 0372 incorrectly stated that entire recording was conducted by Beecham whereas parts not specified above were from a 1936 performance conducted by Reiner; UORC 302 incorrectly dated 1938
London June 1937 (22 June)	LPO Covent Garden Chorus Flagstad, Branzell, Melchior, Schöffler, S.Nilssen	Act 1 Unpublished test pressings Act 2 LP: Anna ANNA 1051 LP: Discocorp RR 223 Act 3 LP: Discocorp RR 223

Tristan und Isolde, Liebestod

London December 1952	RPO Flagstad	LP: Ed Smith EJS 399 CD: Eklipse EKRCD 24 Both issues incorrectly dated 1948

Wesendonk-Lieder

London December 1952	RPO Flagstad	LP: Rococo 5382 CD: Eklipse EKRCD 24 Rococo incorrectly dated 1951; Eklipse incorrectly dated 1948

Oberon, Overture

London ca. 1912	Beecham SO	78: Odeon X 84 LP: Beecham Society WHS 102-104 CD: Symposium 1096-1097 Abridged version
London ca. 1916	Beecham SO	78: Columbia L 1104 LP: Beecham Society WHS 102-104
London December 1937 and July and October 1938	LPO	78: Columbia LX 746 78: Columbia (USA) 69410D LP: World Records SHB 100 CD: Pearl GEMMCD 9094 CD: Dutton CDLX 7009

Der Freischütz, Overture

London November 1935	LPO	Unpublished and incomplete test pressing
London November 1936	LPO	78: Columbia LX 601 78: Columbia (USA) 68986D CD: Dutton CDLX 7009

WEINBERGER

Under the spreading chestnut tree

London December 1939	LPO	Unpublished test pressing

MISCELLANEOUS

British National anthem

London May 1937	LPO Covent Garden Chorus Turner	LP: Beecham Society WSA 521-522 Performed to mark opening of Covent Garden Coronation season
Edinburgh August 1956	RPO Edinburgh Choral Union	LP: Beecham Society WSA 504-505
London May 1959	RPO	LP: World Records SHB 100

BEECHAM TALKS

Beecham introduces the works in his 1939 Radio Luxemburg concert

London
March 1939

CD: Symposium 1096-1097

Beecham talks about Delius A Mass of Life

BBC
June 1951

LP: World Records SHB 32

Beecham talks about 20th century music and about Delius Irmelin

BBC
November 1953

LP: BBC Records REGL 350
LP: Arabesque 8080

Beecham talks about Sibelius

BBC
November 1955

LP: BBC Records REGL 350
LP: Arabesque 8080

Beecham talks about Mozart

Washington
February 1956

LP: World Records SHB 100
Edited version of a public lecture

Beecham talks about the recording of La Bohème

New York　　　　　　　　　　　　　　　LP: Victor SRL 12-28
1956　　　　　　　　　　　　　　　　　Promotional record distributed
　　　　　　　　　　　　　　　　　　　in USA only

Beecham on the changing world of music

Washington　　　　　　　　　　　　　　LP: World Records SHB 100
February 1957　　　　　　　　　　　　 Edited version of a public lecture

Beecham talks about Ethel Smyth

BBC　　　　　　　　　　　　　　　　　LP: BBC Records REGL 350
April 1958　　　　　　　　　　　　　　LP: Arabesque 8080

Beecham on his own life and work

BBC　　　　　　　　　　　　　　　　　LP: BBC Records REGL 350
May 1959　　　　　　　　　　　　　　　LP: Arabesque 8080

Beecham talks to Edmund Tracey about his Delius biography

BBC TV　　　　　　　　　　　　　　　 LP: World Records SHB 32
November 1959

This listing represents only a selection of recordings of Beecham speaking

Note on Beecham's Columbia 78 rpm recordings: in addition to the catalogue numbers shown in this discography, these were widely distributed in overseas territories with different catalogue numbers (France, Germany, Italy, Canada, Argentina etc.)

Sir Adrian Boult
1889-1983

with valuable assistance
from Alan Sanders

Discography compiled by John Hunt

ALFORD

Colonel Bogey, March

| London | LPO | LP: World Records T 750/ST 750 |
| August 1967 | | LP: EMI CFP 173 |

ARNE

Rule Britannia

| London | BBCSO | 78: HMV B 8553/B 9420 |
| January 1937 | | |

ARNOLD

Eight English Dances

| London | LPO | LP: Decca LW 5166/ACL 113/ECS 646 |
| November 1954 | | CD: Decca 425 6612 |

AUBER

Masaniello, Overture

| London | BBCSO | 78: HMV DB 2364 |
| November 1934 | | 78: Victor M 746 |

BACH

6 Brandenburg Concerti BWV 1046-1051

London
April, September
and December
1972
LPO
LP: EMI SLS 866

Concerto in D minor BWV 1052 for piano and orchestra

London
February 1958
LPO
Katin
Decca unpublished

Concerto in C minor BWV 1061 for 2 pianos and orchestra

London
October 1936
BBCSO
A. Schnabel
K.U. Schnabel
78: HMV DB 3041-3043/
    DB 8242-8244 auto
78: Victor M 357
LP: Victor LCT 1140
LP: Rococo 2060
CD: Pearl GEMMCD 9399

Concerto in A minor BWV 1041 for violin and orchestra

London
April 1953
Philharmonia
Menuhin
HMV unpublished

Orchestral Suite No 3 BWV 1068

London
May 1933
BBCSO
78: HMV DB 1963-1965/
    DB 7540-7542 auto
78: Victor M 214
Coupled with Prelude BWV 1019

Air (Orchestral Suite No 3)

London
November 1959
and May 1960
Covent Garden
Orchestra
45: Decca CEP 736/SEC 5119
LP: Decca SPA 155/SPA 366

Fantasia and Fugue in C minor, orchestrated Elgar

London October 1949	LPO	HMV unpublished
London May, June and August 1973	LPO	LP: EMI ASD 2970

Prelude from Violin Sonata BWV 1019, orchestrated Pick-Mangianelli

London May 1933	BBCSO	78: HMV DB 1965/DB 7542 78: Victor M 214 Coupled with Orchestral Suite No 3

The Wise Virgins, Ballet arranged by Walton

London October 1954	LPO	LP: Decca LXT 5028/LW 5157 LP: Decca ACL 218/ECS 657

Mass in B minor: Excerpt (Qui sedes)

London October 1952	LPO Ferrier	45: Decca 45-71138/CEP 722 LP: Decca LXT 2757/LXT 5382 LP: Decca LW 5083/414 6231 CD: Decca 414 6232 CD: Decca 433 4742/433 8022
London February and May 1960 Re-recording for stereo of the orchestral accompaniment to 1952 version	LPO	LP: Decca SXL 2234/SDD 286 LP: Decca SPA 531/AKF 1-7

Mass in B minor: Excerpt (Agnus Dei)

London October 1952	LPO Ferrier	45: Decca 45-71138/CEP 722 LP: Decca LXT 2757/LXT 5382 LP: Decca LW 5083/414 6231 CD: Decca 414 6232 CD: Decca 433 4742/433 8022
London February and May 1960 Re-recording for stereo of the orchestral accompaniment to 1952 version	LPO	LP: Decca SXL 2234/SDD 286 LP: Decca SPA 322/SPA 531/AKF 1-7

Saint John Passion: Excerpt (Es ist vollbracht)

London October 1952	LPO Ferrier Sung in English	45: Decca 45-71112/CEP 721 LP: Decca LXT 2757/LXT 5382 LP: Decca LW 5083/414 6231 CD: Decca 414 6232 CD: Decca 433 4742/433 8022
London February and May 1960 <u>Re-recording for stereo of the</u> <u>orchestral accompaniment to 1952</u> <u>version</u>	LPO	LP: Decca SXL 2234/SDD 286 LP: Decca SPA 531/AKF 1-7

Saint Matthew Passion: Excerpt (Blute nur, du liebes Herz)

London December 1956	LPO Flagstad Sung in English	LP: Decca LXT 5316

Saint Matthew Passion: Excerpt (Buss und Reu)

London October 1952	LPO Ferrier Sung in English	45: Decca CEP 721 LP: Decca LXT 2757/LXT 5382 LP: Decca LW 5083/414 6231 CD: Decca 414 6232 CD: Decca 433 4742/433 8022
London February and May 1960 <u>Re-recording for stereo of the</u> <u>orchestral accompaniment to 1952</u> <u>version</u>	LPO	LP: Decca SXL 2234/SDD 286 LP: Decca SPA 531/AKF 1-7

Bist du bei mir

London December 1956	LPO Flagstad Sung in English	LP: Decca LXT 5316

Jesu bleibet meine Freude (Cantata No 147)

London December 1956	LPO Flagstad Sung in English	45: Decca CEP 540 LP: Decca LXT 5316

Schafe können sicher weiden (Cantata No 208)

London December 1956	LPO Flagstad Sung in English	45: Decca CEP 540 LP: Decca LXT 5316/SPA 322
London November 1959 and May 1960	Covent Garden Orchestra	45: Decca CEP 736/SEC 5119 LP: Decca SPA 155/SPA 366 <u>Arrangement by Bantock</u>

J.C. BACH

Allegro (Piano Concerto in A)

London May 1952	LPO Collet	HMV unpublished
London July 1955	LPO Collet	78: HMV HMS 79 LP: HMV HLP 19 LP: Victor LM 6137 Recorded for HMV's History of Music series

C.P.E. BACH

Symphony in F

London May 1952	LPO	78: HMV HMS 77 LP: HMV HLP 18 LP: Victor LM 6137 Recorded for HMV's History of Music series

Works by J.C.Bach and/or C.P.E.Bach also recorded by Boult and New SO for RCA/Readers' Digest in July 1960 but tapes were destroyed at the conductor's request

BANTOCK

Hebridean Symphony

Birmingham January 1925	CBSO	Columbia unpublished
Glasgow 1968	BBC Scottish SO	CD: Intaglio INCD 7041

BARSUKOV

Piano Concerto No 2

London March 1965	New Philharmonia Barsukov	LP: Pathé DTX 344/ASTX 344 LP: Everest LPBR 6167/SDBR 3167

BARTOK

Divertimento for strings

Walthamstow April 1955	LPO	LP: Nixa NCL 16011 LP: Westminster XWN 18327 LP: Turnabout TV 34154

Music for strings, percussion and celesta

Walthamstow April 1955	LPO	LP: Nixa NCL 16011 LP: Westminster XWN 18327/LAB 7021 LP: Turnabout TV 34154

Rhapsody No 2 for violin and orchestra

London February 1952	LPO Menuhin	HMV unpublished

LPO is described as Philharmonic Promenade Orchestra on many of Boult's recordings for the Nixa and Westminster labels

BAX

The Garden of Fand

London January 1972	LPO	LP: Lyrita SRCS 62 LP: Musical Heritage HNH 4034/ MHS 1769 CD: Lyrita SRCD 231

Mediterranean

London January 1972	LPO	LP: Lyrita SRCS 62 LP: Musical Heritage HNH 4034/ MHS 1769 CD: Lyrita SRCD 231

Northern Ballad No 1

London January 1972	LPO	LP: Lyrita SRCS 62 LP: Musical Heritage HNH 4034/ MHS 1769 CD: Lyrita SRCD 231

November Woods

London November 1967	LPO	LP: Lyrita SRCS 37 LP: Musical Heritage HNH 4038/ MHS 1229 CD: Lyrita SRCD 231

Tintagel

London November 1954	LPO	LP: Decca LXT 5015/ACL 113/ECS 647
London January 1972	LPO	LP: Lyrita SRCS 62 LP: Musical Heritage HNH 4034/ MHS 1769 CD: Lyrita SRCD 231

BEETHOVEN

Symphony No 1

London July and December 1950	LPO	HMV unpublished

Symphony No 3 "Eroica"

Walthamstow June 1957	LPO	LP: Vanguard VRS 1012/VSD 2002/SRV 359-362 LP: Top Rank XRC 6001 LP: Fontana BIG 411/BIG 311 LP: Allegro ALL 818
Walthamstow December 1961	LPO	LP: Somerset Fidelity 15700/555 LP: Pye GGL 0154/GSGL 10154/MAL 562

Symphony No 5

Walthamstow June 1957	LPO	LP: Vanguard VRS 1013/VSD 2003/SRV 359-362 LP: Top Rank XRC 6002

Symphony No 6 "Pastoral"

Walthamstow June 1957	LPO	LP: Vanguard VRS 1014/VSD 2004/SRV 359-362 LP: Top Rank XRC 6003 LP: Fontana BIG 423/BIG 323 LP: Allegro ALL 814
London August 1972	BBCSO	CD: Radio Classics BBCRD 9114
London April and May 1977	LPO	LP: EMI ASD 3456

Symphony No 7

Walthamstow June 1957	LPO	LP: Vanguard VRS 1015/VSD 2005/SRV 359-362 LP: Top Rank XRC 6004 LP: Fontana GIG 424/BIG 324 LP: Allegro ALL 813

Symphony No 8

London July 1932	BBCSO	78: HMV DB 1764-1766/ DB 7122-7124 auto 78: Victor M 181 CD: Beulah PD 6/IPD 12

Piano Concerto No 3

Bedford August 1944	BBCSO Solomon	78: HMV DB 6196-6199/8973-8976 auto CD: Dutton CDLX 7015 CD: EMI CHS 565 5032

Piano Concerto No 4

London January 1953	BBCSO Hess	LP: Rococo 2041

Violin Concerto

London January 1952	LPO Ricci	LP: Decca LXT 2750/ACL 5
London September 1970	New Philharmonia Suk	LP: EMI ASD 2667 LP: EMI 1C 063 02120/1C 037 02120 LP: Vanguard SRV 353SD CD: EMI CES 568 5202

Violin Romance No 1

London February 1959	RPO Menuhin	HMV unpublished

Violin Romance No 2

London February 1959	RPO Menuhin	HMV unpublished
London April 1967	LPO Bress	LP: World Records T 730/ST 730
London August 1972	BBCSO Bean	CD: Radio Classics BBCRD 9114

Coriolan, Overture

London October 1933	BBCSO	78: HMV DB 2101 78: Victor 11-909
Walthamstow June 1957	LPO	LP: Vanguard VRS 1012/SRV 359-362 LP: Vanguard VSD 2002/VSD 2029 LP: Top Rank XRC 6001/BUY 036 LP: Fontana BIG 413/BIG 313 LP: Allegro ALL 818
London September 1970	New Philharmonia	LP: EMI ASD 2667 LP: EMI 1C 063 02120/1C 037 02120

Egmont, Overture

London April 1933	BBCSO	78: HMV DB 1925
Walthamstow June 1957	LPO	LP: Vanguard VRS 1015/SRV 359-362 LP: Vanguard VSD 2005/VSD 2029 LP: Top Rank XRC 6004/BUY 036 LP: Fontana BIG 413/BIG 313
London August 1972	BBCSO	CD: Radio Classics BBCRD 9114

Fidelio, Overture

Walthamstow June 1957	LPO	LP: Vanguard VRS 1014/SRV 359-362 LP: Vanguard VSD 2004/VSD 2029 LP: Top Rank XRC 6003/BUY 036 LP: Fontana BIG 413/BIG 313

Die Geschöpfe des Prometheus, Overture

London August 1969	BBCSO	CD: Radio Classics BBCRD 9114

Grosse Fuge

London August 1968	New Philharmonia	CD: Intaglio INCD 7361

Leonore No 3, Overture

Walthamstow June 1957	LPO	LP: Vanguard VRS 1013/SRV 359-362 LP: Vanguard VSD 2003/VSD 2029 LP: Top Rank XRC 6002/BUY 036 LP: Fontana BIG 413/BIG 313

Die Ruinen von Athen, Overture

London January 1957	Philharmonia	45: HMV 7ER 5129

Die Ruinen von Athen, Turkish March

London January 1957	Philharmonia	45: HMV 7ER 5129

BERKELEY

Violin Concerto

London April 1971	Menuhin Festival Orchestra Menuhin	LP: EMI ASD 2759/EX 29 08643

Magnificat

London 1969	LPO BBC Chorus and Choral Society	CD: Intaglio INCD 7281

BERLIOZ

Béatrice et Bénédict, Overture

Walthamstow August 1956	LPO	45: Nixa NEC 23000 LP: Westminster XWN 18524/LAB 7054 LP: Pye CCL 30160/GGC 4084 LP: Pye GSGC 14084/GSGC 15012

Benvenuto Cellini, Overture

Walthamstow August 1956	LPO	LP: Westminster XWN 18523/LAB 7054 LP: Pye CCL 30159/GGC 4083 LP: Pye GSGC 14083/GSGC 15012

Le carnaval romain, Overture

London October 1933	BBCSO	78: HMV DB 2078
Walthamstow August 1956	LPO	45: Nixa NEC 23000 LP: Westminster XWN 18523 LP: Pye CCL 30160/GGC 4083 LP: Pye GSGC 14083/GSGC 15012 LP: Pye MAL 1142/GH 515

Le corsaire, Overture

Walthamstow August 1956	LPO	LP: Westminster XWN 18524/LAB 7051 LP: Pye CCL 30159/GGC 4084 LP: Pye GSGC 14084/GSGC 15012

Les francs juges, Overture

London December 1936	BBCSO	78: HMV DB 3131-3132 78: Victor DM 803
Walthamstow August 1956	LPO	LP: Westminster XWN 18523/LAB 7053 LP: Pye CCL 30159/GGC 4083 LP: Pye GSGC 14083/GSGC 15012

Le roi Lear, Overture

London December 1936	BBCSO	78: HMV DB 3093-3094 78: Victor DM 803 LP: BBC Records BBC 4001 78 version coupled with Borodin Polovtsian March
Walthamstow August 1956	LPO	LP: Westminster XWN 18524/LAB 7053 LP: Pye CCL 30160/GGC 4084 LP: Pye GSGC 14084

Rob Roy, Overture

Walthamstow August 1956	LPO	LP: Westminster XWN 18524/LAB 7051 LP: Pye CCL 30160/GGC 4084 LP: Pye GSGC 14084/GSGC 15012

Waverley, Overture

Walthamstow August 1956	LPO	LP: Westminster XWN 18523/LAB 7054 LP: Pye CCL 30159/GGC 4083 LP: Pye GSGC 14083/GSGC 15012

BLISS

Music for strings

London March and June 1937	BBCSO	78: HMV DB 3527-3529/ DB 8342-8344 auto 78: Victor M 464 LP: BBC Records BBC 4001 CD: VAI Audio VAIA 10672
London November 1973 and February 1974	LPO	LP: EMI ASD 3020

Piano Concerto

Liverpool January 1943	Liverpool PO Solomon	78: HMV C 3348-3352/7583-7587 auto LP: World Records SH 125 LP: EMI RLS 701

Rout, for soprano and orchestra

Hayes July 1921	British SO Power	78: HMV D 574

BORODIN

Polovtsian March (Prince Igor)

London January 1937	BBCSO	78: HMV DB 3094 78: Victor 36-324 Coupled with Berlioz Le roi Lear Overture

BRAHMS

Symphony No 1

Walthamstow November 1954	LPO	LP: Nixa NCL 16000 LP: Westminster XWN 18104 LP: Pye MAL 730 CD: Precision PVCD 8388
Walthamstow October 1959	LPO	LP: Somerset Fidelity 14000/555 LP: Pye GGL 0105/GSGL 0105 LP: Europa E 402 LP: Musical Heritage MHS 3502
London March 1972	LPO	LP: EMI ASD 2871/SLS 5009

Symphony No 2

Walthamstow November 1954	LPO	LP: Nixa NCL 16001 LP: Westminster XWN 18132 LP: Pye MAL 731 LP: Everest SDBR 3148 CD: Precision PVCD 8389
London January and April 1971	LPO	LP: EMI ASD 2746/SLS 5009 LP: Angel 37032 LP: EMI SXLP 30529

Symphony No 3

Walthamstow November 1954	LPO	LP: Nixa NCL 16002 LP: Westminster XWN 18194 LP: Pye MAL 732 CD: Precision PVCD 8390
London August 1970	LSO	LP: EMI ASD 2660/SLS 5009 Third movement LP: EMI SEOM 13/YKM 5012

Symphony No 4

Walthamstow November 1954	LPO	LP: Nixa NCL 16003 LP: Westminster XWN 18246 LP: Pye MAL 733 CD: Precision PVCD 8391
London March 1972	LPO	LP: EMI ASD 2901/SLS 5009 LP: Angel 37034

Piano Concerto No 1

London November 1932	BBCSO Backhaus	78: HMV DB 1839-1843/ DB 7307-7311 auto 78: Victor M 209 LP: Discocorp RR 315 LP: EMI EX 29 03433 CD: Biddulph LWH 017

Piano Concerto No 2

London November 1935	BBCSO Schnabel	78: HMV DB 2696-2701/ DB 7997-8002 auto 78: Victor M 305 LP: HMV COLH 82 LP: World Records SH 109 LP: EMI 1C 181 52348-52349M CD: Pearl GEMMCD 9399
London March 1958	Philharmonia Kentner	LP: HMV ALP 1704/ASD 268 LP: Capitol G 7133/SG 7133 LP: EMI MFP 2053

Violin Concerto

London December 1971	LSO Menuhin	EMI unpublished First movement only recorded

Serenade No 1

London July 1932	BBCSO		HMV unpublished Minuets 1 and 2 only recorded
London Date uncertain	BBCSO		CD: Intaglio INCD 7431
London May, July and October 1977 & January and April 1978	LPO		LP: EMI SLS 5137

Serenade No 2

London May, July and October 1977 & January and April 1978	LPO	LP: EMI SLS 5137 LP: Angel 37648

Alto Rhapsody

Walthamstow November 1954	LPO Chorus Sinclair	LP: Nixa NCL 16002/NCL 16004 LP: Westminster XWN 18035 LP: Pye MAL 732/GSGC 15021 CD: Precision PVCD 8390
London December 1970	LPO Alldis Choir Baker	LP: EMI ASD 2746/ASD 3260/SLS 5009 LP: Angel 37032/37199 LP: EMI SXLP 30529/1C 065 02758 CD: EMI CDC 747 8542

Academic Festival Overture

London December 1950	LPO	78: HMV DB 9670-9671 Coupled with Hungarian Dances Nos 17 and 18
Walthamstow November 1954	LPO	LP: Nixa NCL 16001/NCL 16004 LP: Westminster XWN 18035 LP: Pye MAL 730/GSGC 15021 CD: Precision PVCD 8389
London July 1967	LPO	LP: World Records T 730/ST 730 LP: EMI CFP 158
London March 1972	LPO	LP: EMI ASD 2901/SLS 5009/SEOM 15 LP: Angel 37034

Tragic Overture

London May 1932	BBCSO	78: HMV DB 1803-1804 78: Victor 11533-11534 Coupled with Hungarian Dances Nos 19, 20 and 21
Walthamstow November 1954	LPO	LP: Nixa NCL 16000/NCL 16004 LP: Westminster XWN 18035 LP: Pye MAL 730/GSGC 15021 CD: Precision PVCD 8388
London August 1970	LSO	LP: EMI ASD 2660/SLS 5009

Haydn Variations

Walthamstow November 1954	LPO	LP: Nixa NCL 16003/NCL 16004 LP: Westminster XWN 18035 LP: Pye MAL 733/GSGC 15021 CD: Precision PVCD 8391
London May, July and October 1977 & January and April 1978	LPO	LP: EMI SLS 5137

Hungarian Dances No 17 and 18

London December 1950	LPO	78: HMV DB 9670 Coupled with Academic Festival Overture

Hungarian Dances Nos 19, 20 and 21

London October 1932	BBCSO	78: HMV DB 1804 Coupled with Tragic Overture

BRIAN

Gothic Symphony

London October 1966	BBCSO Various Choirs Sheppard, Minty, Dowd, Stalman	LP: Aries LP 2601

BRIDGE

Cherry ripe (Old English Songs)

London	LPO	LP: Lyrita SRCS 73
January 1974		LP: Musical Heritage HNH 4078

Lament for string orchestra

London	LPO	LP: Lyrita SRCS 73
January 1974		LP: Musical Heritage HNH 4078

Rosemary (Three Sketches)

London	LPO	LP: Lyrita SRCS 73
September 1975		LP: Musical Heritage HNH 4078

Sally in our alley (Old English Songs)

London	LPO	LP: Lyrita SRCS 73
January 1974		LP: Musical Heritage HNH 4078

Sir Roger de Coverley

London	LPO	LP: Lyrita SRCS 73
January 1974		LP: Musical Heritage HNH 4078

Suite for string orchestra

London	LPO	LP: Lyrita SRCS 73
November 1973		LP: Musical Heritage HNH 4078

BRITTEN

Peter Grimes, 4 Sea Interludes and Passacaglia

Walthamstow   LPO   LP: Westminster XWN 18601/LAB 7057
August 1956   LP: Pye GGC 4059/GSGC 14059

Variations & Fugue on a theme of Purcell (Young Person's Guide to the Orchestra

Walthamstow   LPO   LP: Westminster XWN 18372/LAB 7056
August 1956   LP: Westminster XWN 18601/18737
                                     XWN also contains narration by
                                     Boult and rehearsal sequence

BRUCH

Violin Concerto No 1

London March 1956	LPO Elman	LP: Decca LXT 5222
London December 1971	LSO Menuhin	LP: EMI ASD 2852/1C 063 02332 LP: Angel 36920 LP: EMI EG 29 04911 CD: EMI CES 568 5242

Violin Concerto No 2

London December 1971	LSO Menuhin	LP: EMI ASD 2852/1C 063 02332 LP: Angel 36920

Kol Nidrei

London July 1967	LPO Bunting	LP: World Records T 698/ST 698 LP: EMI CFP 158

Scottish Fantasy

London January 1957	Philharmonia Rabin	LP: Columbia 33CX 1538 LP: Columbia (Germany) C 90964 LP: Angel 35484/60342 CD: EMI CZS 764 1232
London May 1958	LPO Campoli	LP: Decca LXT 5453/SXL 2026 LP: Decca ADD 110/SDD 110/ECS 775 CD: Beulah 2PD 10

BUSONI

Eine Lustspiel-Ouvertüre

London May 1962	Philharmonia	CD: Intaglio INCD 7461

BUTTERWORTH

The Banks of Green Willow

London November 1954	LPO	LP: Decca LXT 5015/ACL 224/ECS 647
Barking November 1969	LPO	CD: Radio Classics BBCRD 9119
Walthamstow June 1973	LPO	LP: Lyrita SRCS 69 LP: Musical Heritage HNH 4005/ MHS 3638

English Idyll No 1

Hayes March 1922	British SO	HMV unpublished
Walthamstow June 1973	LPO	LP: Lyrita SRCS 69 LP: Musical Heritage HNH 4005/ MHS 3638

English Idyll No 2

Walthamstow June 1973	LPO	LP: Lyrita SRCS 69 LP: Musical Heritage HNH 4005/ MHS 3638

A Shropshire Lad

Hayes November 1920	British SO	78: HMV D 520 Abridged version
Manchester March 1942	Hallé	78: HMV C 3287 LP: EMI ED 29 10921 CD: VAI Audio VAIA 10672
London November 1954	LPO	LP: Decca LXT 5015/LW 5175 LP: Decca ACL 224/ECS 647
Walthamstow June 1973	LPO	LP: Lyrita SRCS 69 LP: Musical Heritage HNH 4005/ MHS 3638

CHAUSSON

Poème for violin and orchestra

London February 1952	LPO Menuhin	78: HMV DB 9759-9760 LP: EMI EX 29 08643

CHOPIN

Piano Concerto No 1

London February 1954	LPO Gulda	LP: Decca LXT 2925/ACL 94
Vienna March 1959	VPO Hesse-Bukowska	LP: Westminster WST 14048 LP: CBS (USA) MS 161

Piano Concerto No 2

Vienna March 1959	VPO Hesse-Bukowska	LP: Westminster WST 14049/WGS 8190

Funeral March, orchestrated by Elgar

London May 1932	BBCSO	78: HMV DB 1722 78: Victor 11-533 LP: EMI ED 29 03551 CD: EMI CDH 763 1342

CLARKE

Trumpet Voluntary

London August 1967	LPO Webb	LP: World Records T 698/ST 698 LP: EMI CFP 158

COATES

The Three Bears, Fantasy

London   LPO   LP: Lyrita SRCS 107
December 1976

Calling all workers, March

London   BBC Concert   CD: Radio Classics BBCRD 9106
June 1975   Orchestra

The Dam Busters, March

London   LPO   LP: World Records T 750/ST 750
August 1967   LP: EMI CFP 173

London   LPO   CD: AS-Disc AS 534
April 1969

London   LPO   LP: Lyrita SRCS 71
August 1973   LP: Musical Heritage HNH 4076

London   BBC Concert   CD: Radio Classics BBCRD 9106
June 1975   Orchestra

The Three Elizabeths, Suite

London   BBC Concert   CD: Radio Classics BBCRD 9106
June 1975   Orchestra

London   LPO   LP: Lyrita SRCS 107
November 1976

Evening in town (From Meadow to Mayfair)

London   LPO   LP: Lyrita SRCS 107
December 1976

The Green Hills o' Somerset; Stonecracker John

London   BBC Concert   CD: Radio Classics BBCRD 9106
June 1975   Orchestra
                Wallace

In the country (From Meadow to Mayfair)

London   LPO   LP: Lyrita SRCS 107
December 1976

The Jester at the wedding, Suite

London June 1975	BBC Concert Orchestra	CD: Radio Classics BBCRD 9106

London Suite: Covent Garden; Westminster; Knightsbridge

London June 1975	BBC Concert Orchestra	CD: Radio Classics BBCRD 9106

The Merrymakers, Overture

London June 1975	BBC Concert Orchestra	CD: Radio Classics BBCRD 9106
London November 1976	LPO	LP: Lyrita SRCS 107

Summer Days, Suite

London November 1976	LPO	LP: Lyrita SRCS 107

WALFORD DAVIES

Royal Air Force March

London August 1967	LPO	LP: World Records T 750/ST 750 LP: EMI CFP 173

DELIBES

Coppélia, Ballet Suite

Walthamstow March 1955	LPO	LP: Nixa NCL 16009 LP: Westminster XWN 18241 LP: Pye GGL 0188/MAL 677 Excerpts LP: Westminster LAB 7027

Naila, Waltz

Walthamstow April 1955	LPO	LP: Nixa NCL 16009 LP: Westminster XWN 18241 LP: Pye GGL 0188/MAL 677

Sylvia, Ballet Suite

Walthamstow March 1955	LPO	LP: Nixa NCL 16009 LP: Westminster XWN 18241/LAB 7027 LP: Pye GGL 0188/MAL 677

DELIUS

Marche caprice

London August 1973	New Philharmonia	LP: Lyrita SRCS 71 LP: Musical Heritage HNH 4076

DOHNANYI

Piano Concerto No 2

London September 1956	RPO Dohnanyi	LP: HMV ALP 1514 LP: Angel 35538

Variations on a Nursery Song

London May 1954	LPO Katchen	LP: Decca LXT 2862/LXT 5374 LP: Decca ACL 65/ECS 668 LP: Everest SDBR 3280
London September 1956	RPO Dohnanyi	LP: HMV ALP 1514 LP: Angel 35538
London January 1959	LPO Katchen	LP: Decca LXT 5550/SXL 2176 LP: Decca ADD 428/SDD 428

DUNCAN

Jubilate, arranged by Woodgate

London April 1957	LPO Flagstad	45: Decca CEP 517/SEC 5002 LP: Decca LXT 5392/SXL 2049 LP: Decca ADD 107/SDD 107

DVORAK

Cello Concerto

London April 1957	RPO Rostropovich	LP: HMV ALP 1595/ASD 358 LP: Capitol G 7109/SG 7109 LP: Angel 60136 LP: EMI SXLP 30176/1C 053 01294

ELGAR

Cello Concerto

London October 1945	BBCSO Casals	78: HMV DB 6338-6341/ DB 9043-9046 auto LP: World Records SH 121 LP: EMI HLM 7110 CD: EMI CDH 763 4982
London October 1972	LPO Tortelier	LP: EMI ASD 2906 LP: Angel 37029 LP: EMI SLS 270003/EX 29 06173 CD: EMI CDU 565 0492

Violin Concerto

London October 1954	LPO Campoli	LP: Decca LXT 5014/ACL 312/ECS 675
London December 1965	New Philharmonia Menuhin	LP: EMI ALP 2259/ASD 2259 LP: Angel 36330 LP: EMI SXLP 29 0001/EX 29 06173 CD: EMI CDM 764 7252
London April 1969	LPO Menuhin	CD: AS-Disc AS 534
London April and June 1977 and January 1978	LPO Haendel	LP: EMI ASD 3598

Symphony No 1

London September and October 1949	LPO	78: HMV DB 21024-21029/ DB 9456-9461 auto LP: HMV ALP 1052 LP: Victor LHMV 1036 LP: EMI RLS 7716
Walthamstow December 1967	LPO	LP: Lyrita SRCS 37/REAM 1 LP: Musical Heritage MHS 1285
London September and October 1976	LPO	LP: EMI ASD 3330/EX 29 06173 LP: Angel 37240 CD: EMI CDC 747 2042/CDM 764 0132

Symphony No 2

Bedford August and October 1944	BBCSO	78: HMV DB 6190-6195/ DB 8967-8972 auto LP: EMI ED 29 03551 CD: EMI CDH 763 1342
Walthamstow August 1956	LPO	LP: Nixa NCL 16018 LP: Westminster XWN 18373 LP: Pye GGC 4002/GSGC 14002 LP: Pye GSGC 15008 CD: Precision PVCD 8382
Glasgow September 1963	Scottish National Orchestra	LP: Waverley LLP 1021/SLLP 1022 LP: EMI CFP 172
Walthamstow January 1968	LPO	LP: Lyrita SRCS 40/REAM 2 LP: Musical Heritage MHS 1335
London November 1975 and January 1976	LPO	LP: EMI ASD 3266/EX 29 06173 LP: Angel 37218 CD: EMI CDM 764 0142

Introduction and Allegro for strings

London March 1937	BBCSO	78: HMV DB 3198-3199 78: Victor M 635 LP: EMI ED 29 07251 CD: EMI CDH 763 0972 CD: VAI Audio VAIA 10672 78 version coupled with Sospiri
London August 1961	LPO	LP: World Records T 158/ST 158 LP: EMI CFP 40022
London December 1972	LPO	LP: EMI ASD 2906/EX 29 06173 LP: Angel 37029 CD: EMI CDU 565 0492

Enigma Variations

London March 1936	BBCSO	78: HMV DB 2800-2802/ DB 8068-8070 auto 78: Victor M 475 CD: VAI Audio VAIA 10672
London September 1953	LPO	LP: HMV ALP 1153 LP: Victor LHMV 7 LP: EMI RLS 7716 Nimrod LP: HMV CLP 1840
London August 1961	LPO	LP: World Records T 158/ST 158 LP: EMI CFP 40022
London August 1970	LSO	LP: EMI ASD 2750/EX 29 06173 LP: Angel 36799 CD: EMI CDC 747 2062 CD: EMI CDM 764 0152/CDM 764 7482 Excerpts LP: EMI SEOM 17/HQS 1283/YKM 5013

Chanson de matin

London February 1954	LPO	78: Decca X 574 45: Decca 45-71088 LP: Decca LW 5174/ACL 113/ECS 646 LP: Decca DPA 537-538/SPA 576
London April 1967	LPO	LP: EMI ASD 2356/YKM 5013 CD: EMI CDC 747 2042/CDM 764 0132

Chanson de nuit

London February 1954	LPO	78: Decca X 574 45: Decca 45-71088 LP: Decca LW 5174/ACL 113/ECS 646 LP: Decca DPA 537-538
London April 1967	LPO	LP: EMI ASD 2356/HQS 1283 LP: EMI YKM 5013/EX 29 06173 CD: EMI CDC 747 2042/CDM 764 0132

Bavarian Dances

London October 1954	LPO	LP: Decca LW 5174/ACL 113/ECS 646 Nos 1 and 2 only 45: Decca 45-71067
London April 1967	LPO	LP: EMI ASD 2356/ED 29 11291 No 3 only LP: EMI HQS 1283

The Apostles

London	LPO	LP: EMI SLS 976
October, November	LP Choir	CD: EMI CMS 764 2062
and December 1973	Armstrong, Watts,	Side 6 of LP set contained
& July 1974	Tear, Luxon,	talk on the work by Boult
	Grant, Carol Case	

The Dream of Gerontius

London	New Philharmonia	LP: EMI SLS 987
May and	LP Choir	CD: EMI CDS 747 2088
July 1975	Watts, Gedda,	
	Lloyd	

The Dream of Gerontius, Prelude

London	BBCSO	78: HMV DB 2194
March 1934		LP: EMI ED 29 10921
		CD: EMI CDH 763 1342
		CD: VAI Audio VAIA 10672

The Kingdom

London	LPO	LP: EMI SLS 939
December 1968	LP Choir	CD: EMI CMS 764 2092
and February	M.Price, Minton,	Excerpts
1969	Young, Shirley-Quirk	LP: EMI SEOM 6/SEOM 11

The Music Makers

London	LPO	LP: EMI ALP 2311/ASD 2311
December 1966	LP Choir	LP: Vanguard (USA) 71225
	Baker	CD: EMI CDS 747 2088

4 Choral Songs op 53

London	BBC Chorus	LP: Elgar Society ELGS 002
February 1967		LP: EMI ED 29 08181

2 Choral Songs op 71

London	BBC Chorus	LP: Elgar Society ELGS 002
February 1967		LP: EMI ED 29 08181

2 Choral Songs op 73

London	BBC Chorus	LP: Elgar Society ELGS 002
February 1967		LP: EMI ED 29 08181

Death on the Hills

London	BBC Chorus	LP: Elgar Society ELGS 002
February 1967		LP: EMI ED 29 08181

Go, song of mine

London	BBC Chorus	LP: Elgar Society ELGS 002
February 1967		LP: EMI ED 29 08181

Pomp and Circumstance, March No 1

London June 1955	LPO	45: HMV 7EB 6026/7EP 7100 LP: HMV ALP 1379/RLS 7716
London July 1960	New SO	LP: Readers Digest RDM 1007/2533 LP: Readers Digest RDS 5007/6533 CD: Chesky CD 53
London January 1977	LPO	LP: EMI ASD 3388/EX 29 06173 LP: Angel 37436 CD: EMI CDC 747 2062/CDM 764 0152 CD: EMI WHS 568 4102

Pomp and Circumstance, March No 2

London June 1955	LPO	45: HMV 7EB 6026/7EP 7100 LP: HMV ALP 1379/RLS 7716
London December 1976	LPO	LP: EMI ASD 3388 LP: Angel 37436 CD: EMI CDC 747 2062/CDM 764 0152

Pomp and Circumstance, March No 3

London May 1953	LPO	78: HMV DB 21588 45: HMV 7ER 5039 LP: EMI RLS 7716
London June 1955	LPO	45: HMV 7EB 6027 LP: HMV ALP 1379
London December 1976	LPO	LP: EMI ASD 3388 LP: Angel 37436 CD: EMI CDC 747 2062/CDM 764 0152

Pomp and Circumstance, March No 4

London June 1955	LPO	LP: HMV ALP 1379/RLS 7716
London October 1976	LPO	LP: EMI ASD 3388 LP: Angel 37436 CD: EMI CDC 747 2062/CDM 764 0152

Pomp and Circumstance, March No 5

London June 1955	LPO	45: HMV 7EB 6027 LP: HMV ALP 1379/RLS 7716
London October 1976	LPO	LP: EMI ASD 3388 LP: Angel 37436 CD: EMI CDC 747 2062/CDM 764 0152

Carillon

London February 1974	LPO	LP: EMI ASD 3050/ESD 7167

Cockaigne, Overture

Walthamstow August 1956	LPO	LP: Westminster XWN 18526/LAB 7056
London September 1970 and February 1971	LPO	LP: EMI ASD 2822/ESD 7167 LP: EMI EX 29 06173 CD: EMI CDM 764 0142

Dream Children

London September 1955	LPO	LP: HMV ALP 1379/RLS 7716
London February 1974	LPO	LP: EMI ASD 3050/ESD 7167

Elegy for strings

London February 1974	LPO	LP: EMI ASD 3050/SEOM 24

Empire March

London January 1977	LPO	LP: EMI ASD 3388 LP: Angel 37436

Falstaff

London July 1950	LPO	78: HMV DB 6903-6906 LP: EMI RLS 7716
Walthamstow August 1956	LPO	LP: Nixa NCT 17003 LP: Westminster XWN 18256/LAB 7052 LP: Pye GGC 4059/GSGC 14059
London May, June and August 1973	LPO	LP: EMI ASD 2970

Froissart, Overture

London September 1955	LPO	LP: HMV ALP 1379/RLS 7716
London September 1970 and February 1971	LPO	LP: EMI ASD 2822/ESD 7167 CD: EMI CDU 565 0492

Funeral March (Grania and Diarmid)

London February 1974	LPO	LP: EMI ASD 3050

Imperial March

London April 1937	BBCSO	78: HMV DB 3163 78: Victor M 929 LP: EMI ED 29 60921 CD: EMI CDH 763 1342 CD: VAI Audio VAIA 10672 <u>78 issues coupled with Meyerbeer</u> <u>Coronation March</u>
London December 1976	LPO	LP: EMI ASD 3388 LP: Angel 37436

In the South, Overture

London June 1955	LPO	LP: HMV ALP 1359/RLS 7716
London September 1970 and February 1971	LPO	LP: EMI ASD 2822/ESD 7167 CD: EMI CDU 565 0492

Meditation (The Light of Life)

London February 1974	LPO	LP: EMI ASD 3050/ED 29 11291

Nursery Suite

London June and September 1955	LPO	LP: HMV ALP 1359/RLS 7716

Polonia, Symphonic Prelude

London   LPO   LP: EMI ASD 3050
February 1974

The Sanguine Fan, Ballet

London   LPO   LP: EMI ASD 2970
May, June and
August 1973

Serenade for strings

Bromley   Bromley String   LP: P 142L
May 1964   Orchestra   Private issue for Royal
                                     College of Music

London   LPO   LP: EMI ASD 2906/EX 29 06173
March 1972   LP: Angel 37029
                                 CD: EMI CDC 747 2042/CDM 764 0132

Sospiri

London   BBCSO   78: HMV DB 3199
March 1937   78: Victor M 635
                                 LP: Elgar Society ELG 001
                                 LP: EMI ED 29 10921
                                 CD: EMI CDH 763 1342
                                 CD: VAI Audio VAIA 10672
                                 78 issues coupled with
                                 Introduction and Allegro

Triumphal March (Caractacus)

London   LPO   LP: EMI ASD 3050/ESD 7167
February 1974   LP: EMI ED 29 11291

The Wand of Youth, Suite No 1

London   LPO   LP: HMV ALP 1153/RLS 7716
May 1953   LP: Victor LHMV 7
                                 Excerpts
                                 45: HMV 7ER 5110

London   LPO   LP: EMI ASD 2356/ED 29 11291
April 1967   Excerpts
                                 LP: EMI SEOM 6/SEOM 15

The Wand of Youth, Suite No 2

London   LPO   LP: EMI ASD 2356/ED 29 11291
April 1967   Excerpts
                                 LP: EMI HQS 1283/SEOM 6/SEOM 15

FALLA

Ritual Fire Dance (El amor brujo)

London August 1967	LPO	LP: World Records T 698/ST 698 LP: EMI CFP 158

FINZI

The Fall of the leaf

London October 1974	LPO	LP: Lyrita SRCS 84

Introit for violin and orchestra

Barking November 1969	LPO Jarvis	CD: Radio Classics BBCRD 9119
London September 1975	LPO Friend	LP: Lyrita SRCS 84

Prelude

London September 1975	LPO	LP: Lyrita SRCS 84

Nocturne

London October 1974	LPO	LP: Lyrits SRCS 84

Romance

London January 1977	LPO	LP: Lyrita SRCS 84

A Severn Rhapsody

London January 1977	LPO	LP: Lyrita SRCS 84

3 Soliloquies (Incidental music to Love's Labours Lost)

London January 1977	LPO	LP: Lyrita SRCS 84

FRANCK

Symphony in D minor

Watford June 1959	Philharmonia	LP: Readers Digest RDM 6/RDS 6 LP: RCA GL 25004 LP: Quintessence PMC 7050

Variations symphoniques

London 1923	British SO Tyrer	78: Edison Bell VF 599-600
London December 1955	LPO Curzon	45: Decca CEP 524 LP: Decca LXT 5547/SXL 2173 CD: Decca 425 0822

GERSHWIN

Cuban Overture

| London | LPO | LP: World Records T 698/ST 698 |
| August 1967 | | LP: EMI CFP 158 |

GLINKA

Russlan and Ludmilla, Overture

| London | LPO | LP: World Records T 665/ST 665 |
| October 1966 | | |

GLUCK

Alceste, Overture

| London | BBCSO | 78: HMV DB 3129 |
| January 1937 | | 78: Victor 12-041 |

GOUNOD

O divine redeemer

London	LPO	45: Decca CEP 517/SEC 5002
April 1957	Flagstad	LP: Decca LXT 5392/SXL 2049
		LP: Decca ADD 107/SDD 107
		LP: Decca DPA 615-616

GRAINGER

Childrens' March (Over the hills and far away)

London	LPO	LP: Lyrita SRCS 71
November 1973		LP: Musical Heritage HNH 4076

GRIEG

Piano Concerto

London	LPO	LP: World Records T 559/ST 559
November 1965	Cherkassky	LP: EMI SMFP 57002

GRUBER

Silent night

London	LPO	45: Decca CEP 517/SEC 5002
April 1957	Flagstad	LP: Decca LXT 5392/SXL 2049
		LP: Decca ADD 107/SDD 107

HADLEY

One Morning in Spring, Rhapsody for small orchestra

London	LPO	LP: Lyrita SRCS 106
June 1973		

HANDEL

Music for the Royal Fireworks, arranged by Harty

| London | LPO | 78: HMV DB 6968-6969 |
| October 1949 | | 45: HMV 7ER 5103 |

Water Music, arranged by Harty

Walthamstow	LPO	LP: Nixa NCL 16017
May 1955		LP: Westminster XWN 18115
		LP: Pye GSGC 15026

Overture in D minor, arranged by Elgar

London	LPO	LP: EMI ASD 2822
September 1970		
and February		
1971		

15 Organ Concerti

Great Packington   LPO   LP: CBS 77358
July 1957   Power Biggs CD: Sony M3YK 45825
                                                Selections
                                                LP: Columbia (USA) ML 5839/
                                                            MS 6161/MS 6439
                                                LP: Philips ABL 3260-3261/
                                                             SABL 148-149
                                                LP: Philips ABE 10227/SABE 2007
                                                LP: CBS 72447/71051

Acis and Galatea

Watford June 1959	Philomusica St Anthony Singers Sutherland, Pears, Galliver, Brannigan	LP: Oiseau Lyre OL 50179-50180/ SOL 60011-60012 LP: Decca 414 3101 CD: Decca 436 2272

Acis and Galatea: Excerpt (As when the dove laments her love)

London May 1959	LSO De los Angeles	LP: EMI ASD 4193

Acis and Galatea: Excerpts (Lo, here my love; Love in her eyes sits playing)

London November 1959 and May 1960	Covent Garden Orchestra McKellar	LP: Decca LK 4380/SKL 4121/SPA 562 LP: Contour CC 7559

Dank sei dir Herr, attributed to Handel

London December 1956	LPO Flagstad Sung in English	LP: Decca LXT 5316 CD: Decca 436 2342

Il Floridante: Excerpt (Alma mia)

London May 1959	LSO De los Angeles	HMV unpublished

Jeptha: Excerpts (Deeper and deeper still; Waft her, angels; For ever blessed)

London November 1959 and May 1960	Covent Garden Orchestra McKellar	LP: Decca LK 4380/SKL 4121 LP: Contour CC 7559 CD: Decca 433 0032

Judas Maccabaeus: Excerpt (So shall the lute and harp awake)

London	LSO	LP: EMI ASD 4193
May 1959	De los Angeles	

Judas Maccabaeus: Excerpt (Father of Heaven)

London
October 1952

LPO
Ferrier

45: Decca CEP 723
LP: Decca LXT 2757/LXT 5382
LP: Decca LW 5076/414 6231
CD: Decca 414 6232/433 4742/433 8022

London
February and
May 1960
Re-recording for
stereo of the
orchestral
accompaniment to
1952 version

LPO

LP: Decca SXL 2234/SDD 286/SDD 433
LP: Decca SPA 531/SPA 566/AKF 1-7

Judas Maccabaeus: Excerpts (How vain is man; Sound an alarm)

London
November 1959
and May 1960

Covent Garden
Orchestra
McKellar

LP: Decca LK 4380/SKL 4121
LP: Decca SPA 297/SPA 566
LP: Contour CC 7559
CD: Decca 433 0032

Messiah

London January 1954	LPO LP Choir Vyvyan, Procter, Maran, Brannigan	LP: Decca LXT 2921-2924 LP: Decca ACL 118-120/ECS 613-615 Excerpts 45: Decca 45-71080/45-71082 45: Decca 45-71101/CEP 519 LP: Decca LXT 2989/LXT 5383 LP: Decca LW 5225/LW 5342 LP: Decca ACL 197/ECS 566/ECS 791
London May and August 1961	LSO LSO Chorus Sutherland, Bumbry, McKellar, Ward	LP: Decca MET 218-220/SET 218-220 LP: Decca D104 D3 CD: Decca 433 0032 Excerpts LP: Decca LXT 5685/SXL 2316 LP: Decca LXT 6009-6010/ SXL 6009-6010 LP: Decca LXT 6191/SXL 6191 LP: Decca BR 8508/JB 80/SPA 100 LP: Decca SPA 297/SPA 355 LP: Decca SPA 448/411 8411 CD: Decca 417 8792

Messiah: Excerpts (He shall feed his flock; I know that my redeemer liveth)

London December 1956	LPO Flagstad	LP: Decca LXT 5316 CD: Decca 436 2342

Messiah: Excerpt (He was despised)

London October 1952	LPO Ferrier	45: Decca CEP 550 LP: Decca LXT 2757/LXT 5382 LP: Decca LW 5225/LW 5076 LP: Decca PA 172/414 6231 CD: Decca 433 4742/433 8022
London February and May 1960 <u>Re-recording for stereo of the orchestral accompaniment to 1952 version</u>	LPO	45: Decca SEC 5099 LP: Decca SXL 2234/SDD 286 LP: Decca SPA 448/SPA 531/AKF 1-7

Messiah: Excerpt (O thou that tellest glad tidings)

London	LPO	45: Decca 45-71038/CEP 550
October 1952	Ferrier	LP: Decca LXT 2757/LXT 5382
		LP: Decca LW 5076/414 6231
		LP: Decca 414 6232/433 4742/433 8022

London	LPO	45: Decca SEC 5099
February and		LP: Decca SXL 2234/SDD 286/AKF 1-7
May 1960		LP: Decca SPA 172/SPA 297/SPA 531
<u>Re-recording for stereo of the orchestral accompaniment to 1952 version</u>		LP: Decca DPA 551-552

Messiah: Excerpts (Comfort ye, my people; Every valley shall be exalted)

London	Covent Garden	45: Decca DFE 6623/STO 133
November 1959	Orchestra	LP: Decca LK 4380/SKL 4121
and May 1960	McKellar	LP: Contour CC 7559

Radamisto: Excerpt (Gods all powerful)

London	LPO	LP: Decca LXT 5316
December 1956	Flagstad	CD: Decca 433 2342

Rodelinda: Excerpt (Art thou troubled?)

London	LPO	Decca unpublished
December 1956	Flagstad	

Samson: Excerpt (Return, o God of Hosts)

London October 1952	LPO Ferrier	45: Decca 45-71038/CEP 723 LP: Decca LXT 2757/LXT 5382 LP: Decca LW 5076/414 6231 CD: Decca 414 6232/433 4742/433 8022
London February and May 1960 <u>Re-recording for</u> <u>stereo of the</u> <u>orchestral</u> <u>accompaniment to</u> <u>1952 version</u>	LPO	LP: Decca SXL 2234/SDD 286 LP: Decca SPA 531/AKF 1-7

Semele: Excerpt (O sleep, why dost thou leave me?)

London December 1956	LPO Flagstad	LP: Decca LXT 5316 CD: Decca 436 2342

Semele: Excerpt (Where'er you walk)

London November 1959 and May 1960	Covent Garden Orchestra McKellar	LP: Decca LK 4380/SKL 4121 LP: Decca SPA 566/DPA 615-616 LP: Contour CC 7559

Serse: Excerpt (Ombra mai fù)

London April 1957	LPO Flagstad	Decca unpublished
London November 1959 and May 1960	Covent Garden Orchestra McKellar	45: Decca DFE 6623/STO 133 LP: Decca LK 4380/SKL 4121/SPA 562 LP: Contour CC 7559

Tolomeo: Excerpt (Non lodero col labbro)

London November 1959 and May 1960	Covent Garden Orchestra McKellar	45: Decca DFE 6623/STO 133 LP: Decca LK 4380/SKL 4121/SPA 566 LP: Contour CC 7559

HAYDN

Cello Concerto in D

London October 1945	BBCSO Casals	HMV unpublished

Symphony No 104 "London"

Wembley February 1959	LPO	LP: Classics Club X 86 LP: Concert Hall YM 2161/SMS 2161 LP: Concert Hall M 2088/SMS 2910 LP: Perfect (USA) 15003/13003

German Dances Nos 1, 6 and 7

London May 1952	LPO	HMV unpublished
London July 1955	LPO	78: HMV HMS 78 LP: HMV HLP 19 LP: Victor LM 1637 Recorded for HMV's History of Music series

HINDEMITH

Symphony in E flat

Walthamstow August 1958	LPO	LP: Everest LPBR 6008/SDBR 3008 CD: Everest EVC 9009

Symphonic Metamorphoses on themes by Weber

Walthamstow August 1958	LPO	Everest unpublished

Trauermusik

Bromley May 1964	Bromley String Orchestra	LP: P 142L Private issue for Royal College of Music

HOLST

The Planets

Bedford January 1945	BBCSO Chorus	78: HMV DB 6227-6233/ DB 8994-9000 auto 45: Victor WHMV 1002 LP: Victor LHMV 1002 LP: EMI ED 29 07251 CD: EMI CDH 763 0972 <u>Excerpts</u> 45: HMV 7P 203/7P 204
Walthamstow September 1953	LPO LP Choir	LP: Nixa NLP 903 LP: Westminster XWN 18252/WL 5235 LP: Pye GGL 01721/GH 503 LP: Pye MAL 617/MALS 617 LP: Hallmark HMA 207 LP: Everest SDBR 3443 CD: Everyman EVCD 26
Vienna March 1959	VPO Akademiechor	LP: Westminster XWN 18919 LP: Westminster WST 14067/WGS 8160 LP: Whitehall WH 20033/WHS 20033 LP: World Records T 254/ST 254 LP: CBS (USA) MS 171 <u>Orchestra described on label as</u> <u>Vienna State Opera Orchestra</u>
London July and November 1966	New Philharmonia Ambrosian Singers	LP: EMI ALP 2301/ASD 2301/ESD 7135 LP: Angel 36420 <u>Excerpt</u> LP: EMI SEOM 1
London May, June and July 1978	LPO Mitchell Singers	LP: EMI ASD 3649/1C 069 06908 CD: EMI CDM 764 7482

Beni Mora, Oriental Suite

Walthamstow   LPO   LP: Lyrita SRCS 56
January 1971   CD: Lyrita SRCD 222

A Choral Fantasy

London   LPO   CD: Intaglio INCD 7401
August 1967   Alldis Choir
                   Coster

A Choral Symphony

London   LPO   LP: EMI SAN 354/ED 29 03781
March 1974   LP Choir   LP: Angel 37030
                   Palmer   CD: EMI CDM 565 1282

Country Song (2 Songs without words)

London   LPO   Decca unpublished
March 1961

Egdon Heath

London   LPO   LP: Decca LXT 6006/SXL 6006/JB 49
March 1961   CD: Decca 440 3182

A Fugal Overture

London   LPO   LP: Lyrita SRCS 37
November 1967   LP: Musical Heritage HNH 4038
                                               CD: Lyrita SRCD 222

Hammersmith, Prelude and Scherzo

London   LPO   CD: Intaglio INCD 7281
1967

Walthamstow   LPO   LP: Lyrita SRCS 56
January 1971   CD: Lyrita SRCD 222

The Hymn of Jesus

London March 1962	BBCSO BBC Chorus	LP: Decca LXT 6006/SXL 6006/JB 49 CD: Decca 421 3812

Japanese Suite

Walthamstow March 1970	LSO	LP: Lyrita SRCS 50 LP: Musical Heritage MHS 1919 CD: Lyrita SRCD 222

March (Suite No 1, arranged by Jacob)

London November 1973	LPO	LP: Lyrita SRCS 71 LP: Musical Heritage HNH 4076

Marching Song (2 Songs without words)

Hayes November 1921	British SO	HMV unpublished
London December 1956	LPO	Decca unpublished

The Perfect Fool, Ballet music

London November 1954	LPO	LP: Decca LXT 5015/LW 5175 LP: Decca ACL 113/ECS 657
London March 1961	LPO	LP: Decca LXT 6006/SXL 6006/JB 49 LP: Decca DDS 505/DPA 627-628 CD: Decca 440 3182

Scherzo (from an unfinished symphony)

London December 1955	LPO	Decca unpublished
Walthamstow January 1971	LPO	LP: Lyrita SRCS 56 CD: Lyrita SRCD 222

A Somerset Rhapsody

Walthamstow July 1956	LPO	RCA/Decca unpublished
Walthamstow January 1971	LPO	LP: Lyrita SRCS 56 CD: Lyrita SRCD 222

Royal Albert Hall
(Manager: C. S. Taylor)

The BBC presents 51st Season of

HENRY WOOD PROMENADE CONCERTS

Conductors
SIR ADRIAN BOULT   BASIL CAMERON

Associate Conductor
CONSTANT LAMBERT

Organist: Berkeley Mason

Thursday 9 August at 7

WAGNER—SIBELIUS CONCERT

Conductor: SIR ADRIAN BOULT

OVERTURE, The Flying Dutchman	*Wagner*
(a) ELIZABETH'S PRAYER } (Tannhäuser)	*Wagner*
(b) ELIZABETH'S GREETING	
GOOD FRIDAY MUSIC (Parsifal)	*Wagner*
FORGING SONGS (Siegfried)	*Wagner*
(a) Mime the Craftsman (b) Nothung! Nothung!	
ENTRANCE OF THE GODS (The Rhinegold)	*Wagner*

INTERVAL

Conductor: CONSTANT LAMBERT

NIGHT RIDE AND SUNRISE	*Sibelius*
TONE POEM for Soprano and Orchestra, Luonnotar	*Sibelius*
SYMPHONY No. 3, in C	*Sibelius*

EVA TURNER

WALTER WIDDOP

THE LONDON SYMPHONY ORCHESTRA
Leader: George Stratton

Wednesday, 29 October 1947 at 8

Symphony No. 41, in C (Jupiter) (K.551) — MOZART
1756-1791

Symphonic Poem, Till Eulenspiegel — STRAUSS
(Conducted by the Composer) — Born 1864

INTERVAL

The Planets — HOLST
1874-1934

THE BBC WOMEN'S CHORUS
Chorus Master: Leslie Woodgate

THE BBC SYMPHONY ORCHESTRA
Leader: Paul Beard

Conductors:
SIR ADRIAN BOULT
RICHARD STRAUSS

IRELAND

Piano Concerto

London	LPO	LP: Lyrita SRCS 36
November 1967	Parkin	LP: Musical Heritage MHS 1429

Legend for piano and orchestra

London	LPO	LP: Lyrita RCS 32/SRCS 32
December 1965	Parkin	LP: Musical Heritage MHS 1317

Concertino Pastorale for strings

London	LPO	LP: Lyrita RCS 31/SRCS 31
December 1965		LP: Musical Heritage MHS 1498

These things shall be

London	LPO	LP: Lyrita SRCS 36
November 1967	LP Choir	LP: Musical Heritage MHS 1429
	Carol Case	

A London Overture

London	LPO	LP: Lyrita RCS 31/SRCS 31
December 1965		LP: Musical Heritage MHS 1498

Mai-Dun, Symphonic Rhapsody

London	LPO	LP: Lyrita RCS 32/SRCS 32
December 1965		LP: Musical Heritage MHS 1317

Elegy and Minuet (A Downland Suite)

London   LPO   LP: Lyrita RCS 31/SRCS 31
December 1965   LP: Musical Heritage MHS 1498

Epic March

London   LPO   LP: Lyrita RCS 31/SRCS 31
December 1965   LP: Musical Heritage MHS 1498

The Forgotten Rite, Prelude

London   LPO   LP: Lyrita RCS 32/SRCS 32
December 1965   LP: Musical Heritage MHS 1317

The Holy Boy

London   LPO   LP: Lyrita RCS 31/SRCS 31
December 1965

The Overlanders, Suite of film music arranged by Mackerras

Walthamstow   LPO   LP: Lyrita SRCS 45
January 1970   LP: Musical Heritage MHS 1481

The Overlanders, 2 Symphonic Studies arranged by Bush

Walthamstow   LPO   LP: Lyrita SRCS 45
January 1970   LP: Musical Heritage MHS 1481

Satyricon, Overture

London   LPO   LP: Lyrita RCS 32/SRCS 32
December 1965   LP: Musical Heritage MHS 1317

Scherzo & Cortège on themes from Julius Caesar, arranged by Bush

Walthamstow   LPO   LP: Lyrita SRCS 45
January 1970   LP: Musical Heritage MHS 1481

Tritons, Symphonic Prelude

Walthamstow   LPO   LP: Lyrita SRCS 45
January 1970   LP: Musical Heritage MHS 1481

HOWELLS

Concerto for strings

London LPO LP: EMI ASD 3020
November 1973
and February
1974

Corydon's Dance & Scherzo in Arden (Music for a Prince)

London   New Philharmonia   LP: Lyrita SRCS 69
September 1973   LP: Musical Heritage HNH 4005/
                                        MHS 3638

Elegy for viola, string quartet and string orchestra

London   New Philharmonia   LP: Lyrita SRCS 69
September 1973   LP: Musical Heritage HNH 4005/
                                        MHS 3638

Merry Eye

London   New Philharmonia   LP: Lyrita SRCS 69
September 1973   LP: Musical Heritage HNH 4005/
                                        MHS 3638

Procession

London   LPO   LP: Lyrita SRCS 71
November 1973   LP: Musical Heritage HNH 4076

HUMPERDINCK

Hänsel und Gretel, Overture

Hayes November 1921	British SO	78: HMV D 591
London July 1932	BBCSO	78: HMV DB 1758 78: Victor 11-929 CD: Beulah IPD 12

Hänsel und Gretel, Dream Pantomime

Hayes March 1922	British SO	78: HMV D 617 Coupled with Witches' Ride
London May 1933 and November 1934	BBCSO	78: HMV DB 2366 78: Victor 11-832

Hänsel und Gretel, Witches' Ride

Hayes March 1922	British SO	78: HMV D 617 Coupled with Dream Pantomime

KHACHATURIAN

Piano Concerto in D flat

Walthamstow December 1958	LPO Katz	LP: Pye CCL 30151/GGC 4013/GSGC 14013

LALO

Cello Concerto

London November 1953	LPO Nelsova	LP: Decca LXT 2906/ACL 244

LIADOV

Kikimora

Manchester March 1942	Hallé	78: HMV C 3288 78: Victor 11-8729 CD: Dutton CDAX 8010

LIDDLE

Abide with me

London April 1957	LPO Flagstad	LP: Decca LXT 5392/SXL 2049 LP: Decca ADD 107/SDD 107

LISZT

Les Préludes

| London
July 1960 | New SO | LP: Readers Digest RDM 1007
LP: Readers Digest RDS 5007/RDS 9638
LP: Quintessence PMC 7050
CD: Chesky CD 53 |

Piano Concerto No 1

| London
1923 | British SO
Tyrer | 78: Edison Bell VF 557-558
Excerpt
LP: Decca ZPR 123/DPA 3041-3042 |
| Vienna
March 1959 | VPO
Farnardi | LP: Westminster WST 14125
LP: Whitehall WH 20036/WHS 20036
LP: EMI 1C 045 90350 |

Piano Concerto No 2

| Vienna
March 1959 | VPO
Farnardi | LP: Westminster WST 14125
LP: Whitehall WH 20036/WHS 20036
LP: EMI 1C 045 90350 |

Hungarian Fantasia for piano and orchestra

| Walthamstow
March 1956 | LPO
Farnardi | LP: Westminster XWN 18242/LAB 7018 |

Totentanz for piano and orchestra

| Walthamstow
March 1956 | LPO
Farnardi | LP: Westminster XWN 18242/LAB 7018 |

LITOLFF

Scherzo (Concerto symphonique)

London December 1955	LPO Curzon	Decca unpublished
Walthamstow December 1958	LPO Curzon	LP: Decca LXT 5547/SXL 2173 CD: Decca 425 0822
London January 1967	LPO Cherkassky	LP: World Records T 796/ST 796 LP: EMI SMFP 57004

MAHLER

Symphony No 1

Walthamstow August 1958	LPO	LP: Everest LPBR 6005/S 4565 LP: Everest SDBR 3005/SDBR 3359 LP: World Records CM 31/SCM 31 CD: Everest EVC 9022

Symphony No 3

London November 1947	BBCSO Various Choirs Ferrier	Unpublished radio broadcast

Kindertotenlieder

Vienna May 1957	VPO Flagstad	LP: Decca LXT 5395/SXL 2224 LP: Decca BR 3031/ECS 780 CD: Decca 414 6242/440 4912

Lieder eines fahrenden Gesellen

London July 1950	LPO Thebom	78: HMV DB 9576-9577 45: Victor WDM 1627 LP: Victor LM 1203
Vienna May 1957	VPO Flagstad	45: Decca CEP 680/SEC 5079 LP: Decca LXT 5395/SXL 2224/ECS 780 CD: Decca 414 6242/440 4912
London October 1958	Philharmonia C.Ludwig	LP: Columbia 33CX 1671/SAX 2321 LP: World Records T 703/ST 703 LP: EMI SXLP 143 6521 CD: EMI CDM 769 4992

MENDELSSOHN

Symphony No 3 "Scotch"

Walthamstow November 1954	LPO	LP: Nixa NCL 16005 LP: Westminster XWN 18239/LAB 7040 LP: Pye MAL 676

Symphony No 4 "Italian"

Walthamstow November 1954	LPO	LP: Nixa NCL 16005 LP: Westminster XWN 18243/LAB 7008 LP: Pye MAL 676
London October 1966	LPO	LP: World Records T 680/ST 680

Violin Concerto

London January 1957	Philharmonia Rabin	LP: Columbia 33CX 1597 LP: Angel 35572 CD: EMI CZS 764 1232
London May 1958	LPO Campoli	LP: Decca LXT 5453/SXL 2026 LP: Decca ADD 110/SDD 110 LP: Decca ECS 775/DDS 505
London October 1966	LPO M.Smith	LP: World Records T 680/ST 680

Violin Concerto in D minor op posth.

London April 1953	Philharmonia Menuhin	LP: HMV ALP 1085 LP: Electrola E 90057

A Midsummer Night's Dream, complete incidental music

Walthamstow   LPO   LP: Nixa NCT 17009
March 1955   LP: Westminster XWN 18244/
                                         XWN 18243/LAB 7038
                                     LP: Pye MAL 683
                                     Excerpts
                                     45: Nixa NEC 23008

A Midsummer Night's Dream, Overture

London   BBCSO   78: HMV DB 6242-6243
October 1945   Coupled with Wedding March

A Midsummer Night's Dream, Nocturne

London   BBCSO   78: HMV DA 1318
April 1933   78: Victor 4312

A Midsummer Night's Dream, Wedding March

London   BBCSO   78: HMV DB 6243
October 1945   Coupled with Overture

Die Hochzeit des Camacho, Overture

Walthamstow   LPO   Nixa unpublished
March 1955

Meeresstille glückliche Fahrt, Overture

Walthamstow   LPO   LP: Westminster XWN 18163/XWN 18244
March 1955

The Hebrides, Overture

London October 1933	BBCSO	78: HMV DB 2100 78: Victor 11-886
Walthamstow May 1955	LPO	LP: Westminster XWN 18163/XWN 18244
London July 1960	New SO	LP: Readers Digest RDM 1007/RDM 2547 LP: Readers Digest RDS 1007/ RDS 6547/RDS 9281 CD: Chesky CD 53

Ruy Blas, Overture

London November 1934	BBCSO	78: HMV DB 2365 78: Victor M 746
Walthamstow March 1955	LPO	LP: Westminster XWN 18163

Die schöne Melusine, Overture

Walthamstow May 1955	LPO	LP: Westminster XWN 18163

Son and Stranger, Overture

Walthamstow May 1955	LPO	Nixa unpublished

Elijah: Excerpt (O rest in the Lord)

London January 1954	LPO Procter	45: Decca 45-71082
London April 1957	LPO Flagstad	Decca unpublished

Saint Paul: Excerpt (Jerusalem)

London April 1957	LPO Flagstad	LP: Decca LXT 5392/SXL 2049 LP: Decca ADD 207/SDD 207

Hear my prayer

London April 1957	LPO Flagstad	LP: Decca LXT 5392/SXL 2049 LP: Decca ADD 207/SDD 207

MEYERBEER

Coronation March (Le prophète)

London April 1937	BBCSO	78: HMV DB 3163 78: Victor M 929 Coupled with Elgar Imperial March

MOERAN

Symphony in G minor

London August 1973	New Philharmonia	LP: Lyrita SRCS 70 LP: Musical Heritage HNH 4014

Sinfonietta

London November 1967	LPO	LP: Lyrita SRCS 37 LP: Musical Heritage HNH 4038/ MHS 1229

Cello Concerto

Walthamstow February 1969	LPO Coetmore	LP: Lyrita SRCS 43 LP: Musical Heritage MHS 1411

Overture for a Masque

Walthamstow February 1969	LPO	LP: Lyrita SRCS 43 LP: Musical Heritage MHS 1411

Rhapsody No 2 in E

Walthamstow February 1969	LPO	LP: Lyrita SRCS 43 LP: Musical Heritage MHS 1411

MONN

Allegro (Cello Concerto in G minor)

London May 1952	LPO Pleeth	HMV unpublished
London July 1955	LPO Pleeth	78: HMV HMS 78 LP: HMV HLP 19 LP: Victor LM 6137 Recorded for HMV's History of Music series

MOZART

Symphony No 32

Bedford August 1944	BBCSO	78: HMV DB 6172

Symphony No 34

Tanglewood 1966	Boston SO	CD: Intaglio INCD 7211

Symphony No 35 "Haffner"

Wembley February 1959	LPO	LP: Concert Hall M 2103 LP: Concert Hall SMS 2103/SMS 5028 LP: Perfect (USA) 15003/13003
London September and October 1974 and April 1975	LPO	LP: EMI ASD 3158

Symphony No 39

Tanglewood 1966	Boston SO	CD: Intaglio INCD 7211

Symphony No 40

Vienna March 1959	VPO	LP: Westminster XWN 18942 LP: Westminster WST 14126/WGS 8160 LP: Vanguard S 193 LP: EMI 1C 045 90316

Symphony No 41 "Jupiter"

London May 1933	BBCSO	78: HMV DB 1966-1969/ DB 7543-7546 auto 78: Victor M 203 Coupled with Schauspieldirektor Overture
London September and October 1974 and April 1975	LPO	LP: EMI ASD 3158

Eine kleine Nachtmusik

Vienna March 1959	VPO	LP: Westminster XWN 18942 LP: Westminster WST 14126/WGS 8160 LP: Vanguard S 193 LP: EMI 1C 045 90316

Concerto for 2 pianos K365

London October 1936	BBCSO A.Schnabel K.U.Schnabel	78: HMV DB 3033-3035/ DB 8216-8218 auto 78: Victor M 484 LP: Victor LCT 1140 LP: HMV COLH 90 LP: EMI EX 29 00723 CD: Arabesque Z 6590 CD: EMI CHS 763 7032

Piano Concerto No 5

Tanglewood 1966	Boston SO Frager	CD: Intaglio INCD 7211

Piano Concerto No 17

London September 1973	LSO Previn	LP: EMI ASD 2951/1C 063 02458 LP: Angel 37002

Piano Concerto No 20

London February 1959	Philharmonia A.Fischer	LP: Columbia 33CX 1686/SAX 2335 LP: EMI SXLP 30148/1C 037 00496 CD: EMI CDZ 767 0002/CES 568 5292

Piano Concerto No 23

London	Philharmonia	LP: Columbia 33CX 1686/SAX 2335
February 1959	A.Fischer	LP: EMI SXLP 30148/1C 037 00496
		CD: EMI CDZ 767 0002/CES 568 5292

Piano Concerto No 24

London	LSO	LP: EMI ASD 2951/1C 063 02458
September 1973	Previn	LP: Angel 37002

Horn Concerto No 3

Bristol	BBCSO	78: HMV DB 3973-3974
April 1940	A.Brain	78: Victor M 829
		LP: Victor LM 6130
		CD: EMI CDH 764 1982

Così fan tutte, Overture

London	BBCSO	78: HMV DB 2190/DB 3814
March 1934		78: Victor M 794
		Coupled with Schumann Manfred Overture

Der Schauspieldirektor, Overture

London	BBCSO	78: HMV DB 1969/DB 7543
May 1933		78: Victor M 203
		Coupled with Symphony No 41

Die Zauberflöte, Overture

London	LPO	LP: World Records T 730/ST 730
April 1967		

Exsultate jubilate

London	LSO	LP: EMI ASD 4193
May 1959	De los Angeles	

Ch'io mi scordi di te, concert aria

London	LSO	LP: EMI ASD 4193
May 1959	De los Angeles	
	Moore	

Il rè pastore: Excerpt (L'amerò sarò costante)

London	LSO	HMV unpublished
May 1959	De los Angeles	

MUSSORGSKY

Night on Bare Mountain

London July 1960	New SO	LP: Readers Digest RDM 1007/RDS 5004 LP: Readers Digest RDM 2547/RDS 6547 CD: Chesky CD 53

NICOLAI

Die lustigen Weiber von Windsor, Overture

London March 1934	BBCSO	78: HMV DB 2195 78: Victor M 746
London December 1950	LPO	78: HMV DB 21223 45: HMV 7R 109/7ER 5039

OFFENBACH

Orphée aux enfers, Overture

Bedford April 1945	BBCSO	HMV unpublished

PARRY

Blest pair of sirens

London July 1948	LSO Oxford Bach Choir	78: HMV C 3820-3821
London December 1966	LPO LP Choir	LP: EMI ALP 2311/ASD 2311 LP: Vanguard 71225 CD: EMI CDM 565 1072
London April 1969	LPO LP Choir	CD: AS-Disc AS 534

Elegy for Brahms

London July, October and December 1978	LPO	LP: EMI ASD 3725 CD: EMI CDM 565 1072

England

London April 1969	LPO	CD: AS-Disc AS 534

English Suite for strings

Walthamstow March 1970	LSO	LP: Lyrita SRCS 48 LP: Musical Heritage MHS 1483 CD: Lyrita SRCD 220

Jerusalem

London	LPO	45: Decca SEC 5002
April 1957	Flagstad	LP: Decca LXT 5392/SXL 2049
		LP: Decca ADD 107/SDD 107

Lady Radnor's Suite

Walthamstow	LSO	LP: Lyrita SRCS 48
March 1970		LP: Musical Heritage MHS 1483
		CD: Lyrita SRCD 220

March (Incidental music to The Birds)

London	LPO	LP: Lyrita SRCS 71
August 1973		LP: Musical Heritage HNH 4076
		CD: Lyrita SRCD 220

Overture to an unwritten tragedy

Walthamstow	LSO	LP: Lyrita SRCS 48
March 1970		LP: Musical Heritage MHS 1483
		CD: Lyrita SRCD 220

Symphonic Variations

Walthamstow	LSO	LP: Lyrita SRCS 48
March 1970		LP: Musical Heritage MHS 1483
		CD: Lyrita SRCD 220
London	LPO	LP: EMI ASD 3725
July, October and		CD: EMI CDM 565 1072
December 1978		

Symphony No 5

London	LPO	LP: EMI ASD 3725
July, October and		CD: EMI CDM 565 1072
December 1978		

PONCHIELLI

Dance of the Hours (La Gioconda)

London	LPO	LP: World Records T 730/ST 730
July 1967		

PROKOFIEV

Piano Concerto No 1

Walthamstow December 1958	LPO Katz	LP: Nixa CCL 30151 LP: Pye GGC 4013/GSGC 14013

Lieutenant Kijé, Suite

Paris June 1955	Paris Conservatoire Orchestra	LP: Decca LXT 5119/BR 3074 LP: Decca ACL 159/SPA 229 LP: Decca DPA 617-618 CD: Decca 421 0192/433 6122

The Love of 3 Oranges, Suite

London June 1955	LPO	LP: Decca LXT 5119/LW 5296/ACL 159

PUCCINI

Tosca: Excerpt (Vissi d'arte)

London January 1948	BBCSO Grandi	LP: Bongiovanni GB 1037

PURCELL

Soul of the World (Ode to Saint Cecilia)

London May 1951	Festival Orchestra and Choir	78: HMV DB 21273 Recorded at opening concert of Royal Festival Hall

RACHMANINOV

Symphony No 2

Walthamstow July 1956	LPO	LP: Victor LM 2106 LP: RCA RB 16026/VIC 1139/VICS 1139 LP: Decca ECS 594/DDS 505

Symphony No 3

Walthamstow July 1956	LPO	LP: Victor LM 2185/LSC 2185 LP: RCA RB 16147/SB 2035 LP: Decca ECS 574

Piano Concerto No 1

London February 1958	LPO Katin	LP: Decca LXT 5447/SXL 2034 LP: Decca ADD 188/SDD 188/SPA 169

Piano Concerto No 2

London June 1955	LPO Curzon	LP: Decca LXT 5178/ACL 322/ECS 753

Rhapsody on a theme of Paganini

London May 1954	LPO Katchen	LP: Decca LXT 2862/LXT 5374 LP: Decca ACL 65/ECS 668 LP: Everest SDBR 3280
London May 1959	LPO Katchen	LP: Decca LXT 5550/SXL 2176 LP: Decca BR 3505/SWL 8505 LP: Decca ADD 428/SDD 428/SPA 505 Excerpt LP: Decca SPA 310

RAVEL

Tzigane for violin and orchestra

London January 1957	Philharmonia Rabin	LP: Columbia 33CX 1597 LP: Angel 35572 CD: EMI CZS 764 1232

RESPIGHI

Feste romane

Walthamstow April 1955	LPO	LP: Westminster XWN 18240/LAB 7012

Rossiniana

Walthamstow April 1955	LPO	LP: Westminster XWN 18240/LAB 7041

RIMSKY-KORSAKOV

Capriccio espagnol

London April and May 1974	LPO	LP: EMI ASD 3093 LP: Angel 37227

Dance of the Tumblers (The Snow Maiden)

London October 1966	LPO	LP: World Records T 665/ST 665

Procession of the Nobles (Mlada)

London April and May 1974	LPO	LP: EMI ASD 3093 LP: Angel 37227

Russian Easter Festival, Overture

London May 1957	LPO	LP: Victor LM 2185 LP: RCA RB 16147/SB 2035 LP: Decca ECS 573/DDS 505

RODGERS

Guardalcanal March

London   LPO   LP: World Records T 750/ST 750
July 1967

ROSSINI

La boutique fantasque, selection arranged by Respighi

Hayes   British SO   78: HMV D 572
June 1921

Matinées musicales, arranged by Britten

Walthamstow   LPO   LP: Nixa NCT 17008
August 1956   LP: Westminster XWN 18601/LAB 7055

Soirées musicales, arranged by Britten

Walthamstow   LPO   LP: Nixa NCT 17008
August 1956   LP: Westminster XWN 18601/LAB 7055

March (Soirés musicales, arranged by Britten)

London   LPO   LP: Lyrita SRCS 71
November 1973   LP: Musical Heritage HNH 4076

RUBBRA

Symphony No 6

London   RPO   CD: Intaglio INCD 7311
1971

Symphony No 7

Walthamstow   LPO   LP: Lyrita SRCS 41/SRCS 119
October 1968   LP: Musical Heritage MHS 1397
                                             CD: Lyrita SRCD 235

SAINT-SAENS

Cello Concerto No 1

London	LPO	LP: Decca LXT 2906/ACL 244
November 1953	Nelsova	

Havanaise for violin and orchestra

London	LPO	HMV unpublished
February 1952	Menuhin	

Introduction and Rondo Capriccioso for violin and orchestra

London	LPO	HMV unpublished
February 1952	Menuhin	

Bacchanale (Samson et Dalila)

London	BBCSO	78: HMV DB 2077
October 1933		

Danse macabre

London	LPO	LP: World Records T 698/ST 698
August 1967		LP: EMI CFP 158

Wedding Cake Caprice for piano and orchestra

London	LPO	LP: World Records T 698/ST 698
August 1967	Prior	LP: EMI CFP 158

SARASATE

Zigeunerweisen for violin and orchestra

London April 1967	LPO Bress	LP: World Records T 728/ST 728

SCARLATTI

The Good-humoured Ladies, ballet arranged by Tommasini

Hayes November 1920 and July 1921	British SO	78: HMV D 521 and D 573

SCHUBERT

Symphony No 4 "Tragic"

Wembley February 1959	LPO	LP: Concert Hall M 2139/AM 2248 LP: Concert Hall SMS 2248/ SMS 2462/SMS 2942 LP: Perfect (USA) 15010/13010

Symphony No 8 "Unfinished"

London 1923	British SO	Edison Bell VF 540-542

Symphony No 9 "Great"

London December 1934	BBCSO	78: HMV DB 2415-2420/ DB 7819-7824 auto 78: Victor M 268
Walthamstow November 1954	LPO	LP: Nixa NCL 16006 LP: Westminster XWN 18026 LP: Pye MAL 682
London March 1972	LPO	LP: EMI ASD 2856/SXLP 30558

Wanderer Fantasy, arranged by Liszt for piano and orchestra

London March 1956	LPO Farnardi	LP: Westminster XWN 18242

SCHUMANN

Symphony No 1 "Spring"

Walthamstow August 1956	LPO	LP: Nixa NCT 17004 LP: Westminster XWN 18670 LP: Pye GGC 4066/GSGC 14066/GGCD 302

Symphony No 2

Walthamstow August 1956	LPO	LP: Nixa NCT 17005 LP: Westminster XWN 18670 LP: Pye GGC 4066/GSGC 14066/GGCD 302

Symphony No 3 "Rhenish"

Walthamstow August 1956	LPO	LP: Nixa NCT 17006 LP: Westminster XWN 18671/LAB 7062 LP: Pye GGC 4067/GSGC 14067/GGCD 302

Symphony No 4

Walthamstow August 1956	LPO	LP: Nixa LCT 17007 LP: Westminster XWN 18671 LP: Pye GGC 4067/GSGC 14067/GGCD 302

Piano Concerto

London January 1957	LPO Dorfman	Decca unpublished
London November 1965	LPO Cherkassky	LP: World Records T 559/ST 559 LP: EMI SMFP 57002

Manfred Overture

London March 1934	BBCSO	78: HMV DB 2189-2190 78: Victor 11713-11714

SEARLE

Symphony No 1

London January 1960	LPO	LP: Decca LXT 5588/SXL 2232 LP: Lyrita SRCS 72 LP: Musical Heritage MHS 3490

SHOSTAKOVICH

Symphony No 6

Walthamstow August 1958	LPO	LP: Everest LPBR 6007/SDBR 3007 LP: World Records CM 28/SCM 28 CD: Everest EVC 9005

Symphony No 12 "The Year 1917"

Date not confirmed	BBCSO	CD: Intaglio INCD 7431

SIBELIUS

Violin Concerto

London June 1955	LPO Menuhin	LP: HMV ALP 1350 LP: Victor LM 1946 LP: EMI EX 29 08643 CD: EMI CDM 763 9872

The Bard

London January 1936	BBCSO	HMV unpublished
Walthamstow June 1956	LPO	LP: Nixa NCL 16024 LP: Vanguard VRS 489/SRV 365-366SD LP: Pye GGCD 305 CD: Precision PVCD 8397

En saga

Walthamstow June 1956	LPO	LP: Nixa NCL 16023 LP: Vanguard VRS 489/SRV 365-366SD LP: Pye GGCD 305 CD: Precision PVCD 8397

Finlandia

Walthamstow June 1956	LPO	LP: Nixa NCL 16024 LP: Vanguard VRS 490/SRV 365-366SD LP: Pye GGCD 305

Lemminkainen's Return

Walthamstow June 1956	LPO	LP: Nixa NCL 16023 LP: Vanguard VRS 489/SRV 365-366SD LP: Pye GGCD 305 CD: Precision PVCD 8397

Night Ride and Sunrise

London January 1936	BBCSO	78: HMV DB 2795-2796/ DB 8063-8066 auto 78: Victor M 311 LP: BBC Records BBC 4001
Walthamstow June 1956	LPO	LP: Nixa NCL 16024 LP: Vanguard VRS 490/SRV 365-366SD LP: Pye GGCD 305

The Oceanides

London January 1936	BBCSO	78: HMV DB 2797/8061-8062 auto 78: Victor M 311 LP: World Records SH 237
Walthamstow June 1956	LPO	LP: Nixa NCL 16024 LP: Vanguard VRS 490/SRV 365-366SD LP: Pye GGCD 305

Pohjola's Daughter

Walthamstow June 1956	LPO	LP: Nixa NCL 16023 LP: Vanguard VRS 489/SRV 365-366SD LP: Pye GGCD 305 CD: Precision PVCD 8397

Romance in C

Bristol April 1940	BBCSO	78: HMV DB 3972 78: Victor 13-499

The Swan of Tuonela

Walthamstow June 1956	LPO	LP: Nixa NCL 16023 LP: Vanguard VRS 489/SRV 365-366SD LP: Pye GGCD 305 CD: Precision PVCD 8397

Tapiola

Walthamstow June 1956	LPO	LP: Nixa NCL 16024 LP: Vanguard VRS 490/SRV 365-366SD LP: Pye GGCD 305

The Tempest, Prelude

Walthamstow June 1956	LPO	LP: Nixa NCL 16024 LP: Vanguard VRS 490/SRV 365-366SD LP: Pye GGCD 305

SIMPSON

Symphony No 1

London January 1956	LPO	LP: HMV BLP 1092/HQM 1010

SMETANA

The Bartered Bride, Suite (Overture, Polka, Furiant & Dance of the Comedians)

London October 1966	LPO	LP: World Records T 665/ST 665 LP: EMI SXLP 30199

The Moldau (Má Vlast)

London October 1966	LPO	LP: World Records T 665/ST 665 LP: EMI SXLP 30199/SLS 5073

SMYTH

The Dance

London March 1939	Light Symphony Orchestra	HMV unpublished

Entente cordiale, Interlude

London March 1939	Light Symphony Orchestra	78: HMV DB 3762 78: Victor 18-115

Fête galante, Minuet

London March 1939	Light Symphony Orchestra	78: HMV DB 3762 78: Victor 18-155 LP: EMI ED 29 10921

2 Interlinked French Folk Melodies

London March 1939	Light Symphony Orchestra	78: HMV DB 3762 78: Victor 18-155 LP: EMI ED 29 10921

These recordings of works by Dame Ethel Smyth were taken over by HMV after having been recorded privately

SOUSA

4 Marches: El capitan; Liberty Bell; Stars and Stripes for ever; Washington Post

London August 1967	LPO	LP: World Records T 750/ST 750 LP: EMI CFP 173

STAMITZ

Symphony in E flat

London May 1952	LPO	HMV unpublished
London July 1955	LPO	78: HMV HMS 75 LP: HMV HLP 18 LP: Victor LM 6137 Recorded for HMV's History of Music series

STANFORD

Funeral March (Incidental music to Becket)

London August 1973	LPO	LP: Lyrita SRCS 71 LP: Musical Heritage HNH 4076 CD: Lyrita SRCD 219

RICHARD STRAUSS

Don Quixote

London April 1968	New Philharmonia Du Pré	EMI unpublished Other sessions for this work were conducted by Klemperer and Barenboim, but both remained incomplete

4 Songs with orchestra: Liebeshymnus; Ruhe, meine Seele; Das Rosenband; Muttertändelei

London June 1975	LPO Baker	LP: EMI ASD 3260/1C 065 02758 LP: Angel 37199 CD: EMI CDC 747 8542

JOHANN STRAUSS FATHER

Radetzky March

London   LPO   LP: World Records T 730/ST 730
July 1967

STRAVINSKY

Circus Polka

London   LPO   LP: World Records T 698/ST 698
July 1967   LP: EMI CFP 158

SULLIVAN

Di Ballo, Overture

London   New SO   LP: Readers Digest RDM 1007/RDS 5007
July 1960   LP: Readers Digest RDM 2541/RDS 6541
                                         CD: Chesky CD 53

SUPPÉ

Beautiful Galathea, Overture

Walthamstow April 1955	LPO	LP: Nixa NCL 16012 LP: Westminster XWN 18238

Boccaccio, Overture

Walthamstow April 1955	LPO	LP: Nixa NCL 16012 LP: Westminster XWN 18238/LAB 7033 CD: EMI CDM 764 1962

Fantinitza, Overture

Walthamstow April 1955	LPO	LP: Nixa NCL 16012 LP: Westminster XWN 18238/LAB 7033 CD: EMI CDM 764 1962

Jolly Robbers;   Pique Dame, Overtures

Walthamstow April 1955	LPO	Nixa unpublished

Light Cavalry, Overture

London November 1934	BBCSO	78: HMV DB 2362 78: Victor M 746
Walthamstow April 1955	LPO	LP: Nixa NCL 16012 LP: Westminster XWN 18238/ XWN 18274/LAB 7033

Morning Noon and Night in Vienna, Overture

Walthamstow April 1955	LPO	LP: Nixa NCL 16012 LP: Westminster XWN 18238/ XWN 18274/LAB 7041

Poet and Peasant, Overture

Walthamstow April 1955	LPO	LP: Nixa NCL 16012 LP: Westminster XWN 18238/LAB 7033
London July 1967	LPO	LP: World Records T 730/ST 730

TCHAIKOVSKY

Symphony No 3 "Polish"

London February and November 1956	LPO	LP: Decca LXT 5297/ECS 636

Symphony No 5

Walthamstow May 1959	LPO	LP: Somerset Fidelity 10000/537 LP: Pye GGL 0027/GSGL 10027/MAL 553 LP: Musical Heritage MHS 3564

Symphony No 6 "Pathétique"

Walthamstow May 1959	LPO	LP: Somerset Fidelity 10100/538 LP: Pye GGL 0036/GSGL 10036/MAL 559 LP: Musical Heritage MHS 1369

Piano Concerto No 1

Walthamstow March 1955	LPO Badura-Skoda	LP: Nixa NCL 16013 LP: Westminster XWN 18162 LP: Pye MALS 1355
London January 1967	LPO Cherkassky	LP: World Records T 796/ST 796 LP: EMI SMFP 57004

Concert Fantasia for piano and orchestra

London February 1958	LPO Katin	LP: Decca LXT 5447/SXL 2034 LP: Decca ADD 188/SDD 188/SPA 169

Violin Concerto

London June 1954	LPO Elman	LP: Decca LXT 2970/ACL 25/ECS 596
London February 1959	RPO Menuhin	HMV unpublished
London April 1967	LPO Bress	LP: World Records T 683/ST 683

Sérénade mélancolique for violin and orchestra

London February 1959	RPO Menuhin	HMV unpublished

Suite No 3

Paris June 1955	Paris Conservatoire Orchestra	LP: Decca LXT 5099/ECS 766 Theme and Variations LP: Decca ECS 636
London June 1974	LPO	LP: EMI ASD 3135

Capriccio italien

Bristol April 1940	BBCSO	78: HMV DB 3956-3957 CD: Beulah 1PD 12
Paris June 1955	Paris Conservatoire Orchestra	Decca unpublished
Wembley February 1959	LPO	LP: Musical Masterpieces MMS 176 LP: Perfect (USA) 15001/13001
London April and May 1974	LPO	LP: EMI ASD 3093 LP: Angel 37227

1812 Overture

London April 1952	LPO	LP: Decca LXT 2696/ACL 10/ECS 540
London February 1967	LPO Coldstream Guards' Band	LP: World Records T 683/ST 683 LP: Odyssey 3216 0238 CD: EMI CDU 565 0532

The Nutcracker, Ballet suite

London 1923	British SO	Edison Bell VF 1060 and 1062
London July 1960	New SO	LP: Readers Digest RDM 1012 LP: Readers Digest RDS 5012/RDS 9388 LP: Quintessence PMC 7010 CD: Chesky CD 53
London August 1967	RPO	LP: Columbia TWO 183 LP: Capitol SP 8690 LP: Angel 60176 LP: EMI CFP 40369 Also includes Pas de deux

The Sleeping Beauty, Ballet Suite

London   RPO
August 1967

LP: Columbia TWO 183
LP: Capitol SP 8690
LP: Angel 60176
LP: EMI CFP 40369
Excerpts
LP: EMI YKM 5004

Swan Lake, Ballet suite

London   New SO
July 1960

LP: Readers Digest RDM 1012
LP: Readers Digest RDS 5012/RDS 9385
LP: Quintessence PMC 7010
Excerpt
LP: Readers Digest RDS 9288

Eugene Onegin, Polonaise

London   BBCSO
January 1937

78: HMV DB 3132
78: Victor 36-324

Francesca da Rimini

Paris   Paris Conservatoire
June 1955   Orchestra

Decca unpublished

Gopak (Mazeppa)

London April and May 1974	LPO	LP: EMI ASD 3093 LP: Angel 37227 CD: EMI CDU 565 0532

Hamlet, Fantasy Overture

London January 1952	LPO	LP: Decca LXT 2696/ACL 10/ECS 540
Walthamstow August 1959	LPO	LP: Somerset Fidelity 11600 LP: Pye GGL 0089/GGD 0089/GGL 0279 LP: Pye GSGL 10089/GSGD 10089 LP: Pye MAL 570/MAL 604

Marche slave

Bristol April 1940	BBCSO	78: HMV DB 3971 78: Victor 6513
London January 1967	LPO	LP: World Records T 683/ST 683 LP: Odyssey 3216 0238 LP: Quintessence PMC 7002
London April and May 1974	LPO	LP: EMI ASD 3093 LP: Angel 37227 CD: EMI CDU 565 0532

Romeo and Juliet, Fantasy Overture

Walthamstow August 1959	LPO	LP: Somerset Fidelity 11600
London October 1966	LPO	LP: World Records T 683/ST 683 LP: EMI SXLP 30199/SLS 5073 LP: Odyssey 3216 0238 LP: Quintessence PMC 7045 CD: EMI CDU 565 0532

Serenade for strings

London June 1937	BBCSO	78: HMV DB 3303-3305/ DB 8773-8775 auto 78: Victor M 556 CD: Beulah IPD 12

TEIKE

Old Comrades, March

London   LPO   LP: World Records T 750/ST 750
August 1967   LP: EMI CFP 173

TELEMANN

Viola Concerto in G

Bromley   Bromley String   LP: P 142L
May 1964   Orchestra   Private issue for Royal
                Coulling   College of Music

TOMLINSON

Passepied

Bromley   Bromley String   LP: P 142L
May 1964   Orchestra   Private issue for Royal
                                  College of Music

VAUGHAN WILLIAMS

Symphony No 1 "A Sea Symphony"

London December 1953	LPO LP Choir Baillie, Cameron	LP: Decca LXT 2907-2908/ACL 247- 248 LP: Decca ECS 583/414 6421 CD: Decca 425 6582
London September 1968	LPO LP Choir Armstrong Carol Case	LP: EMI ASD 2349-2350/ESD 7104 LP: Angel 3739 LP: EMI SLS 780/SLS 822 LP: EMI SLS 154 7083 CD: EMI CDC 747 2122/CDM 764 0162 <u>Scherzo</u> LP: EMI SEOM 12

Symphony No 2 "A London Symphony"

London January 1952	LPO	LP: Decca LXT 2693/ACL 290/ECS 616 CD: Decca 430 3662
London February and March 1971	LPO	LP: EMI ASD 2740/ED 29 03311 LP: Angel 36838 LP: SLS 822/SLS 154 7083 CD: EMI CDC 747 2132/CDM 764 0172

Symphony No 3 "A Pastoral Symphony"

London December 1952	LPO Ritchie	LP: Decca LXT 2787/ACL 311/ECS 607 CD: Decca 430 0602
London February 1968	New Philharmonia M.Price	LP: EMI ASD 2392/ED 29 04081 LP: Angel 36532 LP: EMI SLS 822/SLS 154 7083 CD: EMI CDC 747 2142/CDM 764 0182

Symphony No 4

London December 1953	LPO	LP: Decca LXT 2909/ACL 315/ECS 612 CD: Belart 461 1172
London January and February 1968	New Philharmonia	LP: EMI ASD 2375/ED 29 04171 LP: Angel 36557 LP: EMI SLS 822/SLS 154 7083 CD: EMI CDC 747 2142/CDM 764 0182

Symphony No 5

London December 1953	LPO	LP: Decca LXT 2910/ACL 311/ECS 607
Wembley April 1969	LPO	LP: EMI ASD 2538/ED 29 04181 LP: Angel 36998 LP: EMI SLS 822/SLS 154 7083 LP: EMI CDC 747 2142/CDM 764 0182

Symphony No 6

London February 1949 and February 1950	LSO	78: HMV C 3873-3876/7755-7758 auto 45: Victor WHMV 1040 LP: HMV BLP 1001 LP: Victor LHMV 1040 LP: EMI ED 29 02581 CD: EMI CDH 763 3082 February 1950 session needed to record composer's revision of third movement; ED 29 02581 and CDH 763 3082 contain both versions of that movement
London December 1953	LPO	LP: Decca LXT 2911/ACL 289/ECS 602 CD: Belart 461 1172 First movement LP: Decca SPA 217
London February 1967	New Philharmonia	LP: EMI ASD 2329/ED 29 04081 LP: Angel 36469 LP: EMI SLS 822/SLS 154 7083 CD: EMI CDC 747 2152/CDM 764 0192 Also issued on LP by Time Life

Symphony No 7 "Sinfonia Antartica"

London December 1953	LPO LP Choir Ritchie, Gielgud	LP: Decca LXT 2912/ACL 291/ECS 577 CD: Decca 425 1572
London November 1969	LPO LP Choir Burrowes	LP: EMI ASD 2631 LP: Angel 36763 LP: EMI SLS 822/SLS 154 7083 CD: EMI CDM 764 0202

Symphony No 8

London September 1956	LPO	LP: Decca LXT 5314/SXL 2207 LP: Decca ADD 199/SDD 199/ECS 644 CD: Decca 425 1572
London September and December 1968 and March 1969	LPO	LP: EMI ASD 2469/ED 29 02391 LP: Angel 36625 LP: EMI SLS 822/SLS 154 7083 CD: EMI CDC 747 2172/CDM 764 0212

Symphony No 9

Walthamstow August 1958	LPO	LP: Everest LPBR 6006/SDBR 3006 LP: World Records T 144/ST 144 CD: Everest EVC 9001 Includes spoken introduction by Sir Adrian Boult
London December 1969	LPO	LP: EMI ASD 2581/ED 29 02391 LP: Angel 36742 LP: EMI SLS 822/SLS 154 7083 CD: EMI CDC 747 2172/CDM 764 0212

Concerto accademico

London February 1952	LPO Menuhin	LP: EMI EH 29 12761 CD: EMI CDH 763 8282

Concerto for 2 pianos and orchestra

London December 1968	LPO Vronsky, Babin	LP: EMI ASD 2469/ASD 2914 LP: Angel 36625 LP: EMI ED 29 06531

Concerto grosso for string orchestra

London April and October 1975	LPO	LP: EMI ASD 3286 LP: Angel 37211

Dona nobis pacem

London April 1973	LPO LP Choir Armstrong Carol Case	LP: EMI ASD 2962/SLS 5082 LP: Angel 36972

English Folk Song Suite, arranged by Jacob

Walthamstow September 1953	LPO	LP: Nixa NLP 905 LP: Westminster XWN 18248/WL 5270 LP: Vanguard VRS 1093 LP: Pye GSGC 15019/GH 652 CD: Precision PVCD 8396
Vienna March 1959	VPO	LP: Westminster XWN 18928 LP: Westminster WST 14111/WGS 8111 LP: World Records T 391/ST 391
London August 1970	LSO	LP: EMI ASD 2570 LP: Angel 36799/37276 CD: EMI CDM 764 0222

Fantasia on a theme of Thomas Tallis

Bristol April 1940	BBCSO	78: HMV DB 3958-3959 78: Victor M 769 LP: BBC Records BBC 4001 LP: EMI ED 29 08001 CD: VAI Audio VAIA 10672
Walthamstow September 1953	LPO	LP: Nixa NLP 905 LP: Westminster XWN 18248/XWN 18249 LP: Westminster XWN 18250 LP: Westminster WL 5270/LAB 7048 CD: Precision PVCD 8396
Vienna March 1959	VPO	LP: Westminster XWN 18928 LP: Westminster WST 14111/WGS 8111 LP: World Records T 391/ST 391
Walthamstow November 1969	LPO	LP: Lyrita SRCS 41/REAM 1 LP: Musical Heritage MHS 1397
Cheltenham July 1972	New Philharmonia	CD: Radio Classics BBCRD 9119
London April and October 1975	LPO	LP: EMI ASD 3286 LP: Angel 37211 CD: EMI CDM 764 0172

Orchestra described on the labels of Boult's Vaughan Williams recordings for Westminster as Vienna State Opera Orchestra

Fantasia on Greensleeves

London September 1953	LPO	LP: Nixa NLP 903 LP: Westminster XWN 18248/XWN 18249 LP: Westminster XWN 18250 LP: Westminster WL 5270/LAB 7048 LP: Vanguard VRS 1093 LP: Pye GSGC 15019 CD: Precision PVCD 8396
Vienna March 1959	VPO	LP: Westminster XWN 18928 LP: Westminster WST 14111/WGS 8111 LP: World Records T 391/ST 391
London August 1970	LSO	LP: EMI ASD 2750/ED 29 06531 LP: Angel 36799/36902 CD: EMI CDM 764 0222

Fantasia quasi variazione on Old 104th Psalm Tune

London December 1969	LPO LP Choir Katin	LP: EMI ASD 2581/SLS 822 LP: Angel 36742/37276

Flos campi

London June 1946	Philharmonia BBC Chorus Primrose	78: HMV DB 6353-6355/ DB 9112-9114 auto LP: EMI EH 29 12761 CD: EMI CDH 763 8282

In the Fen Country

London February 1968	New Philharmonia	LP: EMI ASD 2393/SLS 822 LP: Angel 36532/36902 CD: EMI CDM 764 0222

Job

London January 1946	BBCSO	78: HMV DB 6289-6293/ DB 9042-9046 auto LP: EMI ED 29 08001
London January 1954	LPO	LP: Decca LXT 2937/ACL 313/ECS 676 CD: Belart 461 1222
London November 1958	LPO	LP: Everest LPBR 6019/SDBR 6019 CD: Everest EVC 9006
London August 1970	LSO	LP: EMI ASD 2673 LP: Angel 36773 Excerpts LP: EMI SEOM 12
London October 1972	LPO	CD: Intaglio INCD 7411

The Lark ascending

London October 1952	LPO Pougnet	LP: Parlophone PMB 1003 LP: EMI ED 29 02581 CD: EMI CDH 763 3082
London March 1967	New Philharmonia Bean	LP: EMI ASD 2329/ASD 2847/SLS 822 LP: Angel 36469/36902 CD: EMI CDM 764 0222

A Norfolk Rhapsody

Walthamstow September 1953	LPO	LP: Nixa NLP 905 LP: Westminster XWN 28248/WL 5270 LP: Pye GH 652 LP: Vanguard VRS 1093 CD: Precision PVCD 8396
London February 1968	New Philharmonia	LP: EMI ASD 2375/ASD 2847 LP: Angel 36557/36902 LP: EMI SLS 822/SLS 154 7083 LP: EMI ED 29 04171 CD: EMI CDM 764 0222

Old King Cole, ballet for orchestra

Walthamstow September 1953	LPO	LP: Westminster XWN 18249 LP: Westminster XWN 18251/WL 5228 LP: Pye GSGC 15019
London October 1954	LPO	LP: Decca LW 5151/ACL 315/ECS 612

On Wenlock Edge

London October 1972	LPO R.Lewis	CD: Intaglio INCD 7411

Partita for double string orchestra

London November 1956	LPO	LP: Decca LXT 5314/SXL 2207 LP: Decca ADD 199/SDD 199/ECS 644 CD: Decca 430 3662
London April and October 1975	LPO	LP: EMI ASD 3286 LP: Angel 37211

The Pilgrim's Progress

London November 1970 and January 1971	LPO LP Choir W.Evans, Dickerson, Partridge, J.Noble, Herincx, Keyte, Shaw, Shirley-Quirk	LP: EMI SLS 959/SLS 143 5133 LP: Angel 3785 CD: EMI CMS 764 2122 Excerpts LP: EMI SEOM 12/SEOM 15 SLS 959 included rehearsal sequence

Serenade to Music

London May 1951	Festival Orchestra and Chorus	78: HMV DA 7040-7041 LP: EMI ED 29 10921 Recorded at opening concert of Royal Festival Hall
London November 1969	LPO Burrowes, Armstrong, Longfield, Hayward, Hodgson, Jennings, Minty, Dickinson, Partridge, Dickerson, W.Evans, Bowen, Angas, Carol Case, J.Noble, Keyte	LP: EMI ASD 2538/ASD 2847 LP: Angel 36698/36902 LP: EMI SLS 822/SLS 5082 CD: EMI CDM 764 0222

Song of Thanksgiving (originally known as Thanksgiving for Victory)

London November 1944	BBCSO BBC Choruses Suddaby, Dyall	CD: Intaglio INCD 7571
London December 1951	LPO Luton Choirs Dolemore, Speaight	78: Parlophone SW 8138-8139 LP: Parlophone PMB 1003 LP: EMI ED 29 02581 CD: EMI CDH 763 3082

Towards the Unknown Region

London April 1973	LPO LP Choir	LP: EMI ASD 2962/SLS 5082 LP: Angel 36972

5 Tudor Portraits

Manchester	BBC Northern Orchestra & Singers Harrison, P.Walker	CD: Intaglio INCD 7571

The Wasps, Suite

London September 1953	LPO	LP: Westminster XWN 18250 LP: Westminster XWN 18251/WL 5228 Overture LP: Westminster LAB 7048 LP: Pye GSGC 15019 CD: Everest EVC 9006
London December 1953	LPO	LP: Decca LXT 2907/LW 5277 LP: Decca ACL 248/ECS 601 CD: Belart 461 1222 Overture LP: Decca ECS 647
London September 1968	LPO	LP: EMI ASD 2440/ASD 2914/SLS 780 LP: Angel 3739/37276 LP: EMI ED 29 06531 CD: EMI CDM 764 0202 Excerpts LP: EMI SEOM 12/SEOM 15 LP: EMI ED 29 04181/SLS 154 7083

The Wasps, March

London September 1973	New Philharmonia	LP: Lyrita SRCS 71 LP: Musical Heritage HNH 4076

VERDI

Macbeth: Excerpt (Vieni t'affretta)

London January 1948	BBCSO Grandi	Unpublished radio broadcast

VIVALDI

Violin Concerto in C "Il piacere"

London April 1953	Philharmonia Menuhin	LP: HMV HLP 16 Recorded for HMV's History of Music series

WAGNER

A Faust Overture

London   LPO   LP: EMI ASD 3071
January 1974

Der fliegende Holländer, Overture

London   Festival Symphony   78: Vocalion KO 5296
March 1927   Orchestra

London   LPO   LP: EMI ASD 3071
January 1974   CD: EMI CZS 762 5392

Götterdämmerung, Dawn and Siegfried's Rhine Journey

London   LPO   LP: EMI ASD 2934
December 1972   LP: Angel 36998
                                           LP: EMI 2C 181 50352-50353
                                           CD: EMI CZS 762 5392

Götterdämmerung, Siegfried's Funeral March

London   LPO   LP: EMI ASD 2934
December 1972   LP: Angel 36998
                                           LP: EMI 2C 181 50352-50353
                                           CD: EMI CZS 762 5392

Lohengrin, Prelude

London December 1971	New Philharmonia	LP: EMI ASD 2812 LP: Angel 36871 LP: EMI 2C 181 50352-50353 CD: EMI CZS 762 5392

Lohengrin, Act 3 Prelude

London December 1971	New Philharmonia	LP: EMI ASD 2812 LP: Angel 36871 LP: EMI 2C 181 50352-50353 CD: EMI CZS 762 5392

Die Meistersinger von Nürnberg, Overture

London April 1933	BBCSO	78: HMV DB 1924
London December 1971	New Philharmonia	LP: EMI ASD 2812 LP: Angel 36871 LP: EMI 2C 181 50352-50353 CD: EMI CZS 762 5392

Die Meistersinger von Nürnberg, Act 3 Prelude

London December 1971	New Philharmonia	LP: EMI ASD 2812 LP: Angel 36871 LP: EMI 2C 181 50352-50353 CD: EMI CZS 762 5392

Die Meistersinger von Nürnberg, Procession of the Masters

London March 1927	Festival Symphony Orchestra	78: Vocalion KO 5302

Parsifal, Prelude

London   LSO   LP: EMI ASD 3000
January 1973   LP: Angel 37090
                                CD: EMI CZS 762 5392

Parsifal, Act 3 Prelude

London   LSO   LP: EMI ASD 3000
January 1973   LP: Angel 37090
                                CD: EMI CZS 762 5392

Parsifal, Transformation Music

London   LSO   LP: EMI ASD 3000
January 1973   LP: Angel 37090
                                CD: EMI CZS 762 5392

Parsifal, Good Friday Music

London   BBCSO   78: HMV DB 1677
April 1932 and
April 1933

London   LSO   LP: EMI ASD 3000
January 1973   LP: Angel 37090
                                CD: EMI CZS 762 5392

Das Rheingold, Entry of the Gods into Valhalla

London   LPO   LP: EMI ASD 3071
January 1974   CD: EMI CZS 762 5392

Rienzi, Overture

London   LPO   LP: EMI ASD 3071
January 1974   CD: EMI CZS 762 5392

Siegfried, Forest Murmurs

London   LPO   LP: EMI ASD 2934
December 1972   LP: Angel 36998
                                LP: EMI 2C 181 50352-50353
                                CD: EMI CZS 762 5392

Siegfried Idyll

Hayes December 1921 and February & March 1922	British SO	HMV unpublished
London January 1973	LSO	LP: EMI ASD 3000 LP: Angel 37090

Tannhäuser, Overture

London December 1971	New Philharmonia	LP: EMI ASD 2812 LP: Angel 36871 LP: EMI 2C 181 50352-50353 CD: EMI CZS 762 5392

Tannhäuser, Act 3 Prelude

London December 1972	LPO	LP: EMI ASD 2934 LP: Angel 36998 LP: EMI 2C 181 50352-50353

Tannhäuser, Entry of the Guests

London January 1974	LPO	LP: EMI ASD 3071 CD: EMI CZS 762 5392

Tristan und Isolde, Prelude

London July 1932	BBCSO	78: HMV DB 1757
London December 1971	New Philharmonia	LP: EMI ASD 2812 LP: Angel 36871 LP: EMI 2C 181 50352-50353 CD: EMI CZS 762 5392

Tristan und Isolde, Act 3 Prelude

London December 1972	LPO	LP: EMI ASD 2934 LP: Angel 36998 LP: EMI 2C 181 50352-50353 CD: EMI CZS 762 5392

Die Walküre, Ride of the Valkyries

London December 1972	LPO	LP: EMI ASD 2934 LP: Angel 36998 LP: EMI 2C 181 50352-50353 CD: EMI CZS 762 5392

Wesendonk-Lieder

London June 1975	LPO Baker	LP: EMI ASD 3260/!C 065 02758 LP: Angel 37199 CD: EMI CDC 747 8542

Im Treibhaus (Wesendonk-Lieder)

London October 1958	Philharmonia C.Ludwig	Columbia unpublished

J.F.WAGNER

Under the Double Eagle, March

London August 1967	LPO	LP: World Records T 750/ST 750 LP: EMI CFP 173

WALTON

Belshazzar's Feast

Walthamstow	LPO	LP: Nixa NLP 904
September 1953	LP Choir	LP: Westminster XWN 18251/WL 5248
	Noble	LP: Pye MALS 1337

Symphony No 1

Walthamstow	LPO	LP: Nixa NCL 16020
August 1956		LP: Westminster XWN 18374
		LP: Pye GGC 4008/GSGC 14008
		LP: Everest SDBR 3448
		CD: Precision PVCD 8377

Cello Concerto

London	LPO	CD: Intaglio INCD 7281
1967	Tortelier	

Crown Imperial, Coronation March

London	BBCSO	78: HMV DB 3164
April 1937		78: Victor 12-031
		LP: EMI ED 29 10921
		CD: VAI Audio VAIA 10672
London	LPO	LP: EMI ASD 3388/1C 063 02889
January 1977		LP: Angel 37436

March (Film music to Hamlet)

London	LPO	LP: Lyrita SRCS 71
November 1973		LP: Musical Heritage HNH 4076

Orb and Sceptre, Coronation March

London	LPO	LP: EMI ASD 3388/1C 063 02889
January 1977		LP: Angel 37436

Portsmouth Point, Overture

London	BBCSO	78: HMV DA 1540
December 1936		LP: EMI ED 29 10921
		CD: VAI Audio VAIA 10672
London	LPO	LP: Decca LXT 5028/LW 5195
October 1954		LP: Decca ACL 224/ECS 647
		CD: Decca 425 6612
London	LPO	LP: World Records T 698/ST 698
July 1967		LP: EMI CFP 158

Scapino, Overture

London	LPO	LP: Decca LXT 5028/LW 5195
October 1954		LP: Decca ACL 313/ECS 647
		CD: Decca 425 6612

Siesta

London	LPO	LP: Decca LXT 5028/LW 5195
October 1954		LP: Decca ACL 224/ECS 647
		CD: Decca 425 6612

WARLOCK

An Old Song

London June 1973	LPO	Lyrita unpublished

WEBER

Euryanthe, Overture

London January 1937	BBCSO	78: HMV DB 3130

Der Freischütz, Overture

London March 1927	Festival Symphony Orchestra	78: Vocalion KO 5299
London April and October 1932	BBCSO	78: HMV DB 1678

Oberon, Overture

Bedford April 1945	BBCSO	HMV unpublished

WIENIAWSKI

Violin Concerto No 1

London January 1957	Philharmonia Rabin	LP: Columbia 33CX 1538 LP: Angel 35484/60342 CD: EMI CZS 764 1232

Violin Concerto No 2

London March 1956	LPO Elman	LP: Decca LXT 5222/ECS 596

WILLIAMSON

Organ Concerto

Guildford November 1974	LPO Williamson	LP: Lyrita SRCS 79 LP: Musical Heritage MHS 3586

Violin Concerto

London January 1971	LPO Menuhin	LP: EMI ASD 2759/SLS 5085

WOLF

Italian Serenade

London January 1957	Philharmonia	45: HMV 7ER 5129

WOLF-FERRARI

I Gioielli della madonna, Intermezzo

London July 1967	LPO	LP: World Records T 698/ST 698 LP: EMI CFP 158

ZIMMERMANN

Anchors Aweigh, March

London August 1967	LPO	LP: World Records T 750/ST 750 LP: EMI CFP 173

MISCELLANEOUS

The British Grenadiers

London January 1937	BBCSO	78: HMV B 8553/B 9420
London August 1967	LPO	LP: World Records T 750/ST 750 LP: EMI CFP 158 LP: CBS 61684

God Save the King

London April 1932	BBCSO	HMV unpublished
London January 1937	BBCSO	78: HMV B 8553

The Instruments of the Orchestra

London June 1967	LPO members	LP: EMI MFP 2092/CFP 40074 Spoken commentary by Boult

Liliburlero March, arranged by Alford

London August 1967	LPO	LP: World Records T 750/ST 750 LP: EMI CFP 173

National Anthems of the Allies: Greece, Czechoslavakia, France, Poland, Belgium, Holland, Norway and Jugoslavia

London April and May 1941	BBCSO	78: HMV C 3232 Transferred from BBC recordings

O come all ye faithful, arranged by Woodgate

London April 1957	LPO Flagstad	45: Decca CEP 517/SEC 5002 LP: Decca LXT 5392/SXL 2049 LP: Decca ADD 107/SDD 107

Royal Festival Hall
(General Manager: T. E. Bean, C.B.E.)
Monday, 1st March, 1965, at 8

MOZART   Overture, Figaro

BRAHMS   Piano Concerto No. 2 in B flat

HOLST   The Planets

BOULT   New Philharmonia Orchestra
Leader: Hugh Bean

GEZA ANDA

Members of the New Philharmonia Chorus (Chorus Master: Wilhelm Pitz)

Sir John Barbirolli
1899-1970

with valuable assistance
from Malcolm Walker

Discography compiled by John Hunt

Sir John Barbirolli

ADAMS

The Holy City

London September 1932	Orchestra Crooks	78: HMV DB 1798 78: Victor 7854 45: HMV 7P 249 LP: EMI MRS 5185 LP: EMI (Australia) OXLP 7524 LP: World Records SH 427 CD: Claremont GSE 785050 <u>78 issues coupled with The Star of Bethlehem</u>

The Star of Bethlehem

London September 1932	Orchestra Crooks	78: HMV DB 1798 78: Victor 7854 45: HMV 7P 249 LP: EMI (Australia) OXLP 7639 LP: World Records SH 427 CD: Claremont GSE 785050 <u>Coupled with The Holy City</u>

ALBINONI

Oboe Concerti in B flat and D

London June 1959	Pro Arte Orchestra Rothwell	LP: Vanguard SRV 191/SRV 191SD LP: Pye GGC 4023/GSGC 14023 LP: Pye GSGC 2003 CD: Nixa NIXCD 6004

ARENSKY

Variations on a theme of Tchaikovsky

London   LSO   LP: EMI ALP 2099/ASD 646/ASD 2830
September 1964   LP: Angel 36269
                                                 LP: EMI SXLP 30239
                                                 Excerpts
                                                 45: EMI 7EG 8958

AUBER

Fra Diavolo, Overture

London   LPO   78: HMV C 2644
July 1933

BACH

Piano Concerto in F BWV 1056, first movement only

London   Orchestra   78: HMV C 2456
September 1932   Arnaud   Coupled with Raff La fileuse

Concerto in C for 2 pianos BWV 1064

London   Orchestra   78: HMV C 2648-2649
December 1933   Bartlett, Robertson

Violin Concerto in E BWV 1042

London   Orchestra   78: HMV DB 1871-1873/
December 1932   Elman   DB 7382-7384 auto
                                                 CD: Pearl GEMMCD 9388

Cello Sonata in G BWV 1029

London July 1929	Barbirolli, cello Bartlett	78: National Gramophonic Society NGS 133-134

Cello Suite in C BWV 1009, Sarabande only

Manchester December 1961	Barbirolli, cello	LP: Barbirolli Society BS 02 Performed at Barbirolli's Golden Jubilee celebration

Schafe können sicher weiden, arranged by Barbirolli (Cantata No 208)

New York December 1940	NYPO	78: Columbia (USA) X 207 Coupled with Brahms Academic Festival Overture
London May 1969	Hallé	LP: EMI ASD 2496/SEOM 10 LP: EMI ESD 154 5831 CD: EMI CFPCD 4580

Saint Matthew Passion: Excerpt (Du lieber Heiland, du)

London April 1929	Orchestra Offers	78: HMV DB 1761 Coupled with Elgar Where corals lie (Sea Pictures)

Cantatas Nos 21 and 68, 2 unspecified arias

London October 1935	LPO Souez	HMV unpublished

BALFE

The Bohemian Girl, Overture

London October 1933	Orchestra	78: HMV C 2635 LP: EMI SLS 796

BAX

Symphony No 3

Manchester December 1943	Hallé	78: HMV C 3380-3385/7593-7598 auto LP: EMI EX 29 01073 CD: EMI CDH 763 9102 <u>Barbirolli's first recording with Hallé Orchestra</u>

Violin Concerto

London April 1937	LPO Heifetz	HMV unpublished <u>Recording incomplete</u>

Garden of Fand

Manchester June 1956	Hallé	LP: Nixa CCT 31000 LP: Mercury MG 50115/SR 90115 LP: Pye GGC 4061/GSGC 14061 LP: Pye GSGC 15017/GSGC 2059 CD: Precision PVCD 8380 CD: Nixa NIXCD 6003

Tintagel

London December 1965	LSO	LP: EMI ALP 2305/ASD 2305/ESD 7092 LP: Angel 36415 CD: EMI CDC 747 9842/CDM 565 1102

BEETHOVEN

Symphony No 1

Manchester December 1957	Hallé	LP: Nixa CCL 30132/CSCL 70001 LP: Vanguard SRV 146/SRV 146SD LP: Pye GGC 4081/GSGC 14081 CD: Precision PVCD 8373

Symphony No 3 "Eroica"

London May 1967	BBCSO	LP: EMI ASD 2348/SXLP 30209 LP: Angel 36461 <u>Third movement</u> LP: EMI SEOM 1

Symphony No 5

New York April 1938	NYPO	Unpublished radio broadcast
London May 1947	Hallé	78: HMV C 3716-3719/7718-7721 auto 45: Victor WBC 1018 LP: Victor LBC 1018

Symphony No 7

Manchester March 1945	Hallé	HMV unpublished Recording incomplete
Manchester December 1969	Hallé	Unpublished private recording Barbirolli's 70th birthday concert

Symphony No 8

Manchester   Hallé
January 1958

LP: Nixa CCL 30132/CSCL 70001
LP: Vanguard SRV 146/SRV 146SD
LP: Pye GGC 4081/GSGC 14081
CD: Precision PVCD 8373

Piano Concerto No 4

New York   NYPO
October 1941   Hoffmann

LP: International Piano Library
    IPL 503
CD: Intaglio INCD 7651

Piano Concerto No 5 "Emperor"

Manchester   Hallé
April 1959   Katz

LP: Nixa CCL 30152/CSCL 70019
LP: Vanguard SRV 138/SRV 138SD
LP: Pye GC 4044/GSGC 14044
LP: Pye GSGC 15015/GSGC 2028

Violin Concerto

London   LPO
June 1936   Kreisler

78: HMV DB 2927-2932/
    DB 8210-8215 auto
78: Victor M 325
LP: HMV COLH 11
LP: World Records H 101
CD: Pearl GEMMCDS 9362
CD: Biddulph LAB 001-3

Egmont, Overture

London   Hallé
April 1949

78: HMV DB 21139
45: HMV 7P 233

Fidelio: Excerpt (Abscheulicher, wo eilst du hin?)

London   Orchestra
May 1928   Leider

78: HMV D 1497
78: Victor 7118
LP: HMV COLH 132
LP: Preiser LV 30
LP: EMI 1C 147 30785-30786
CD: Preiser 89004

Leonore No 3, Overture

Manchester   Hallé
April 1959

LP: Nixa CCL 30156
LP: Pye GGL 0302/GGC 4089/GSGC 14089
LP: Pye GSGC 2038/GH 508

BELLINI

Norma: Excerpt (Casta diva)

London	LPO	78: HMV DB 2720
October 1935	Souez	78: Victor 36286
		LP: Orion ORS 7293

Norma: Excerpt (Deh! Proteggimi o Dio!)

London	Orchestra	HMV unpublished
June 1929	Minghini-Cattaneo	

BENJAMIN

Overture to an Italian comedy

New York	NYPO	Unpublished radio broadcast
April 1941		

BERLIOZ

Symphonie fantastique

Manchester January 1947	Hallé		78: HMV C 3563-3569/7664-7770 auto
Manchester September 1959	Hallé		LP: Pye GGC 4005/GSGC 14005 LP: Pye GSGC 15010/GSGC 2025 LP: Vanguard SRV 181/SRV 181SD CD: EMI CDM 763 7622/CDU 568 0272
London April 1969	Hallé		CD: Hunt CD 731

La Damnation de Faust, Suite (Hungarian March; Dance of the Sylphs; Will o' the Wisps)

Manchester   Hallé   LP: Nixa CCT 31005
May 1957   LP: Pye GGC 4095/GSGC 14095
                                                                                CD: EMI CDM 763 7622/CDM 767 8352

Benvenuto Cellini, Overture

New York October 1938	NYPO	Unpublished radio broadcast

Le Carnaval romain, Overture

New York November 1940	NYPO	78: Columbia (USA) 11670D 45: Fontana CFE 15029 LP: Columbia (USA) HL 7121 LP: CBS 72691 78 version coupled with Smetana Bartered Bride Overture
London December 1966	Hallé	LP: Barbirolli Society SJB 103 CD: EMI CDM 763 7622

Les Nuits d'été

London December 1967	New Philharmonia Baker	LP: EMI ASD 2444/SLS 5013 LP: Angel 36505 CD: EMI CDM 769 5442 Vilanelle LP: EMI SEOM 8/SEOM 24 LP: EMI CFP 41 44871

BISHOP

Lo! Here the gentle lark

London	Orchestra	78: HMV DB 2502
May 1935	Pons	78: Victor 8733
		Coupled with Mozart Ach ich
		fühl's (Die Zauberflöte)

BIZET

L'Arlésienne, Suite No 1

London	Hallé	78: HMV DB 21275-21276/
October 1950		DB 9656-9657 auto
		45: Victor WBC 1047
		LP: HMV BLP 1004
		LP: Victor LBC 1047
		CD: Dutton/Barbirolli Society
		CDSJB 1002

Carmen, orchestral selection arranged by Gibilaro

London	Covent Garden	78: HMV C 2056
September 1930	Orchestra	

Carmen: Excerpts (L'amour est un oiseau rebelle; Près des remparts de Séville)

London	Orchestra	78: HMV DB 1303
June 1929	Minghini-Cattaneo	CD: Preiser 89008
	Sung in Italian	

Carmen: Excerpt (La fleur que tu m'avais jetée)

London	Orchestra	LP: Rubini RDA 010
July 1929	Hislop	
	Sung in English	

BRAHMS

Symphony No 1

Vienna December 1967	VPO	LP: EMI ASD 2401 LP: Angel 3732 CD: Toshiba TOCE 7134/Royal 6433

Symphony No 2

New York April 1940	NYPO	78: Columbia (USA) M 412 LP: Columbia (USA) RL 3044
Vienna December 1966	VPO	LP: EMI ASD 2421 LP: Angel 3732 CD: Toshiba TOCE 7135/Royal 6434
Munich April 1970	Bavarian RO	CD: Orfeo C265 921B

Symphony No 3

Manchester May 1952	Hallé	45: Victor WBC 1042 LP: HMV BLP 1015 LP: Victor LBC 1042
Vienna December 1967	VPO	LP: EMI ASD 2432 LP: Angel 3732 CD: Toshiba TOCE 7136/Royal 6434

Symphony No 4

Manchester September 1960	Hallé	LP: Pye GGC 4037/GSGC 14037 LP: Pye GSGC 15014/GSGC 2027 LP: Vanguard SRV 183/SRV 183SD CD: EMI CDM 764 4442
Vienna December 1967	VPO	LP: EMI ASD 2433 LP: Angel 3732 CD: Toshiba TOCE 7137/Royal 6435

Piano Concerto No 1

London August 1967	New Philharmonia Barenboim	LP: EMI ASD 2353/SXLP 30283 LP: Angel 36463 LP: EMI SLS 874/EMX 41 20851 CD: EMI CDM 763 5362

Piano Concerto No 2

London December 1967	New Philharmonia Barenboim	LP: EMI ASD 2413/SLS 874/EMX 2110 LP: Angel 36526 CD: EMI CDM 763 5372

Violin Concerto

London June 1936	LPO Kreisler	78: HMV DB 2915-2919/ DB 8127-8131 auto 78: Victor M 402 LP: HMV COLH 35 LP: World Records SH 115 CD: Pearl GEMMCDS 9362 CD: Biddulph LAB 001-3
New York January 1939	NYPO Huberman	LP: Rococo 2007 <u>This may be a 1944 performance conducted by Rodzinski</u>

Double Concerto

Manchester September 1960	Hallé Campoli, Navarra	LP: Pye GGC 4009/GSGC 14009 LP: Pye GSGC 15016/GSGC 2029 LP: Vanguard SRV 136/SRV 136SD

Haydn Variations

Vienna December 1967	VPO	LP: EMI ASD 2432/ASD 2589 LP: Angel 3732 LP: EMI 1C 187 01010-01011 CD: Toshiba TOCE 7136 CD: EMI CDM 568 1212/Royal 6435

Academic Festival Overture

New York November 1940	NYPO	78: Columbia (USA) X 200 LP: Columbia (USA) ML 2075/ML 5126 <u>78 version coupled with Bach Sheep may safely graze</u>
Manchester September 1960	Hallé	LP: Pye GGC 4009/GSGC 14009 LP: Pye GSGC 15016/GSGC 2029 LP: Vanguard SRV 136/SRV 136SD
Vienna December 1967	VPO	LP: EMI ASD 2433/ASD 2589 LP: Angel 3732 LP: EMI 1C 187 01010-01011 CD: Toshiba TOCE 7137/Royal 6435

Tragic Overture

Vienna December 1967	VPO	LP: EMI ASD 2421/ASD 2589 LP: Angel 3732 LP: EMI 1C 187 01010-01011 CD: Toshiba TOCE 7135 CD: EMI CDM 763 5372/Royal 6433

Ein deutsches Requiem: Excerpt (Ihr habt nun Traurigkeit)

London August 1928	Covent Garden Orchestra & Chorus Austral <u>Sung in English</u>	78: HMV DB 1540 78: Victor 9395 LP: HMV COLH 147 LP: Rubini RDA 005

BRITTEN

Violin Concerto

Manchester April and May 1948	Hallé Olof	HMV unpublished

BRUCH

Violin Concerto No 1

New York April 1942	NYPO Milstein	78: Columbia (USA) M 517 LP: Columbia (USA) ML 2003/ ML 7083/RL 6631 CD: Biddulph LAB 096

BRUCKNER

Symphony No 8

London May 1970	Hallé	CD: Hunt CD 717

BUTTERWORTH

A Shropshire Lad

Manchester June 1956	Hallé	LP: Nixa CCT 31000 LP: Mercury MG 50115/SR 90115 LP: Pye GGC 4061/GSGC 14061 LP: Pye GSGC 15017/GSGC 2059/GH 652 CD: Precision PVCD 8380 CD: Nixa NIXCD 6003

CASALS

Sardana

London March 1928	London School of Cellos	78: HMV (Spain) AF 207 LP: EMI SLS 796 78 version coupled with Mozart O Isis und Osiris (Zauberflöte)

CASTELNUOVO-TEDESCO

Oboe Concerto

Manchester October 1950	Hallé Rothwell	Unpublished private recording

CHABRIER

Espana

Manchester January 1954	Hallé	78: HMV DB 21615 45: HMV 7ER 5026/7P 255 45: Victor ERAB 13 LP: HMV BLP 1068

Habanera

Manchester August 1957	Hallé	Nixa/Pye unpublished

Marche joyeuse

Manchester August 1957	Hallé	45: Nixa CEC 32021 LP: Nixa CCT 31005 LP: Mercury MG 50161/SR 90161 LP: Pye GGC 4076/GSGC 14076 LP: Reader's Digest RDS 8015

CHAUSSON

Poème de l'amour et de la mer

Manchester March 1951	Hallé Ferrier	LP: Decca 414 0951 CD: Decca 433 4722/433 8022

CHOPIN

Piano Concerto No 1

London April 1937	LSO Rubinstein	78: HMV DB 3201-3204/ 　　DB 8290-8293 auto 78: Victor M 418 LP: EMI 1C 053 01172/3C 053 01172 CD: EMI CHS 764 4912
New York April 1940	NYPO Hoffmann	LP: International Piano Library 　　IPL 502

Piano Concerto No 2

London January 1931	LSO Rubinstein	78: HMV DB 1491-1493/ 　　DB 7217-7219 auto 78: Victor M 147 LP: EMI 1C 053 01172/3C 053 01172 CD: EMI CHS 764 4912
London July 1935	Orchestra Cortot	78: HMV DB 2612-2615/ 　　DB 8658-8661 auto 78: Victor M 567 CD: Pearl GEMMCD 9491 CD: EMI CZS 767 3592 CD: Grammophono AB 78501
New York December 1936	NYPO Hoffmann	LP: International Piano Library 　　IPL 501 CD: Danacord HPC 002

CIMAROSA

Oboe Concerto, arranged by Benjamin

London June 1959	Pro Arte Orchestra Rothwell	LP: Vanguard SRV 191/SRV 191SD LP: Pye GGC 4023/GSGC 14023 LP: Pye GSGC 2003 CD: Nixa NIXCD 6004

CLARKE

Trumpet Voluntary

Manchester August 1957	Hallé Lang	LP: Nixa CCL 30129 LP: Mercury MG 50161/SR 90161 LP: Pye GGC 4076/GSGC 14076/GH 515 LP: Reader's Digest RDS 8015

COLLINS

Sir Toby and Sir Andrew, Overture

New York March 1942	NYPO	Unpublished radio broadcast

CORELLI

Christmas Concerto, arranged by Bridge

London January 1927	NGS Chamber Orchestra	78: National Gramophonic Society NGS 69-70/NGS 69A-B

Concerto grosso, arranged by Barbirolli

New York February 1943	NYPO	Unpublished radio broadcast
Rome February 1947	Santa Cecilia Orchestra	78: HMV (Italy) S 10511-10512

Oboe Concerto, arranged by Barbirolli

Manchester June 1946	Hallé Rothwell	78: HMV C 3540/DB 4258 First movement LP: HMV CLP 1840
Manchester May 1957	Hallé Rothwell	LP: Nixa CCL 30127 LP: Pye GGC 4065/GSGC 14065 LP: Pye GSGC 15034/GSGC 2007 CD: Precision PVCD 8378 CD: Nixa NIXCD 6004
London November 1968	New Philharmonia Rothwell	LP: EMI ASD 2496

COTTRAU

Santa Lucia

London March 1933	Orchestra Gigli	78: HMV DB 1902/DB 3907 CD: EMI CHS 763 3962 CD: ASV CDAJA 5122

DEBUSSY

La mer

Manchester September 1959	Hallé	LP: Pye GGC 4010/GSGC 14010 LP: Pye GSGC 15013/GSGC 2011 LP: Vanguard SRV 177/SRV 177SD LP: Reader's Digest RDS 8012 CD: EMI CDM 763 7632
Vienna December 1967	VPO	CD: Hunt CD 731
Paris December 1968	Orchestre de Paris	LP: EMI ASD 2442/EMX 2027 LP: Angel 36583 LP: EMI 1C 187 01010-01011 CD: EMI CZS 762 6692

3 Nocturnes

Paris December 1968	Orchestre de Paris ORTF Choir	LP: EMI ASD 2442/EMX 2027 LP: Angel 36583 LP: EMI 1C 187 01010-01011 CD: EMI CZS 762 6692

Ibéria (Images)

New York February 1938	NYPO	78: HMV DB 3661-3663 78: Victor M 460 CD: Pearl GEMMCDS 9922

Prélude à l'après-midi d'un faune

Manchester December 1953	Hallé	LP: HMV BLP 1058 LP: EMI SLS 796 CD: Dutton/Barbirolli Society CDSJB 1002

Danse sacrée et danse profane

London January 1927	NGS Chamber Orchestra Bartlett	78: National Gramophonic Society NGS 70-71

Petite Suite, arranged by Büsser

New York December 1940	NYPO	78: Columbia (USA) X 207 Coupled with Ravel La valse

Rhapsody No 1 for clarinet and orchestra

New York December 1940	NYPO Goodman	78: Columbia (USA) 11517D

DELIBES

Sylvia, ballet music

London June 1934	Orchestra	78: HMV C 2695-2696
Manchester February 1948	Hallé	78: HMV C 3797-3798

DELIUS

Appalachia

London July 1970	Hallé Ambrosian Singers Jenkins	LP: EMI ASD 2635/ESD 7099 LP: EMI EMX 41 20811 LP: Angel 36756 CD: EMI CMS 565 1192 Barbirolli's final studio recording sessions Rehearsal sequence: LP: EMI SLS 796 CD: EMI CMS 565 1192

2 Aquarelles, arranged by Fenby

London March 1949	Hallé	78: HMV C 3864 LP: EMI EX 29 01073 78 version coupled with Mozart Figaro Overture

Brigg Fair

London July 1970	Hallé	LP: EMI ASD 2635/ESD 7099 LP: EMI EMX 41 20811 LP: Angel 36756 CD: Toshiba TOCE 6411/TOCE 7211 CD: EMI CMS 565 1192 Barbirolli's final studio recording sessions

La Calinda (Koanga)

London August 1968	Hallé	LP: EMI ASD 2477/SEOM 10 LP: Angel 36588 CD: EMI CMS 565 1192

Fennimore and Gerda, Intermezzo

Manchester June 1956	Hallé	LP: Nixa CCL 30108 LP: Pye GGC 4075/GSGC 14075/GSGC 2055 LP: Vanguard SRV 240/SRV 240SD CD: Nixa NIXCD 6003 CD: EMI CMS 565 1192
London August 1968	Hallé	EMI unpublished

Idyll

Manchester	Hallé	LP: Nixa CCL 30108
December 1956	Fisher, Walters	LP: Pye GGC 4075/GSGC 14075/GSGC 2055
		LP: Vanguard SRV 240/SRV 240SD
		CD: Nixa NIXCD 6003

In a summer garden

London	Hallé	LP: EMI ASD 2477
August 1968		LP: Angel 36588
		CD: EMI CMS 565 1192

Intermezzo and Serenade (Hassan)

London	Hallé	LP: EMI ASD 2477
August 1968	Tear	LP: Angel 36588
		CD: EMI CMS 565 1192

Irmelin, Prelude

Manchester	Hallé	45: Nixa CEC 32019
June 1956		LP: Nixa CCL 30108
		LP: Pye GGC 4075/GSGC 14075
		LP: Pye GSGC 14137/GSGC 2055
		LP: Vanguard SRV 240/SRV 240SD
		CD: Nixa NIXCD 6003
London	LSO	LP: EMI ALP 2305/ASD 2305
July 1966		LP: Angel 36415
		LP: EMI ESD 7092/SLS 796
		CD: EMI CDC 747 9842/CMS 565 1192

Late swallows, arranged by Fenby

London	Hallé	LP: EMI ASD 2477/ED 769 5341
August 1968		LP: Angel 36588
		CD: EMI CDM 769 5342/CDEMX 2198
		CD: EMI CMS 565 1192

On hearing the first cuckoo in Spring

Manchester	Hallé	45: Nixa CEC 32019
June 1956		LP: Nixa CCL 30108
		LP: Pye GGC 4075/GSGC 14075
		LP: Pye GSGC 2005/GH 654
		LP: Vanguard SRV 240/SRV 240SD
		LP: Reader's Digest RDS 8016
		CD: Nixa NIXCD 6003
London	Hallé	LP: EMI ASD 2477
August 1968		LP: Angel 36588
		CD: EMI CZS 767 6502/CDU 568 2722
		CD: EMI CDU 555 2432/CMS 565 1192

A Song before sunrise

London June 1929	New SO	78: HMV D 1697 78: Victor 4732 Coupled with In a summer garden not conducted by Barbirolli
London August 1968	Hallé	LP: EMI ASD 2477 LP: Angel 36588 CD: EMI CDCFP 4620/CMS 565 1192

A Song of summer

London February 1950	Hallé	78: HMV DB 9609-9610/ DB 21277-21278 auto Coupled with Mozart Andante (Cassation in G); DB 21277- 21278 not published
London July 1966	LSO	LP: EMI ALP 2305/ASD 2305/ESD 7092 Lp: Angel 36415 CD: EMI CDC 747 9842/CMS 565 1192

Summer night on the river

London January 1927	NGS Chamber Orchestra	78: National Gramophonic Society NGS 72
London August 1968	Hallé	LP: EMI ASD 2477 LP: Angel 36588 CD: EMI CMS 565 1192

Walk to the Paradise Garden (A Village Romeo and Juliet)

Manchester February 1945	Hallé	78: HMV C 3484
Manchester June 1956	Hallé	LP: Nixa CCL 30108 LP: Pye GGC 4075/GSGC 14075 LP: Pye GSGC 14137/GSGC 2055 LP: Vanguard SRV 240/SRV 240SD LP: Reader's Digest RDS 8014 CD: Nixa NIXCD 6003
Boston October 1964	Boston SO	CD: Music and Arts CD 251
London August 1965	LSO	LP: EMI ALP 2305/ASD 2305/ESD 7092 LP: Angel 36415 CD: EMI CDC 747 9842/CDZ 762 5272 CD: EMI CMS 565 1192

D'ERLANGER

Midnight Rose

London June 1934	Orchestra	78: HMV C 2711 <u>Coupled with Grieg Homage March (Sigurd Jorsalfar)</u>

DONIZETTI

Don Pasquale, Overture

Manchester May 1951	Hallé	78: HMV DA 2004 45: HMV 7ER 5009 LP: EMI HQM 1122 CD: EMI CDM 764 1382

L'Elisir d'amore: Excerpt (Una furtiva lagrima)

London March 1933	Orchestra Gigli	78: HMV DB 1901/DB 3906/DB 4592 78: Victor 7194 LP: HMV COLH 118/ALP 1681/RLS 729 CD: EMI CDH 761 0512 CD: Nimbus NI 7817 <u>DB 1901 and 7194 coupled with Handel Ombra mai fù (Serse)</u>

DVORAK

Symphony No 7

Manchester Hallé
August 1957

LP: Nixa CCL 30145
LP: Mercury MG 50159
LP: Pye GGC 4068/GSGC 14068
LP: Pye GSGC 2057/GGCD 304
CD: Nixa NIXCD 1004
CD: EMI CDM 763 7742

Symphony No 8

Manchester Hallé
June 1957

LP: Nixa CCL 30122/CSCL 70002
LP: Mercury MG 50162
LP: Vanguard SRV 133/SRV 133SD
LP: Pye GGC 4069/GSGC 14069/GGCD 304
CD: Nixa NIXCD 1004
CD: EMI CDM 764 1932/CDU 565 0162

Symphony No 9 "From the New World"

Manchester Hallé
April 1959

LP: Nixa CCL 30155
LP: Vanguard SRV 182/SRV 182SD
LP: Pye GGC 4070/GSGC 14070
LP: Pye GSGC 7051/GGCD 304/GH 534
LP: Reader's Digest RDS 8017
CD: Nixa NIXCD 1004
CD: EMI CDM 763 7742

Scherzo capriccioso

Manchester Hallé
June 1957

LP: Nixa CCL 30122/CSCL 70002
LP: Mercury MG 50162
LP: Vanguard SRV 133/SRV 133SD
LP: Pye GGC 4069/GSGC 14069/GH 534
CD: Nixa NIXCD 1004
CD: EMI CDM 764 1932

Serenade in D

Manchester Hallé
August 1957

LP: Nixa CCL 30153
LP: Mercury MG 50041
LP: Pye GGC 4082/GSGC 14082/GSGC 2037
CD: Nixa NIXCD 1004

Legends Nos 4, 6 and 7

Manchester Hallé
September 1958

LP: Nixa CCL 30145
LP: Pye GGC 4068/GSGC 14068
LP: Pye GSGC 2057/GGCD 304/GH 534
CD: Nixa NIXCD 1004
CD: EMI CDM 764 1932

Goin' home

London Orchestra
May 1929 Hislop

HMV unpublished

ELGAR

Symphony No 1

Manchester December 1956	Hallé	LP: Nixa CCL 30102-30103 LP: Pye GGC 4052/GSGC 14052 LP: Pye GSGC 15022/GSGC 2010 CD: Precision PVCD 8379 CD: Nixa NIXCD 6002
London August 1963	Philharmonia	LP: EMI ALP 1989/ASD 540/ASD 2748 LP: Angel 60068 LP: EMI SLS 5030/SXLP 30268 LP: EMI EMX 41 20841 CD: EMI CDM 764 5112
Kings Lynn July 1970	Hallé	CD: Intaglio INCD 7011

Symphony No 2

Manchester June 1954	Hallé	LP: HMV ALP 1242 LP: Victor LBC 1088 LP: Barbirolli Society SJB 101
London April 1964	Hallé	LP: EMI ALP 2061-2062/ASD 610-611 LP: EMI ASD 2749/SLS 5030 LP: Angel 6033 LP: EMI SXLP 30287/EMX 41 20931 CD: EMI CDM 764 7242
Boston September 1964	Boston SO	CD: Music and Arts CD 251 CD: Intaglio INCD 7471

Cello Concerto

Manchester May 1957	Hallé Navarra	LP: Nixa CCL 30103 LP: Pye GGC 4057/GSGC 14057 LP: Pye GSGC 15005/GSGC 2017 CD: Precision PVCD 8384 CD: Nixa NIXCD 1006 CD: EMI CDM 763 9552
London August 1965	LSO du Pré	LP: EMI ALP 2106/ASD 655/ASD 2764 LP: Angel 36438 LP: EMI SLS 895/SLS 154 6963 LP: EMI SLS 5068/EX 769 7071 CD: EMI CDC 747 3292/CMS 763 2832 CD: EMI CMS 769 7072/CZS 568 1192

Introduction and Allegro for strings

London October 1927	NGS Chamber Orchestra	78: National Gramophonic Society NGS 94-95
London January 1929	Barbirolli Chamber Orchestra	78: HMV C 1694-1695 LP: Barbirolli Society SJB 104
London September 1947	Hallé	78: HMV C 3669-3670
Manchester September 1953	Hallé	LP: HMV BLP 1049
Manchester December 1956	Hallé	LP: Pye GSGC 14137/GH 652 LP: Reader's Digest RDS 8014 CD: Nixa NIXCD 6002 CD: EMI CDM 763 9552
London May 1962	Sinfonia of London	LP: EMI ALP 1970/ASD 521/ASD 2762 LP: Angel 36101 LP: EMI SLS 5030/SXLP 30279 LP: ESD 7169/STAMP 1 CD: EMI CDC 747 5372
Manchester December 1969	Hallé	Unpublished private recording Barbirolli's 70th birthday concert

Enigma Variations

London October 1947	Hallé	78: HMV C 3692-3695/7702-7705 auto
Manchester June 1956	Hallé	LP: Nixa CCL 30101 LP: Mercury MG 50125/SR 90125 LP: Vanguard SRV 184/SRV 184SD LP: Pye GGC 4057/GSGC 14057 LP: Pye GSGC 15005/GSGC 2017/GH 654 CD: Precision PVCD 8384 CD: Nixa NIXCD 1006 CD: EMI CDM 763 9552 Nimrod 45: Nixa CEC 32023 LP: Pye GSGC 14137
Turin November 1957	RAI Turin Orchestra	CD: Hunt CDHP 584
London August 1962	Philharmonia	LP: EMI ALP 1998/ASD 548 LP: Angel 36120 LP: EMI SLS 5030/ESD 7169 CD: EMI CDM 769 1852 Nimrod CD: EMI CDU 555 2422/CDU 555 2424

Caractacus: Excerpt (Leap, leap to light)

London September 1928	Orchestra Dawson	78: HMV C 1988 Coupling not conducted by Barbirolli

Caractacus: Excerpt (O my warriors!)

London September 1928	Orchestra Dawson	78: HMV C 1579 LP: EMI HQM 1172/RLS 107 7053 LP: World Records SMA 411 78 version coupled with Mussorgsky Song of the flea

Cockaigne, Overture

London December 1949 and February 1950	Hallé	78: HMV DB 21321-21322/ DB 9633-9634 auto DB 21321-21322 not published
Manchester January 1954	Hallé	LP: HMV BLP 1065
London August 1962	Philharmonia	LP: EMI ALP 1998/ASD 548 LP: Angel 36120 LP: EMI SLS 5030/ESD 7169 CD: EMI CDM 764 5112/CDM 769 5632

Dream Children No 1

London February 1950	Hallé	78: HMV DB 21594 LP: EMI HQM 1122/EX 29 01073 Coupled with Grieg Lyric Piece No 4

The Dream of Gerontius

Turin November 1957	RAI Turin Orchestra RAI Rome Chorus Shacklock, Vickers, Nowakowski	CD: Hunt CDHP 584
Manchester December 1964	Hallé Ambrosian Singers Sheffield Philharmonic Chorus Baker, R.Lewis, Borg	LP: EMI ALP 2101-2102/ASD 648-649 LP: Angel 3660 LP: EMI SLS 770 CD: EMI CMS 763 1852 Excerpts LP: EMI SEOM 7/SEOM 11/YKM 5013 LP: EMI SLS 5275/CFP 4548 CD: EMI CDCFP 4548

Elegy for strings

Manchester January 1947	Hallé	78: HMV B 9567 Coupled with Fauré Nocturne (Shylock Suite)
Manchester December 1956	Hallé	45: Nixa CEC 32023 LP: Pye GSGC 14137 CD: Nixa NIXCD 6003 CD: EMI CDM 763 9552
London July 1966	New Philharmonia	LP: EMI ALP 2292/ASD 2292/ASD 2762 LP: Angel 36403 LP: EMI HQS 1283/SXLP 30456 CD: EMI CDC 747 5372/CDM 764 7242

Falstaff

London June 1964	Hallé	LP: EMI ALP 2062/ASD 611/ASD 2762 LP: Angel 6033 LP: EMI SLS 5030/SXLP 30279 CD: EMI CDM 769 1852

Froissart, Overture

London	New Philharmonia
July 1966	

LP: EMI ALP 2292/ASD 2292/ASD 2762
LP: Angel 36403
LP: EMI SXLP 30279/SXLP 30456
CD: EMI CDM 769 5632

Lullaby (Bavarian Dance No 2)

London   Hallé
May 1947

78: HMV C 3695/C 7705
LP: EMI EX 29 01073

Pomp and Circumstance, March No 1

London   Philharmonia
August 1963

45: EMI 7ER 5230/RES 4310
LP: EMI ALP 2292/ASD 2292/SLS 5030
LP: Angel 36403/3750
LP: EMI YKM 5013/SEOM 24
LP: EMI SXLP 30456/ESD 154 5801
LP: EMI 1C 187 01010-01011
CD: EMI CDM 769 5632/CZS 767 5964
CD: EMI CDCFP 4580/CDCFP 4620

Pomp and Circumstance, March No 2

London   New Philharmonia
July 1966

LP: EMI ALP 2292/ASD 2292/SEOM 10
LP: Angel 36403/3750
LP: EMI SLS 5030/SXLP 30456
LP: EMI 1C 187 01010-01011
CD: EMI CDM 769 5632

Pomp and Circumstance, March No 3

London   New Philharmonia
July 1966

LP: EMI ALP 2292/ASD 2292
LP: Angel 36403/3750
LP: EMI SLS 5030/SXLP 30456
LP: EMI 1C 187 01010-01011
CD: EMI CDM 769 5632

Pomp and Circumstance, March No 4

London   Philharmonia
August 1963

45: EMI 7ER 5230/RES 4310
LP: EMI ALP 2292/ASD 2292/HQS 1283
LP: Angel 36403/3750
LP: EMI SLS 5030/SXLP 30456
LP: EMI 1C 187 01010-01011
CD: EMI CDM 769 5632

Pomp and Circumstance, March No 5

London   New Philharmonia
July 1966

LP: EMI ALP 2292/ASD 2292
LP: Angel 36403/3750
LP: EMI SLS 5030/SXLP 30456
LP: EMI 1C 187 01010-01011
CD: EMI CDM 769 5632

Serenade for strings

London April 1949	Hallé	78: HMV B 9778-9779
London May 1962	Sinfonia of London	45: EMI 7ER 5231/RES 4311 LP: EMI ALP 1970/ASD 521/ASD 2380 LP: Angel 36101 CD: EMI CDC 747 5372

Sea slumber song (Sea Pictures)

London August 1965	LSO Baker	LP: EMI ALP 2106/ASD 655/ASD 2721 LP: EMI SLS 5013 CD: EMI CDC 747 3292/CMS 763 1852
Kings Lynn July 1970	Hallé Meyer	CD: Intaglio INCD 7011

In haven (Sea Pictures)

London August 1965	LSO Baker	LP: EMI ALP 2106/ASD 655 LP: EMI ASD 2721/SLS 5013 CD: EMI CDC 747 3292/CMS 763 1852
Kings Lynn July 1970	Hallé Meyer	CD: Intaglio INCD 7011

Sabbath morning at sea (Sea Pictures)

London April 1929	Orchestra Offers	HMV unpublished
London August 1965	LSO Baker	LP: EMI ALP 2106/ASD 655 LP: EMI ASD 2721/SLS 5013 CD: EMI CDC 747 3292/CMS 763 1852
Kings Lynn July 1970	Hallé Meyer	CD: Intaglio INCD 7011

Where corals lie (Sea Pictures)

London April 1929	Orchestra Offers	78: HMV DB 1761 Coupled with Bach Du lieber Heiland du (Saint Matthew Passion)
London August 1965	LSO Baker	LP: LP ALP 2106/ASD 655/ASD 2721 LP: EMI SLS 5013/SEOM 1/YKM 5013 LP: EMI CFP 40332/CFP 41 44871 CD: EMI CDC 747 3292/CMS 763 1852 CD: EMI CDCFP 40332
Kings Lynn July 1970	Hallé Meyer	CD: Intaglio INCD 7011

The swimmer (Sea Pictures)

London August 1965	LSO Baker	LP: EMI ALP 2106/ASD 655 LP: EMI ASD 2721/SLS 5013 CD: EMI CDC 747 3292/CMS 763 1852
Kings Lynn July 1970	Hallé Meyer	CD: Intaglio INCD 7011

Sospiri

London July 1966	New Philharmonia	LP: EMI ALP 2292/ASD 2292/ASD 2762 LP: Angel 36403 LP: EMI SXLP 30456 LP: EMI CDC 747 5372/CDM 764 7242

FALLA

7 Popular Spanish Songs, arranged by Halffter

| Manchester | Hallé | 45: Nixa CEC 32009 |
| May 1957 | da Gabarin | |

FARNABY

Loth to depart (Improvisations on virginal pieces), arranged by Rubbra

| London | Hallé | 78: HMV DB 21387/DB 9715 |
| December 1950 | | LP: EMI HQM 1122 |

FAURÉ

Pelléas et Mélisande, Suite

| Manchester | Hallé | LP: HMV ALP 1244/HQM 1122 |
| January 1954 | | CD: Dutton/Barbirolli Society CDSJB 1002 |

Nocturne (Shylock Suite)

| Manchester | Hallé | 78: HMV B 9567 |
| April 1947 | | |

FRANCK

Symphony in D minor

New York October 1939	NYPO	Unpublished radio broadcast

Prague
March 1962
	Czech PO	LP: Supraphon SUA 10438/
		     SUAST 50438
		LP: EMI CFP 190
		LP: Crossroads (USA) 2216 0127/
		     2216 0128
		CD: Supraphon 11 06132

Variations symphoniques for piano and orchestra

London December 1963	Philharmonia Ogdon	LP: EMI ALP 1991/ASD 542 LP: Angel 36142 CD: EMI CDZ 762 8592/CZS 767 7722

GERMAN

Nell Gwynn Dances (Pastoral Dance; Country Dance; Torch Dance)

Manchester May 1957	Hallé	LP: Nixa CCL 30129

GIBBONS

Fantasia No 3

London June 1925	Music Society String Quartet, of which Barbirolli was the cellist	78: National Gramophonic Society NGS 29 LP: Barbirolli Society BS 03 Coupled with Fantasy No 9

Fantasia No 6

London June 1925	Music Society String Quartet, of which Barbirolli was the cellist	78: National Gramophonic Society NGS 30 Coupled with Fantasy No 8 and Goossens Jack o' Lantern

Fantasia No 8

London June 1925	Music Society String Quartet, of which Barbirolli was the cellist	78: National Gramophonic Society NGS 30 Coupled with Fantasy No 6 and Goossens Jack o' Lantern

Fantasia No 9

London June 1925	Music Society String Quartet, of which Barbirolli was the cellist	78: National Gramophonic Society NGS 29 LP: Barbirolli Society BS 03 Coupled with Fantasy No 3

GIORDANO

Andrea Chenier: Excerpt (Un di all' azzuro)

London June 1928	Orchestra Zanelli	HMV unpublished
London June 1929	New SO Pertile	78: HMV DB 1118 Coupling not conducted by Barbirolli

GLAZUNOV

Violin Concerto

London March 1934	LPO Heifetz	78: HMV DB 2196-2198/ DB 7696-7698 auto 78: Victor M 218 LP: Victor ARM4-0943 LP: EMI EX 749 3751 CD: Biddulph LAB 026 CD: EMI CDH 764 0302 CD: RCA/BMG 09026 617782/617332 CD: Pearl GEMMCDS 9157

Autumn (The Seasons); Ballabile (Les ruses d'amour)

London April 1930	Covent Garden Orchestra	78: HMV C 1930 78: Victor 11-442

GLUCK

Armide: Excerpt (Ah! Si la liberté)

London May 1928	Orchestra Leider	78: HMV D 1547 78: American Gramophonic Society AGSB 26 LP: HMV COLH 132 LP: Preiser LV 30 LP: EMI 1C 147 30785-30786 CD: Preiser 89004 CD: Pearl GEMMCDS 9926 78 versions coupled with Mozart Or sai chi l'onore (Don Giovanni)

Orfeo ed Euridice: Excerpt (Che farò)

London May 1928	Orchestra Olczewska	78: HMV D 1490 78: Victor 7115 Coupled with Handel Ombra mai fù (Serse)

GOOSSENS

By the tarn

London June 1925	Music Society String Quartet, of which Barbirolli was the cellist	78: National Gramophonic Society NGS 28 Coupling did not involve Barbirolli

Jack o' Lantern

London June 1925	Music Society String Quartet, of which Barbirolli was the cellist	78: National Gramophonic Society NGS 30 Coupled with Gibbons Fantasies Nos 6 and 8

GOUNOD

Petite Symphonie for wind instruments

Manchester September 1958	Hallé soloists	LP: Nixa CCL 30153 LP: Pye GGC 4082/GSGC 14082/GSGC 2037

Faust, orchestral selection

London September 1930	Covent Garden Orchestra	78: HMV C 2055

Faust: Excerpts (Le veau d'or; Vous qui faites l'endormie)

London November 1929	Orchestra Autori Sung in Italian	HMV unpublished

Nazareth

London September 1932	Orchestra Crooks Sung in English	78: HMV DA 1288 78: Victor 1634 45: HMV 7P 333 LP: World Records SH 247 78 version coupled with Nevin The Rosary

GRAINGER

Londonderry Air

Eindhoven December 1944	Hallé	Unpublished private recording Concert for the Armed Forces
London April 1948	Hallé	78: HMV C 3819 Coupled with Vaughan Williams Greensleeves Fantasia
Manchester May 1957	Hallé	45: Nixa CEC 32022

Mock Morris; Molly on the shore; Shepherd's Hey

Manchester May 1957	Hallé	45: Nixa CEC 32022

GRANADOS

3 Spanish songs, unspecified

Manchester May 1957	Hallé de Gabarain	Nixa unpublished

DE GREEF

Flemish Folksong No 2

London May 1930	LSO	HMV unpublished

GRIEG

Piano Concerto

London October 1933	New SO Backhaus	78: HMV DB 2074-2076/ DB 7560-7562 auto 78: Victor M 204 LP: EMI EX 29 03433

Peer Gynt, Incidental music

London January and August 1968	Hallé Ambrosian Singers Armstrong, Clark	LP: EMI TWO 269 LP: Angel 36531 LP: EMI CFP 41 45031/EMX 41 20491 CD: EMI CDM 253 6792/CDE 767 7732 CD: EMI CDEMX 2049 Excerpts LP: EMI ASD 2773

Peer Gynt, Suite No 1

London October 1933	Orchestra	78: HMV C 2640-2641 78: Victor M 404 CD: Koch 3-7077-2
Manchester December 1948	Hallé	78: HMV C 3921-3922/DB 4310-4311 45: Victor WBC 1017 LP: Victor LBC 1017
Manchester August 1957	Hallé	LP: Nixa CCL 30126 LP: Mercury MG 50164/SR 90164 LP: Vanguard SRV 222/SRV 222SD LP: Pye GGC 4077/GSGC 14077 LP: GSGC 15018/GSGC 2004 LP: Pye GH 515/GH 522/GH 643

Symphonic Dance No 1

London December 1929	Covent Garden Orchestra	78: HMV C 1928 Coupled with Symphonic Dance No 2
Manchester August 1957	Hallé	LP: Nixa CCL 30126 LP: Mercury MG 50164/SR 90164 LP: Vanguard SRV 222/SRV 222SD LP: Pye GGC 4077/GSGC 14077 LP: Pye GSGC 15018/GSGC 2004/GH 643

Symphonic Dance No 2

London December 1929	Covent Garden Orchestra	78: HMV C 1928 Coupled with Symphonic Dance No 1
Manchester August 1957	Hallé	LP: Nixa CCL 30126 LP: Mercury MG 50164/SR 90164 LP: Vanguard SRV 222/SRV 222SD LP: Pye GGC 4077/GSGC 14077/GH 643 LP: Pye GSGC 15018/GSGC 2004

Symphonic Dance No 3

Manchester August 1957	Hallé	LP: Nixa CCL 30126 LP: Mercury MG 50164/SR 90164 LP: Vanguard SRV 222/SRV 222SD LP: Pye GGC 4077/GSGC 14077/GH 643 LP: Pye GSGC 15018/GSGC 2004

Symphonic Dance No 4

Manchester August 1957	Hallé	LP: Nixa CCL 30126 LP: Mercury MG 50164/SR 90164 LP: Vanguard SRV 222/SRV 222SD LP: Pye GGC 4077/GSGC 14077/GH 643 LP: Pye GSGC 15018/GSGC 2004

2 Elegiac Melodies

Manchester August 1957	Hallé	LP: Nixa CCL 30126 LP: Mercury MG 50164/SR 90164 LP: Vanguard SRV 222/SRV 222SD LP: Pye GGC 4077/GSGC 14077/GH 643 LP: GSGC 15018/GSGC 2004

Lyric Suite

London August 1969	Hallé	LP: EMI ASD 2773/SXLP 30254 LP: EMI CFP 41 45031 CD: EMI CDM 767 7732/CDE 253 6792 CD: EMI CDEMX 2049/CDCFP 4585

Homage March (Sigurd Jorsalfar)

London June 1934	Orchestra	78: HMV C 2711 Coupled with D'Erlanger Midnight Rose
London August 1969	Hallé	LP: EMI ASD 2773/SXLP 30254 LP: EMI YKM 5006/CFP 41 45031

Secret (Lyric Pieces)

Manchester August 1953	Hallé	78: HMV DB 21594 <u>Coupled with Elgar Dream Children No 1</u>

Norwegian Dances

London May 1970	Hallé	LP: EMI ASD 2773/SXLP 30524 LP: EMI CFP 41 45031 <u>No 2 only</u> LP: EMI SEOM 10

GRIFFES

The White Peacock

New York October 1938	NYPO	Unpublished radio broadcast

GROTHE

Roses and women

London May 1929	Orchestra Hislop	HMV unpublished

HANDEL

Concerto grosso, unspecified

London September 1930	Covent Garden Orchestra	HMV unpublished

Oboe Concerto in B flat, arranged by Rothwell and Mackerras

Manchester September 1958	Hallé Rothwell	LP: Nixa CCL 30149 LP: Pye GGC 4086/GSGC 14086/GSGC 7052 CD: EMI CDM 763 9562

Organ Concerto in B flat

Manchester August 1958	Hallé Chadwick	LP: Nixa CCL 30149 LP: Pye GGC 4086/GSGC 14086/GSGC 7052 CD: EMI CDM 763 9562

Rodrigo, orchestral suite

Manchester September 1958	Hallé	LP: Nixa CCL 30149 LP: Pye GGC 4086/GSGC 14086/GSGC 7052 CD: EMI CDM 763 9562

Judas Maccabaeus: Excerpt (Sound an alarm)

London January 1929	Orchestra Widdop	78: HMV D 1886 LP: EMI HQM 1164 LP: Rococo 5250 LP: Pearl GEMM 218 CD: Pearl GEMMCD 9112 CD: Claremont GSE 785.046 78 version coupled with Thou shalt break them (Messiah)

Messiah: Excerpt (Comfort ye, my people/Ev'ry valley)

London	Orchestra	78: HMV D 1620
January 1929	Widdop	LP: EMI HQM 1164
		CD: Pearl GEMMCD 9112

Messiah: Excerpt (Thou shalt break them)

London	Orchestra	78: HMV D 1886
January 1929	Widdop	LP: EMI HQM 1164
		LP: Rococo 5250
		LP: Pearl GEMM 218
		CD: Pearl GEMMCD 9112
		78 version coupled with Sound an alarm (Judas Maccabaeus)

Serse: Excerpt (Ombra mai fù)

London	Orchestra	78: HMV D 1490
June 1928	Olczewska	78: Victor 7115
		Coupled with Gluck Che farò (Orfeo ed Euridice)

London	Orchestra	78: HMV DB 1901
March 1933	Gigli	78: Victor 7194
		LP: HMV COLH 118/ALP 1681/HLM 7019
		LP: EMI 10 35263/11 01531
		CD: EMI CDH 761 0512
		78 versions coupled with Donizetti Una furtiva lagrima (Elisir d'amore)

Manchester	Hallé	LP: Nixa CCL 30149
September 1958	R.Lewis	LP: Pye GGC 4086/GSGC 14086
		LP: Pye GSGC 7052
		CD: EMI CDM 763 9562

Serse: Excerpt (Quelle che tutta)

Manchester	Hallé	LP: Nixa CCL 30149
September 1958	R.Lewis	LP: Pye GGC 4086/GSGC 14086
		LP: Pye GSGC 7052
		CD: EMI CDM 763 9562

Serse, Suite (Overture, Act III Sinfonia and Gigue, but also including the 2 arias listed above sung by R.Lewis)

Manchester	Hallé	LP: Nixa CCL 30149
September 1958		LP: Pye GGC 4086/GSGC 14086
		LP: Pye GSGC 7052
		CD: EMI CDM 763 9562

HAYDN

Symphony No 83 "La poule"

London Hallé 78: HMV DB 21076-21078/
December 1949   DB 9469-9471 auto
        45: Victor WBC 1060
        LP: HMV ALP 1038
        LP: Victor LBC 1060

Symphony No 88

Manchester Hallé HMV unpublished
August 1953

Symphony No 96 "The Miracle"

Manchester Hallé LP: HMV ALP 1038
April 1952

Symphony No 104 "The London"

London NGS Chamber 78: National Gramophonic Society
November 1927 Orchestra   NGS 98-101
        Coupled with Mozart Andante
        (Cassation in C)

London Barbirolli 78: HMV C 1608-1610/
January-April Chamber Orchestra   C 7228-7230 auto
1928   78: Victor 35981-35983
        LP: Barbirolli Society SJB 104
        CD: Koch 3-7077-2

New York NYPO Unpublished radio broadcast
January 1939

Cello Concerto

London May 1928	Orchestra Suggia	78: HMV DB 1186-1188/D 1518-1520 LP: EMI EH 761 0831 <u>DB 1186-1188 not published</u>
London December 1967	LSO du Pré	LP: EMI ASD 2466/SLS 895/SXLP 30273 LP: Angel 36580 CD: EMI CDC 747 8402/CMS 763 2832 CD: EMI CZS 568 1322

Oboe Concerto in C, attributed

Manchester August 1957	Hallé Rothwell	LP: Nixa CCL 30127 LP: Mercury MG 50041 LP: Pye GGC 4065/GSGC 14065 LP: Pye GSGC 2007 CD: Precision PVCD 8378 CD: Nixa NIXCD 6004

Piano Concerto in D, third movement only

London September 1932	Orchestra Arnaud	78: HMV C 2455 <u>Coupled with Saint-Saens Valse caprice</u>

Die Jahreszeiten: Excerpt (Schon eilet froh der Ackersmann)

London May 1931	LSO Schorr	78: HMV DB 1564 LP: EMI HQM 1243 LP: Rococo 5260 CD: Pearl GEMMCD 9398 <u>78 version coupled with Mendelssohn Herr Gott Abrahams (Elijah)</u>

HEMING

Threnody for a soldier killed in action, arranged and developed by Collins

Manchester March 1945	Hallé	78: HMV C 3427

HILL

Herz am Rhein

London May 1931	Orchestra Schorr	78: HMV DA 1224 Coupled with Loewe Fridericus Rex

HUMPERDINCK

Hänsel und Gretel, Overture

London December 1927	Orchestra	78: Edison Bell X 520
London May 1947	Hallé	78: HMV C 3623
Manchester May 1957	Hallé	45: Nixa CEC 32004 CD: EMI CDM 764 1384

IBERT

Divertissement

Manchester January 1954	Hallé	LP: HMV ALP 1244 CD: Dutton/Barbirolli Society CDSJB 1002

ROYAL FESTIVAL HALL

General Manager: T. E. Bean, C.B.E.

PHILHARMONIA CONCERT SOCIETY

ARTISTIC DIRECTOR:
WALTER LEGGE

PHILHARMONIA ORCHESTRA

PRINCIPAL CONDUCTOR: OTTO KLEMPERER

LEADER: HUGH BEAN

ELGAR

The Dream of Gerontius

ANNA REYNOLDS   RONALD DOWD

DONALD BELL

PHILHARMONIA CHORUS

CHORUS MASTER: WILHELM PITZ

SIR JOHN BARBIROLLI

Sunday, March 24, 1963, at 7.30 p.m.

ROYAL FESTIVAL HALL
General Manager - T. E. Bean, C.B.E.

S. A. GORLINSKY
presents

MONDAY, SEPTEMBER 13th, 1965

A concert to commemorate the Sibelius Centenary

HELSINKI CITY SYMPHONY ORCHESTRA
(*Leader : Naum Levin*)

conducted by

SIR JOHN BARBIROLLI

SIBELIUS PROGRAMME

Symphony No. 7 in C, Op. 105

Violin Concerto in D minor, Op. 47
Allegro moderato
Adagio di molto
Allegro ma non tanto

INTERVAL
(*A warning gong will be sounded for five minutes before the end of the interval.*)

Symphony No. 1 in E minor, Op. 39
Andante ma non troppo—Allegro energico
Andante (ma non troppo lento)
Scherzo (Allegro)
Finale (Quasi una fantasia)

Soloist

HENRYK SZERYNG
(By arrangement with Wilfred Van Wyck Ltd.)

IRELAND

A London Overture

London December 1965	LSO	LP: EMI ALP 2305/ASD 2305/ESD 7092 LP: Angel 36415 CD: EMI CDC 747 9842 CD: EMI CDM 764 7162/CDM 565 1092

The Forgotten Rite, Prelude

London May 1949	Hallé	78: HMV C 3894 LP: EMI EH 29 01073 CD: EMI CDH 763 9102

Mai-Dun, Symphonic rhapsody

London May 1949	Hallé	78: HMV DB 21232-21233/ DB 9651-9652 auto LP: EMI EH 29 01073 DB 21232-21233 not published

These things shall be

Manchester May 1948	Hallé Hallé Choir P.Jones	78: HMV C 3826-3827 LP: EMI EH 29 01073 CD: EMI CDH 763 9102

JAERNEFELT

Praeludium

London October 1933	Orchestra	78: HMV B 8112/DA 4399 78: Victor 4320 <u>Coupled with Berceuse</u>

Berceuse for small orchestra

London May 1933	Orchestra	78: HMV B 8112/DA 4399 78: Victor 4320 <u>Coupled with Praeludium</u>

LALO

2 Aubades

London December 1929	LSO	HMV unpublished

LEHAR

Gold und Silber, Waltz

Manchester April 1952	Hallé	78: HMV DB 21520 45: HMV 7ER 5009/7P 267 45: Victor ERAB 13
Manchester May 1957	Hallé	45: Nixa CEC 32005
London December 1966	Hallé	LP: EMI TWO 180/ESD 7067/SEOM 10 LP: Capitol SP 8698 LP: Angel 3750

LEONCAVALLO

Matinata

London June 1929	Orchestra Hislop	HMV unpublished

I Pagliacci: Excerpt (Vesti la giubba)

London July 1929	Orchestra Hislop	78: HMV DA 1062 LP: Rubini GV 43 LP: Rococo 5283 78 version coupled with Pagliacco non son
London May 1930	LSO Melchior Sung in German	78: Electrola EJ 582 LP: EMI 1C 147 01259-01260 LP: Pearl GEMM 228-229 CD: Danacord DACOD 315-316 CD: Nimbus NI 7816 CD: Preiser 89086 CD: Pearl GEMMCD 9500 Also issued on LP by Preiser and Danacord; 78 version coupled with Meyerbeer O Paradiso (L'Africana)

I Pagliacci: Excerpt (Pagliaccio non son)

London July 1929	Orchestra Hislop	78: HMV DA 1062 LP: Rubini GV 43 LP: Rococo 5283 78 version coupled with Vesti la giubba
London March 1933	Orchestra Gigli	78: HMV DA 1312 LP: HMV COLH 144 LP: EMI RLS 729 CD: EMI CDH 761 0512 CD: Nimbus NI 7856 78 coupling not conducted by Barbirolli

LIADOV

The Enchanted Lake

Manchester December 1953	Hallé	45: HMV 7ER 5026

LISZT

Piano Concerto No 1, first movement only

New York April 1938	NYPO Levitzki	Unpublished radio broadcast

LOEILLET

Trio in B

Beverley Hills January 1941	Barbirolli, cello Rothwell, D.Kennedy	LP: Barbirolli Society BS 03

LOEWE

Fridericus rex

London May 1931	Orchestra Schorr	78: HMV DA 1224 Coupled with Hill Herz am Rhein

LUIGINI

Ballet russe

London December 1929	Covent Garden Orchestra	78: HMV C 1948-1949

MAHLER

Symphony No 1

Manchester June 1957	Hallé	LP: Nixa CCL 30107 LP: Pye GGC 4074/GSGC 14074 LP: Vanguard SRV 223/SRV 223SD CD: Precision PVCD 8385

Symphony No 2 "Resurrection"

Stuttgart June 1970	SDR Orchestra SDR Choirs Donath, Finnilä	CD: Hunt CD 719

Symphony No 3

Berlin March 1969	BPO St Hedwig's Choir West	CD: Hunt CD 719

Symphony No 4

Prague January 1967	BBCSO Harper	CD: Intaglio INCD 7291

Symphony No 5

London July 1969	New Philharmonia	LP: EMI SLS 785 LP: Angel 3760 CD: EMI CDM 769 1862/767 6222 Adagietto LP: EMI SLS 796/ASD 2642 LP: EMI MRS 5141/SEOM 6 CD: EMI CDE 555 2422

Symphony No 5, Adagietto only

New York December 1939	NYPO	Unpublished radio broadcast

Symphony No 6

Berlin January 1966	BPO	CD: Hunt CD 702
London January 1967	New Philharmonia	CD: Hunt CDGI 726
London August 1967 (16 August)	New Philharmonia	Unpublished radio broadcast
London August 1967 (17-18 August)	New Philharmonia	LP: EMI SLS 778/SLS 851 LP: Angel 3725 LP: EMI CFP 41 44243 CD: EMI CZS 767 8162

Symphony No 9

Turin November 1960	RAI Turin Orchestra	LP: Cetra LAR 8 CD: Hunt CDLSMH 34003
Berlin January 1964	BPO	LP: EMI ALP 2047-2048/ ASD 596-597 LP: Angel 3652 LP: EMI SLS 851/CFP 41 44263 CD: EMI CDM 763 1152

Kindertotenlieder

London May 1967	Hallé Baker	LP: EMI ASD 2338/ASD 4409/SLS 5013 LP: Angel 36465 CD: EMI CDC 747 7932/CZS 762 7072

Lieder eines fahrenden Gesellen

London May 1967	Hallé Baker	LP: EMI ASD 2338/ASD 4409/SLS 5013 LP: Angel 36465 CD: EMI CDC 747 7932/CDM 764 4442 CD: EMI CZS 762 7072

Blicke mir nicht in die Lieder (Rückert-Lieder)

London	New Philharmonia	LP: EMI SLS 785/ASD 2721/ASD 4409
July 1969	Baker	LP: Angel 3760
		LP: EMI SLS 5013/SLS 5275
		CD: EMI CDC 747 7932/CZS 762 7072

Ich atmet' einen linden Duft (Rückert-Lieder)

London	New Philharmonia	LP: EMI SLS 785/ASD 2721/ASD 4409
July 1969	Baker	LP: Angel 3760
		LP: EMI SLS 5013/SLS 5275
		CD: EMI CDC 747 7932/CZS 762 7072

Um Mitternacht (Rückert-Lieder)

London	New Philharmonia	LP: EMI SLS 785/ASD 2721/ASD 4409
July 1969	Baker	LP: Angel 3760
		LP: EMI SLS 5013/SLS 5275/HQS 1294
		CD: EMI CDC 747 7932/CZS 762 7072

Liebst du um Schönheit (Rückert-Lieder)

London	New Philharmonia	LP: EMI SLS 785/ASD 2721/ASD 4409
July 1969	Baker	LP: Angel 3760
		LP: EMI SLS 5013/SLS 5275
		CD: EMI CDC 747 7932/CZS 762 7072

Ich bin der Welt abhanden gekommen (Rückert-Lieder)

London	Hallé	LP: EMI ASD 2338/SEOM 8
May 1967	Baker	LP: Angel 36465

London	New Philharmonia	LP: EMI SLS 785/ASD 2721/ASD 4409
July 1969	Baker	LP: Angel 3760
		LP: EMI SLS 5013/SLS 5275
		CD: EMI CDC 747 7932/CZS 762 7072

MALASHKIN

O could I in song tell my sorrow

London	Orchestra	HMV unpublished
June 1928	Chaliapin	
	Sung in English	

MARCELLO

Oboe Concerto in D, arranged by Bonelli

London	Pro Arte Orchestra	LP: Vanguard SRV 191/SRV 191SD
June 1959	Rothwell	LP: Pye GGC 4023/GSGC 14023/GSGC 2003
		CD: Nixa NIXCD 6004

Oboe Concerto in C, arranged by Rothwell

London	Hallé	LP: EMI ASD 2496
September 1968	Rothwell	

Allegretto, arranged by Barbirolli

London	NGS Chamber	78: National Gramophonic Society
October 1927	Orchestra	NGS 97
		Coupled with Purcell Suite for strings

MASCAGNI

Cavalleria rusticana, Intermezzo

London	LSO	78: HMV C 2292
September 1931		Coupled with Rachmaninov Prelude in C sharp minor conducted by Sargent
Manchester	Hallé	LP: Nixa CCL 30147
September 1958		LP: Pye GGC 4016/GSGC 14016/GH 515
		LP: Vanguard SRV 250SD
		LP: Reader's Digest RDS 8011
		CD: EMI CDM 764 1952

Cavalleria rusticana: Excerpt (Voi lo sapete)

London	Orchestra	78: Edison Bell X 523
December 1927	Stiles-Allen	Coupled with Puccini Viene
	Sung in English	la sera (Madama Butterfly)

Cavalleria rusticana: Excerpt (Mamma, quel vino)

London	Orchestra	78: HMV DB 1230
December 1928	Hislop	LP: Rubini GV 43
		CD: Pearl GEMMCD 9956
		78 version coupled with Puccini Che gelida manina (La Bohème)

MASSENET

Manon: Excerpt (En fermant les yeux)

London June 1931	Orchestra Gigli Sung in Italian	78: HMV DA 1216 78: Victor 1656 LP: HMV COLH 118/ALP 1681/RLS 729 CD: EMI CDH 761 0512 CD: Nimbus NI 7817

Sous les tilleuls (Scènes alsaciennes)

Manchester August 1957	Hallé	LP: Mercury MG 50161/SR 90161 LP: Pye GGC 4076/GSGC 14076 LP: Reader's Digest RDS 8015

McEWEN

Peat Reek, for string quartet

London December 1925	Music Society String Quartet, of which Barbirolli was the cellist	78: National Gramophonic Society NGS 52 Coupled with Purcell Fantasia in 3 parts

MENDELSSOHN

Symphony No 4 "Italian"

Manchester February 1948	Hallé	78: HMV C 3758-3760/7726-7728 auto 45: Victor WBC 1021 LP: Victor LBC 1021
Berne April 1961	Hallé	LP: Concert Hall AM 2248/SMS 2248 LP: Concert Hall CM 218/SM 218

The Hebrides, Overture

Manchester April 1948	Hallé	78: HMV C 3770 45: HMV 7R 120/7P 217
Manchester May 1957	Hallé	LP: Nixa CCL 30128 LP: Pye GGL 0301/GSGL 10301 LP: Pye GGC 4095/GSGC 14095/GH 508 CD: EMI CDM 764 1382

Scherzo (A Midsummer Night's Dream)

Manchester September 1944	Hallé	HMV unpublished
Manchester February 1945	Hallé	78: HMV C 3426 Coupled with Wagner Rienzi Overture

Scherzo (Octet)

London May 1949	Hallé	78: HMV C 3944 Coupled with Schubert Rosamunde Overture

Elijah: Excerpt (Lord God of Abraham)

London May 1931	LSO Schorr Sung in German	78: HMV DB 1564 LP: EMI HQM 1243 LP: Rococo 5260 LP: EMI EX 29 01693 CD: Pearl GEMMCD 9398 CD: Memoir CDMOIR 411

MESSAGER

Fortunio: Excerpt (La maison grise)

London	Orchestra	78: HMV B 3154
May 1929	Hislop	LP: Rubini RDA 010
		78 version coupled with
		Rachmaninov To the children

MEYERBEER

L'Africana: Excerpt (O paradiso)

London	LSO	78: Electrola EJ 582
May 1929	Melchior	LP: EMI 1C 147 01259-01260
	Sung in German	LP: Pearl GEMM 228-229
		CD: Danacord DACOD 315-316
		CD: Nimbus NI 7816
		CD: Preiser 89086
		78 version coupled with
		Leoncavallo Vesti la giubba
		(I Pagliacci); also issued
		on LP by Preiser and Danacord

MONN

Cello Concerto in G minor

London	LSO	LP: EMI ASD 2466/SXLP 30273
September 1968	du Pré	LP: Angel 36580
		CD: EMI CMS 763 2832/CZS 568 1322

MOZART

Symphony No 25

New York November 1941	NYPO	78: Columbia (USA) X 217

Symphony No 29

Manchester December 1956	Hallé	LP: Nixa CCL 30106 LP: Pye GGC 4060/GSGC 14060 LP: Pye GSGC 15026/GSGC 2032 LP: Vanguard SRV 180/SRV 180SD CD: EMI CDM 763 9592

Symphony No 34

Turin November 1960	RAI Turin Orchestra	LP: Cetra LAR 8 CD: Hunt CDHP 584

Symphony No 36 "Linz"

London September 1969	LSO	Unpublished radio broadcast

Symphony No 41 "Jupiter"

Manchester December 1956	Hallé	LP: Nixa CCL 30106 LP: Pye GGC 4060/GSGC 14060 LP: Pye GSGC 15026/GSGC 2032 LP: Vanguard SRV 180/SRV 180SD CD: EMI CDM 763 9592

Clarinet Concerto

New York December 1940	NYPO Goodman	Columbia (USA) unpublished

Oboe Concerto, arranged by Paumgartner

Manchester December 1948	Hallé Rothwell	78: HMV C 3954-3955 <u>Last movement only</u> LP: EMI SLS 796

Piano Concerto No 22

London June 1935	Chamber Orchestra Fischer	78: HMV DB 2681-2684/ DB 8015-8018 auto 78: Victor M 316 LP: HMV COLH 94 LP: Victor LCT 6013 LP: EMI 2C 061 01422/29 10851 LP: Turnabout THS 65094 CD: EMI CHS 763 7192

Piano Concerto No 23

London January 1931	LSO Rubinstein	78: HMV DB 1491-1493/ DB 7217-7219 auto 78: Victor M 147 LP: EMI 1C 137 1544273

Piano Concerto No 25

Naples January 1968	Naples SO Ciani	CD: Stradivarius STR 10005 CD: Curcio-Hunt CON 07

Piano Concerto No 27

London May 1934	LSO Schnabel	78: HMV DB 2249-2252/ DB 7733-7736 auto 78: Victor M 240 LP: HMV COLH 67 LP: EMI 1C 053 01341/EX 29 00723 CD: EMI CHS 763 7032 CD: Arabesque Z 6592 CD: Grammofono AB 78531
New York November 1940	NYPO Casadesus	78: Columbia (USA) M 490 LP: Columbia (USA) ML 2186/ML 4791 LP: Columbia 33C 1028

Violin Concerto No 5

London February 1934	LPO Heifetz	78: HMV DB 2199-2202/ DB 7692-7695 auto 78: Victor M 254 LP: Victor ARM4-0943 CD: Biddulph LAB 012 CD: EMI CDH 565 1912 CD: RCA/BMG 09026 617782/617332 CD: Pearl GEMMCDS 9157

Eine kleine Nachtmusik

London March 1928 and January 1929	Barbirolli Chamber Orchestra	78: HMV C 1655-1656 78: Victor 9789-9790/ 36283-36284 auto LP: Barbirolli Society SJB 104 CD: Koch 3-7077-2 78 version coupled with Purcell Hornpipe (The Married Beau)

Andante (Cassation K63)

London February 1950	Hallé	78: HMV DB 21278/DB 9609 Coupled with Delius Song of Summer; DB 21278 not issued

Andante (Cassation K99)

London November 1927	NGS Chamber Orchestra	78: National Gramophonic Society NGS 101 Coupled with Haydn London Symphony

Minuet (Divertimento K251)

Manchester April 1952	Hallé	HMV unpublished

String Quartet No 15 K421

London June 1925	Kutcher String Quartet, of which Barbirolli was cellist	78: Vocalion K 05190-05193 Coupled with Minuet (Quartet K428)

Minuet (String Quartet No 16 K428)

London June 1925	Kutcher String Quartet, of which Barbirolli was cellist.	78: Vocalion K 05193 Coupled with String Quartet No 15

Don Giovanni: Excerpt (Or sai chi l'onore)

London	Orchestra	78: HMV D 1547
May 1928	Leider	78: American Gramophonic Society AGSB 26
		LP: HMV COLH 132/CSLP 503
		LP: Victor LCT 6701
		LP: Preiser LV 30
		LP: EMI 1C 147 30785-30786
		LP: EMI EX 29 05983
		CD: EMI CMS 763 7502
		CD: Preiser 89004
		<u>78 versions coupled with Gluck Ah! Si la liberté (Armide)</u>

Don Giovanni: Excerpt (Madamina!)

London	Orchestra	78: HMV DA 994
June 1928	Chaliapin	78: Victor 1393

Die Entführung aus dem Serail, Overture

London	Barbirolli Chamber	HMV unpublished
January 1928	Orchestra	

Le Nozze di Figaro, Overture

London	Hallé	78: HMV C 3864
March 1949		<u>Coupled with Delius 2 Aquarelles</u>

Die Zauberflöte, Overture

Manchester	Hallé	LP: Nixa CCL 30156
April 1959		LP: Pye GGL 0302/GGC 4089/GSGC 14089
		LP: Pye GSGC 2038/GH 508
		CD: EMI CDM 764 1382

Die Zauberflöte: Excerpt (Ach! Ich fühl's)

London	Orchestra	78: HMV DB 2502
May 1935	Pons	78: Victor 8733
	Sung in French	CD: Pearl GEMMCD 9415
		<u>78 versions coupled with Bishop Lo! Here the gentle lark</u>

Die Zauberflöte: O Isis und Osiris, arranged by Barbirolli

London	London School	78: HMV (Spain) AF 207
March 1928	of Cellos	<u>Coupled with Casals Sardana</u>

MUSSORGSKY

Song of the flea

London September 1928	Orchestra Dawson	78: HMV C 1759 LP: EMI MFP 1144/RLS 107 7053 LP: World Records SMA 411 Coupled with Elgar O my warriors (Caractacus)

NEVIN

The Rosary

London September 1932	Orchestra Crooks	78: HMV DA 1288 78: Victor 1634 45: HMV 7P 333 LP: World Records SH 247 CD: Claremont GSE 785.033 CD: Pearl GEMMCD 9093 78 versions coupled with Gounod Nazareth

NICOLAI

Die lustigen Weiber von Windsor, Overture

Manchester August 1957	Hallé	45: Nixa CEC 32029 LP: Nixa CCL 30129 LP: Mercury MG 50161/SR 90161 LP: Pye GGC 4076/GSGC 14076 LP: Reader's Digest RDS 8015 CD: EMI CDM 764 1382/CDM 764 4442

NIELSEN

Symphony No 4 "Inextinguishable"

Manchester September 1959	Hallé	LP: Nixa CCL 30164/CSCL 70024 LP: Pye GGC 4026/GSGC 14026 LP: Pye GSGC 15025/GSGC 2031 LP: Vanguard SRV 179/SRV 179SD CD: EMI CDM 763 7752

PERGOLESI

3 giorni, attributed

London October 1911	Barbirolli, cello R.Barbirolli, piano	Edison Bell VF 1132 Coupled with Thomé Simple aveu

Oboe Concerto, arranged by Barbirolli

New York September 1940	NYPO Rothwell	Unpublished radio broadcast
London February 1948	Hallé Rothwell	78: HMV C 3731
Manchester May 1957	Hallé Rothwell	LP: Nixa CCL 30127 LP: Pye GGC 4065/GSGC 14065 LP: Pye GSGC 15034/GSGC 2007 CD: Precision PVCD 8378 CD: Nixa NIXCD 6004

PONCHIELLI

Dance of the Hours (La Gioconda)

London May 1933	LSO	78: Electrola EH 835
Manchester August 1957	Hallé	LP: Nixa CCL 30129 LP: Mercury MG 50161/SR 90161 LP: Pye GGC 4076/GSGC 14076/GH 515 LP: Reader's Digest RDS 8015

POPPER

Duet for 2 cellos

Beverley Hills January 1941	Barbirolli, L.Kennedy	LP: Barbirolli Society BS 03

PUCCINI

La Bohème: Excerpt (Si sente meglio?/Che gelida manina!/Sì! Mi chiamano Mimì/O soave fanciulla.......to end Act 1)

Manchester	Hallé	LP: Nixa CCL 30142
August 1958	Lafayette, R.Lewis	LP: GGC 4039/GSGC 14039/GSGC 2036
		CD: Nixa NIXCD 6005
		CD: EMI CDM 764 1952

La Bohème: Excerpt (Vecchia zimarra)

London	Orchestra	HMV unpublished
November 1929	Autori	

La Bohème: Excerpt (Che gelida manina)

London	Orchestra	78: HMV DB 1230
December 1928	Hislop	LP: Rubini GV 43
		CD: Pearl GEMMCD 9956
		Coupled with Mascagni Mamma quel vino (Cavalleria rusticana)

Madama Butterfly

Rome	Rome Opera	LP: EMI SAN 184-186/SLS 927
August 1966	Orchestra & Chorus	LP: Angel 3072
	Scotto, di Stasio,	LP: EMI SLS 100 0813/EX 29 08393
	Bergonzi, Panerai,	CD: EMI CMS 769 6542
	Montarsolo, Palma	Excerpts
		45: EMI 7P 401
		LP: EMI ASD 2326/ASD 3915/SLS 796
		LP: Angel 36567
		LP: EMI SEOM 1/SEOM 3/SEOM 10
		CD: EMI CDM 764 5542/CMS 769 1282
		CD: EMI CDZ 762 8622/565 0272
		CD: EMI CDEMX 9519/CDCFP 4582

Madama Butterfly: Excerpt (Viene la sera....to end Act 1)

Manchester	Hallé	LP: Nixa CCL 30142
August 1958	Lafayette, R.Lewis	LP: Pye GGC 4039/GSGC 14039
		LP: Nixa GSGC 14137/GSGC 2036
		CD: Nixa NIXCD 6005
		CD: EMI CDM 764 1952

Madama Butterfly: Excerpt (Viene la sera)

London	Orchestra	78: Edison Bell X 523
December 1927	Stiles-Allen,	Coupled with Mascagni Voi lo
	D.Jones	sapete (Cavalleria rusticana)
	Sung in English	

Manon Lescaut: Excerpt (Tu! Tu! Amore!)

Manchester	Hallé	LP: Nixa CCL 30142
August 1958	Lafayette, R.Lewis	LP: Pye GGC 4039/GSGC 14039/GSGC 2036
		CD: Nixa NIXCD 6005
		CD: EMI CDM 764 1952

Manon Lescaut, Intermezzo

Manchester	Hallé	LP: Nixa CCL 30147
September 1959		LP: Pye GGC 4016/GSGC 14016/GSGC 14137
		LP: Vanguard SRV 250SD
		LP: Reader's Digest RDS 8011
		CD: EMI CDM 764 1952

Tosca: Excerpt (Recondita armonia)

London	Orchestra	78: HMV DA 1063
July 1929	Hislop	LP: Rubini GV 43
		78 version coupled with
		E lucevan le stelle

Tosca: Excerpt (E lucevan le stelle.....Trionfal di nova speme)

Manchester	Hallé	LP: Nixa CCL 30142
August 1958	Lafayette, R.Lewis	LP: Pye GGC 4039/GSGC 14039/GSGC 2036
		CD: Nixa NIXCD 6005
		CD: EMI CDM 764 1952

Tosca: Excerpt (Elucevan le stelle)

London	Orchestra	78: HMV DA 1063
July 1929	Hislop	LP: Rubini GV 43
		78 version coupled with
		Recondita armonia

Tosca: Excerpt (Tre sbirri)

London June 1929	Covent Garden Orchestra & Chorus Inghilleri	78: HMV D 1701 Coupled with La povera mia cena

Tosca: Excerpt (La povera mia cena)

London June 1929	Covent Garden Orchestra Inghilleri, Dua	78: HMV D 1701 LP: EMI EX 29 01693 78 version coupled with Tre sbirri

Turandot: Excerpts (Non piangere Liù; In questa reggia; Straniero ascolta; Nessun dorma)

London May 1937 (5 May)	LPO Covent Garden Chorus Turner, Favero, Martinelli, Dua, Tomey	LP: Ed Smith EJS 50 CD: EMI CDH 761 0742

Turandot: Excerpts (Signore ascolta; Non piangere Liù; In questa reggia; Straniero ascolta; Nessun dorma)

London May 1937 (10 May)	LPO Covent Garden Chorus Turner, Albanese, Martinelli, Dua, Tomey	LP: Ed Smith EJS 50 LP: Private issue PHCH 100 LP: Legendary LR 110 CD: EMI CDH 761 0742

PURCELL

Dido and Aeneas

London August 1965	English Chamber Orchestra Ambrosian Singers de los Angeles, Harper, Johnson, Tear, Glossop	LP: EMI AN 169/SAN 169 LP: Angel 36359 LP: EMI SXLP 30275/CFP 40359 Excerpts LP: EMI SEOM 2 CD: EMI CDZ 767 2532 CD: EMI CDCFP 4611/555 2422

Suite for strings, arranged by Barbirolli

London October 1927	NGS Chamber Orchestra	78: National Gramophonic Society NGS 96-97 Coupled with Marcello Allergretto
New York February 1938	NYPO	78: HMV DB 3729-3730 78: Victor M 533 CD: Pearl GEMMCDS 9922
Manchester June 1956	Hallé	LP: Nixa CCL 30101 LP: Mercury MG 50125/SR 90125
Boston October 1964	Boston SO	CD: Music and Arts CD 251 CD: Intaglio INCD 7471
London May 1969	Hallé	LP: EMI ASD 2496

Hornpipe (The Married Beau)

London March and July 1928	Barbirolli Chamber Orchestra	78: HMV C 1656 78: Victor 9790/36284 LP: EMI SLS 796 LP: Barbirolli Society SJB 104 CD: Koch 3-7077-2

Fantasy upon 1 note, arranged by Mangeot and Warlock

London   Music Society   78: National Gramophonic Society
February 1926   String Quartet,   NGS 53
                      of which Barbirolli   Coupled with Fantasy in C
                      was the cellist

Fantasy in C, arranged by Mangeot and Warlock

London   Music Society   78: National Gramophonic Society
February 1926   String Quartet,   NGS 53
                      of which Barbirolli   LP: Barbirolli Society BS 03
                      was the cellist   78 version coupled with
                                              Fantasy upon 1 note

Fantasy in C minor, arranged by Mangeot and Warlock

London   Music Society   78: National Gramophonic Society
February 1926   String Quartet,   NGS 51
                      of which Barbirolli   LP: Barbirolli Society BS 03
                      was the cellist

Fantasy in 3 parts, arranged by Mangeot and Warlock

London   Barbirolli, cello   78: National Gramophonic Society
February 1926   Mangeot, Berley   NGS 52
                                              Coupled with McEwen Peat Reek

RACHMANINOV

Piano Concerto No 3

New York	NYPO	LP: International Piano Library
February 1939	Gieseking	IPL 505

To the children

London	Orchestra	78: HMV B 3154
May 1929	Hislop	Coupled with Messager La maison grise (Fortunio)

QUILTER

A Children's Overture

London	LPO	78: HMV C 2603
July 1933		78: Victor 36370
		LP: EMI EX 29 01073

RAFF

La fileuse, arranged by Gibilaro

London	Orchestra	78: HMV C 2456
September 1932	Arnaud	LP: HMV RLP 10/SLS 796

RAVEL

Daphnis et Chloé, Suite No 2

New York December 1939	NYPO	Unpublished radio broadcast <u>This recording may be of the complete ballet</u>
Manchester September 1959	Hallé Hallé Choir	LP: Pye GGC 4010/GSGC 14010 LP: Pye GSGC 15013/GSGC 2011 LP: Vanguard SRV 177/SRV 177SD LP: Reader's Digest RDS 8012 CD: EMI CDM 763 7632

Ma mère l'oye, Suite

Manchester May 1957	Hallé	LP: Nixa CCT 31005 CD: EMI CDM 763 7632

La valse

New York November 1940	NYPO	78: Columbia (USA) X 207 LP: Columbia (USA) RL 3046/HL 7075
Manchester September 1959	Hallé	LP: Pye GGC 4010/GSGC 14010 LP: Pye GSGC 15013/GSGC 2011 LP: Vanguard SRV 177/SRV 177SD LP: Reader's Digest RDS 8012 CD: EMI CDM 763 7632

Shéhérazade

London August 1967	New Philharmonia Baker	LP: EMI ASD 2444/SLS 5013 LP: Angel 36505

RESPIGHI

Fontane di Roma

New York February 1939	NYPO	78: HMV DB 3917-3918 78: Victor M 576 CD: Pearl GEMMCDS 9922

Arie di corte (Ancient Airs and Dances, 3rd suite)

New York February 1938	NYPO	78: HMV DB 3830 78: Victor 17-558 <u>DB 3830 not published</u>

RIMSKY-KORSAKOV

Capriccio espagnol

New York November 1940	NYPO	78: Columbia (USA) X 185 78: Columbia (USA) RL 3046/HL 7075
Manchester December 1953	Hallé	LP: HMV BLP 1058
London April 1961	Hallé	45: Concert Hall M 961/SMS 961

ROSSE

The Merchant of Venice, Suite

London June 1929	Barbirolli Chamber Orchestra	78: HMV C 1731-1732 <u>Doge's March only</u> LP: EMI SLS 796

ROSSINI

Il Barbiere di Siviglia: Excerpt (Una voce poco fa)

London	Orchestra	78: HMV DB 2501
May 1935	Pons	78: Victor 8870
		CD: Pearl GEMMCD 9415
		CD: RCA/BMG 09026 614112

Il Barbiere di Siviglia: Excerpt (La calumnia)

London	Orchestra	HMV unpublished
November 1929	Autori	

Il Barbiere di Siviglia: Excerpt (Largo al factotum)

London	Covent Garden	78: HMV DB 1698
June 1929	Orchestra	Coupled with Verdi Inaffia
	Inghilleri	l'ingola (Otello)

La Gazza ladra, Overture

Rome	Santa Cecilia	78: HMV (Italy) S 10535
February 1947	Orchestra	

Petite messe solennelle

New York	NYPO	LP: Ed Smith UORC 162
April 1939	Westminster Choir	
	Ginster, Castagna,	
	Kullmann, Warren	

Semiramide, Overture

Manchester	Hallé	LP: Nixa CCL 30147
September 1958		LP: Pye GGC 4016/GSGC 14016/GH 508
		LP: Vanguard SRV 250SD
		LP: Reader's Digest RDS 8011
		CD: EMI CDM 764 1382

Stabat mater: Excerpt (Inflammatus)

London August 1928	Covent Garden Orchestra & Chorus Austral	78: HMV D 1506 LP: HMV COLH 147/EX 29 01693 LP: Rubini RDA 005 CD: Memoir CDMOIR 411 CD: Testament SBT 1008

William Tell, Overture

Manchester May 1957	Hallé	LP: Nixa CCL 30129 CD: EMI CDM 764 1382

William Tell, Ballet music arranged by Godfrey

Manchester September 1958	Hallé	LP: Nixa CCL 30147 LP: Pye GGC 4016/GSGC 14016/GH 654 LP: Vanguard SRV 250SD LP: Reader's Digest RDS 8011

RUBBRA

Symphony No 5

London December 1950	Hallé	78: HMV DB 21384-21387/ DB 9715-9718 auto 45: Victor WHMV 1011 LP: Victor LHMV 1011 LP: HMV BLP 1021/HQM 1016

SAINT-SAENS

Le carnaval des animaux

Manchester	Hallé	LP: HMV ALP 1224
February 1954	Rawicz, Landauer	CD: Dutton/Barbirolli Society CDSJB 1002

Le carnaval des animaux: Excerpt (Le cygne)

Manchester	Barbirolli, cello	LP: Barbirolli Society BS 02
December 1961	Fermoy	Performed at Barbirolli's Golden Jubilee celebration

Havanaise for violin and orchestra

London	LSO	78: HMV DB 3211
March 1937	Heifetz	78: Victor 15347
		LP: Victor ARM4-0945
		LP: EMI EX 749 3751
		CD: Biddulph LAB 025
		CD: EMI CDH 764 2512/Pearl GEMMCD 9023
		CD: RCA/BMG 09026 617782/617352

Introduction and Rondo capriccioso for violin and orchestra

London	LSO	78: HMV DB 2580
March 1935	Heifetz	78: Victor 14115
		LP: Victor ARM4-0945
		LP: EMI EX 749 3751
		CD: Biddulph LAB 025
		CD: EMI CDH 764 2512
		CD: RCA/BMG 09026 617782/617352

Samson et Dalila : Excerpts (Mon coeur s'ouvre; Printemps qui commence)

London	Orchestra	78: HMV DB 1332
June 1929	Minghini-Cattaneo Sung in Italian	CD: Club 99 CC 9954

Valse caprice for piano and orchestra

London	Orchestra	78: HMV C 2455
September 1932	Arnaud	LP: HMV RLP 10

SARASATE

Zigeunerweisen for violin and orchestra

London April 1937	LSO Heifetz	78: HMV DB 3212 78: Victor 15246 LP: Victor ARM4-0945 LP: EMI EX 749 3751 CD: Biddulph LAB 025 CD: EMI CDH 764 2512 CD: RCA/BMG 09026 617782/617352

SCHOENBERG

Pelleas und Melisande

London August and September 1967	New Philharmonia	LP: EMI ASD 2459 LP: Angel 36509 CD: EMI CDM 565 0782
London August 1968	Hallé	CD: Intaglio INCD 7171

SCHUBERT

Symphony No 4 "Tragic"

New York January 1939	NYPO	78: HMV DB 3826-3829/ DB 8700-8703 auto 78: Victor M 562

Symphony No 5

Bucharest September 1961	Enesco State Symphony Orchestra	LP: Electrocord ECE 0144 78: Everest SDBR 3411

Symphony No 9 "Great"

Manchester December 1953	Hallé	LP: HMV ALP 1178 LP: Victor LBC 1085
London June 1964	Hallé	LP: EMI ALP 2251/ASD 2251 LP: Angel 36328/60194 LP: EMI SXLP 30267/EMX 2010 CD: EMI CDE 568 1212

Rosamunde, Overture

Manchester April 1948 and London May 1949	Hallé	78: HMV DB 3943-3944/ DB 4294-4295 auto 45: Victor WBC 1047 LP: Victor LBC 1047 78 version coupled with Mendelssohn Scherzo (Midsummer Night's Dream)

Rosamunde, Ballet Music No 2

London October 1933	New SO	78: HMV C 2637 Coupled with Marche Militaire No 1

Marche Militaire No 1 in D

London October 1933	New SO	78: HMV C 2637 Coupled with Rosamunde Overture

5 German Dances and 7 Trios D90

New York February 1939	NYPO	78: HMV DA 1811-1812/ DA 8411-8412 auto 78: Victor 2162-2163

SCHUMANN

Symphony No 4

New York November 1937	NYPO	Unpublished radio broadcast

Cello Concerto

London LPO   78: HMV DB 2244-2246/
May 1934 Piatigorsky   DB 7742-7744 auto
                  78: Victor M 247
                  45: Victor WCT 1119
                  LP: Victor LCT 1119
                  LP: Melodiya M10 44841-44842
                  CD: Pearl GEMMCD 9447
                  CD: Music and Arts CD 674

Violin Concerto

New York   NYPO   78: HMV DB 3435-3438/
February 1938 Menuhin   DB 8448-8451 auto
                  78: Victor M 451
                  45: Victor WCT 28
                  LP: Victor LCT 6
                  LP: EMI EX 29 08643
                  CD: Biddulph LAB 047

SIBELIUS

Symphony No 1

New York April 1942	NYPO	78: Columbia (USA) M 325
Manchester December 1957	Hallé	LP: Nixa CCL 30113 LP: Pye GGC 4058/GSGC 14058/GSGC 2058 LP: Vanguard SRV 132/SRV 132SD CD: EMI CDM 764 1392
London December 1966	Hallé	LP: EMI ASD 2366/SLS 799 LP: Angel 36489 CD: EMI CDM 763 1522/CDEMX 2130

Symphony No 2

New York June 1940	NYPO	78: Columbia (USA) M 423 LP: Columbia (USA) RL 3045
Manchester December 1952	Hallé	LP: HMV ALP 1122 LP: Victor LBC 1084
London October 1963	RPO	LP: Reader's Digest RDM 1028/RDS 5028 LP: RCA GL 25011 CD: Chesky CD 3
London July 1966	Hallé	LP: EMI ALP 2308/ASD 2308/SLS 799 LP: Angel 36425 LP: EMI EMX 2006 CD: EMI CDEMX 2157

Symphony No 3

London May 1969	Hallé	LP: EMI ASD 2648/SLS 799 CD: Toshiba TOCE 6043

Symphony No 4

London May 1969	Hallé	LP: EMI ASD 2494/SLS 799 CD: Toshiba TOCE 6044

Symphony No 5

Manchester May 1957	Hallé	LP: Nixa CCL 30144 LP: Pye GGC 4022/GSGC 14022 LP: Vanguard SRV 137/SRV 137SD CD: EMI CDM 764 1392
London July 1966	Hallé	LP: EMI ASD 2326/SLS 799/EMX 41 20 501 CD: Toshiba

Symphony No 6

London May 1970	Hallé	LP: EMI ASD 2648/SLS 799 CD: Toshiba TOCE 6043

Symphony No 7

London March 1949	Hallé	78: HMV C 3895-3897/7763-7765 auto 45: Victor WHMV 1011 LP: Victor LHMV 1011
London July 1966	Hallé	LP: EMI ASD 2326/SLS 799/EMX 41 20 501 CD: Toshiba
London November 1968	Helsinki PO	CD: Intaglio INCD 7171

Violin Concerto

London November 1968	Helsinki PO Szeryng	CD: Intaglio INCD 7201

Finlandia

London January 1966	Hallé	LP: EMI ALP 2272/ASD 2272/SEOM 10 LP: Capitol SP 8669/Angel 3750 LP: EMI EG 29 02731/EMTVD 50 CD: EMI CDM 769 2052/767 6382 CD: EMI CZS 767 2242/CDS 794 4312 CD: EMI CDU 565 0562

Karelia Suite

London January 1966	Hallé	LP: EMI ALP 2272/ASD 2272 LP: Capitol SP 8669/Angel 60208 LP: EMI ESD 154 5811/EG 29 02731 CD: EMI CDU 565 0562/767 6382 Excerpts 45: EMI 7P 400 LP: EMI SLS 796/SEOM 17/CFP 40294 LP: EMI YKM 5020 CD: EMI CDM 769 2052/CDCFP 4584 CD: EMI CDZ 762 5012/767 5932 CD: EMI CDZ 762 5042/781 4212

Lemminkainen's Return

London   Hallé   LP: EMI ALP 2272/ASD 2272/EG 29 02 731
January 1966   LP: Capitol SP 8669
                                   LP: Angel 60208/6061
                                   CD: EMI CDM 769 2052/767 6382
                                   CD: EMI CDU 565 0562

Pelleas and Melisande, excerpts (1.At the castle gate; 2.A spring in the park; 3.At the spinning wheel; 4.The death of Melisande)

London   Hallé   LP: EMI ASD 2366/SLS 799 (1, 2, 4)
January 1966   LP: EMI SXLP 30162
and July 1967   LP: EMI YKM 5020 (3)
                                   CD: EMI CDEMX 2130
                                   CD: EMI CDM 763 1522/CDZ 767 2252

Pohjola's Daughter

Manchester   Hallé   LP: Nixa CCL 30144
August 1958   LP: Pye GGC 4022/GSGC 14022
                                   LP: Vanguard SRV 137/SRV 137SD
                                   CD: EMI CDM 763 7752

London   Hallé   LP: EMI ALP 2272/ASD 2272/EG 29 02 731
January 1966   LP: Capitol SP 8669
                                   LP: Angel 60208
                                   CD: EMI CDM 763 7752/CDM 769 2052

Rakastava

London   Hallé   LP: EMI ASD 2494/SLS 799
July 1969   LP: EMI SXLP 30162
                                   CD: Toshiba TOCE 6044/TOCE 6428

Romance in C

London   Hallé   LP: EMI ASD 2494/SLS 799
July 1969   CD: Toshiba TOCE 6044/TOCE 6428

Scènes historiques, 1st suite (Overture, Scene and Festivo)

London August 1969	Hallé	LP: EMI SXLP 30162 CD: EMI CDM 763 7752

The Swan of Tuonela

Manchester January 1955	Hallé	LP: HMV ALP 1335
London January 1966	Hallé	LP: EMI ALP 2308/ASD 2308/SLS 799 LP: Angel 36425 LP: EMI SXLP 30162/EMX 2006 CD: EMI CDZ 767 2272/CDEMX 2157

Valse triste

Manchester June 1957	Hallé	LP: Mercury MG 50161/SR 90161 LP: Pye GGC 4076/GSGC 14076 LP: Reader's Digest RDS 8015
London January 1966	Hallé	LP: EMI ALP 2272/ASD 2272/EG 29 0 2731 LP: Capitol SP 8669 LP: Angel 3750/60208 CD: EMI CDM 769 2052/767 6382 CD: EMI CDZ 767 2262/CDZ 767 2532 CD: EMI CDU 565 0562

SMETANA

The Bartered Bride, Overture

New York August 1940	NYPO	78: Columbia (USA) 19903D 45: Fontana CFE 15029 LP: Columbia (USA) HL 7121

SOUSA

Stars and stripes forever, March

Manchester August 1957	Hallé	45: Nixa CEC 32021 LP: Nixa CCL 30129 LP: Mercury MG 50161/SR 90161 LP: Pye GGC 4076/GSGC 14076/GH 522 LP: Reader's Digest RDS 8015

JOHANN STRAUSS FATHER

Radetzky March, arranged by Jacob

Manchester June 1954	Hallé	45: HMV 7ER 5119
Manchester June 1956	Hallé	45: Nixa CEC 32003 LP: Nixa CCL 30130 LP: Mercury MG 50124/SR 90124 LP: Pye GGC 4078/GSGC 14078/GGD 0094 LP: Pye GSGD 10094/GSGC 15024 LP: Pye GSGC 2008/GSGC 2051 LP: Vanguard SRV 237/SRV 237SD LP: Reader's Digest RDS 8016
London December 1966	Hallé	LP: Columbia TWO 180 LP: Capitol SP 8698 LP: Angel 60184 LP: EMI ESD 7067/CFP 41 44991 CD: EMI CDCFP 4499

JOHANN STRAUSS

An der schönen blauen Donau, Waltz

Manchester June 1956	Hallé	LP: Nixa CCL 30130 LP: Mercury MG 50124/SR 90124 LP: Pye GGC 4078/GSGC 14078 LP: Pye GSGC 14137/GSGC 15024 LP: Pye GSGC 2008/GSGC 2051/GH 515 LP: Pye GGD 0094/GSGD 10094 LP: Vanguard SRV 237/SRV 237SD LP: Reader's Digest RDS 8016
London December 1966	Hallé	LP: Columbia TWO 180 LP: Capitol SP 8698 LP: Angel 60184 LP: EMI ESD 7067/CFP 41 44991 CD: EMI CDCFP 4499

Annen Polka

Manchester June 1956	Hallé	LP: Nixa CCL 30130 LP: Mercury MG 50124/SR 90124 LP: Pye GGC 4078/GSGC 14078 LP: Pye GSGC 15024/GSGC 2008 LP: Pye GSGC 2051/GH 515 LP: Pye GGD 0094/GSGD 10094 LP: Vanguard SRV 237/SRV 237SD LP: Reader's Digest RDS 8016

Champagne Polka

London December 1966	Hallé	LP: Columbia TWO 180 LP: Capitol SP 8698 LP: Angel 3750/60184 LP: EMI ESD 7067/CFP 41 44991 CD: EMI CDCFP 4499

Fantasy, arranged by Landauer

Manchester February 1954	Hallé Rawicz, Landauer	LP: HMV ALP 1224/MFP 2137

Die Fledermaus, Overture

Manchester June 1956	Hallé	45: Nixa CEC 32003 LP: Nixa CCL 30130 LP: Mercury MG 50124/SR 90124 LP: Pye GGC 4078/GSGC 14078 LP: Pye GSGC 15024/GSGC 2008 LP: Pye GSGC 2051/GH 522 LP: Vanguard SRV 237/SRV 237SD LP: Reader's Digest RDS 8016

Die Fledermaus: Excerpt (Brüderlein und Schwesterlein)

London December 1930	LSO Covent Garden Chorus Soloists Sung in English	78: HMV C 2107 LP: HMV (Australia) OXLP 7617

Die Fledermaus: Excerpt (Welch ein Fest, welche Nacht voll Freud')

London December 1930	LSO Covent Garden Chorus Soloists Sung in English	78: HMV C 2107 LP: HMV (Australia) OXLP 7629

G'schichten aus dem Wienerwald, Waltz

Eindhoven December 1944	Hallé	Unpublished private recording
Manchester June 1956	Hallé	LP: Nixa CCL 30130 LP: Mercury MG 50124/SR 90124 LP: Pye GGC 4078/GSGC 14078 LP: Pye GSGC 15024/GSGC 2008 LP: Pye GSGC 2051/GGD 0094/GSGD 10094 LP: Vanguard SRV 237/SRV 237SD LP: Reader's Digest RDS 8016

Kaiserwalzer

Manchester January 1955	Hallé	45: HMV 7ER 5119 LP: EMI SLS 796

Perpetuum mobile

Manchester   Hallé
June 1956
                                            45: Nixa CEC 32003
                                            LP: Nixa CCL 30130
                                            LP: Mercury MG 50124/SR 90124
                                            LP: Pye GGC 4078/GSGC 14078
                                            LP: Pye GSGC 15024/GSGC 2008/GSGC 2051
                                            LP: Pye GGD 0094/GSGD 10094
                                            LP: Vanguard SRV 237/SRV 237SD

London   Hallé   LP: Columbia TWO 180
December 1966   LP: Capitol SP 8698
                                            LP: Angel 60184
                                            LP: EMI ESD 7067/CFP 41 44991
                                            CD: EMI CDCFP 4499

Rosen aus dem Süden, Waltz

Manchester   Hallé   78: HMV C 3408
September 1944

Unter Donner und Blitz, Polka

London   Hallé   LP: Columbia TWO 180
December 1966   LP: Capitol SP 8698
                                            LP: Angel 60184
                                            LP: EMI ESD 7067/CFP 41 44991
                                            CD: EMI CDCFP 4499

Der Zigeunerbaron, Overture

Manchester   Hallé   45: Nixa CEC 32004
June 1956   LP: Nixa CCL 30130
                                            LP: Mercury MG 50124/SR 90124
                                            LP: Pye GGC 4078/GSGC 14078
                                            LP: Pye GSGC 15024/GSGC 2008
                                            LP: Pye GSGC 2051/GH 522
                                            LP: Pye GGD 0094/GSGD 10094
                                            LP: Vanguard SRV 237/SRV 237SD

London   Hallé   LP: Columbia TWO 180
December 1966   LP: Capitol SP 8698
                                            LP: Angel 60184
                                            LP: EMI ESD 7067

JOHANN & JOSEF STRAUSS

Pizzicato Polka

Manchester December 1944	Hallé	HMV unpublished
Manchester June 1956	Hallé	45: Nixa CEC 32003 LP: Nixa CCL 30103 LP: Mercury MG 50124/SR 90124 LP: Pye GGC 4078/GSGC 14078 LP: Pye GSGC 15024/GSGC 2008 LP: Pye GSGC 2051/GH 522 LP: Pye GGD 0094/GSGD 10094 LP: Vanguard SRV 237/SRV 237SD LP: Reader's Digest RDS 8016

RICHARD STRAUSS

Ein Heldenleben

London September 1969 (26-27 September)	LSO	LP: EMI ASD 2613/CFP 40325 LP: Angel 36764
London September 1969 (28 September)	LSO	Unpublished radio broadcast

Die Liebe der Danae, symphonic fragment arranged by Krauss

Manchester January 1955	Hallé	LP: HMV ALP 1335

Metamorphosen

London August 1967	New Philharmonia	LP: EMI SLS 778/ASD 2830 CD: EMI CZS 767 8122/767 8162 CD: EMI CDM 565 0782

Oboe Concerto

Place and date unconfirmed	Hallé Rothwell	Unpublished private recording

Der Rosenkavalier, Waltz sequence

Manchester June 1946	Hallé	78: HMV C 3556-3558/7661-7663 auto 78: HMV DB 4240-4242 45: Victor WBC 1017 LP: Victor LBC 1017 78 versions coupled with Wagner Lohengrin Act 3 Prelude
London December 1966	Hallé	LP: Columbia TWO 180 LP: Capitol SP 8698 LP: Angel 60184 LP: EMI ESD 7067

4 letzte Lieder

London September 1969	LSO Schwarzkopf	Unpublished radio broadcast

STRAVINSKY

Concerto in D for string orchestra

Manchester   Hallé   78: HMV C 3733-3734
March 1948

L'oiseau de feu, Suite (1919 version)

New York   NYPO   Unpublished radio broadcast
April 1938

STRICKLAND

Lonesome moonlight

London   Orchestra   HMV unpublished
December 1928   Hislop

SULLIVAN

The Golden Legend: Excerpt (The night is calm)

London   Covent Garden   78: HMV D 1506
August 1928   Orchestra   LP: EMI HLM 7026
                   and Chorus   LP: Rubini RDA 005
                   Austral

The lost chord

London   Orchestra   78: HMV DB 1526
June 1931   Gigli   78: Victor 8767
                                       LP: EMI HLM 7019
                                       CD: Pearl GEMMCD 9033
                                       78 versions coupled with
                                       Tosti Addio

SUPPÉ

The Beautiful Galatea, Overture

Manchester	Hallé	45: Nixa CEC 32018
June 1957		LP: Mercury MG 50160/SR 90160/18094
		LP: Pye GGC 4094/GSGC 14094
		CD: EMI CDM 764 1962

Jolly Robbers, Overture

Manchester   Hallé   LP: Mercury MG 50160/SR 90160/18094
June 1957   LP: Pye GGC 4094/GSGC 14094
                                                 CD: EMI CDM 764 1962

Light Cavalry, Overture

Manchester   Hallé   45: Nixa CEC 32017
June 1957   LP: Mercury MG 50160/SR 90160/18094
                                           LP: Pye GGC 4094/GSGC 14094/GH 515
                                           CD: EMI CDM 764 1962

Morning, Noon and Night in Vienna, Overture

Manchester   Hallé   45: Nixa CEC 32018
June 1957   LP: Mercury MG 50160/SR 90160/18094
                                           LP: Pye GGC 4094/GSGC 14094/GH 522
                                           CD: EMI CDM 764 1962

Pique Dame, Overture

Manchester   Hallé   45: Nixa CEC 32017
June 1957   LP: Mercury MG 50160/SR 90160/180
                                           LP: Pye GGC 4094/GSGC 14094
                                           CD: EMI CDM 764 1962

Poet and Peasant, Overture

Manchester   Hallé   45: HMV 7ER 5034
February 1954   LP: EMI HQM 1122

Manchester   Hallé   LP: Mercury MG 50160/SR 90160/18094
June 1957   LP: Pye GGC 4094/GSGC 14094/GH 515
                                           CD: EMI CDM 764 1962

TCHAIKOVSKY

Symphony No 4

| Manchester
May 1957 | Hallé | LP: Nixa CCL 30116
LP: Pye GGL 0300/GSGL 10300
LP: Pye GGC 4028/GSGC 14028/GGCD 303
LP: Vanguard SRV 135/SRV 135SD
CD: EMI CDM 763 9602 |

Symphony No 5

| New York
Date to be
confirmed | NYPO | CD: Dutton/Barbirolli Society
awaiting publication |

| Manchester
April 1959 | Hallé | LP: Nixa CCL 30154
LP: Pye GGC 4029/GSGC 14029
LP: Pye GSGC 2020/GGCD 303
LP: Vanguard SRV 139/SRV 139SD
CD: EMI CDM 763 9622 |

Symphony No 6 "Pathétique"

| Manchester
August 1958 | Hallé | LP: Nixa CCL 30146
LP: Pye GGC 4030/GSGC 14030
LP: Pye GSGC 2021/GGCD 303
LP: Vanguard SRV 148/SRV 148SD
CD: EMI CDM 763 7762 |

Piano Concerto No 1

| London
June 1932 | LSO
Rubinstein | 78: HMV DB 1731-1734/
DB 7242-7244 auto
78: Victor M 170
LP: EMI 1C 137 1544273
CD: Claremont GSE 785041 |

| London
December 1963 | Philharmonia
Ogdon | LP: HMV ALP 1991/ASD 542
LP: Angel 36142
LP: EMI SXLP 30552
CD: EMI CDM 763 5252 |

Violin Concerto

London December 1929	LSO Elman	78: HMV DB 1405-1408/ DB 7057-7060 auto 78: Victor M 79 LP: Pearl GEMM 270 LP: BBC Enterprises REH 717 CD: BBC Enterprises CD 717 CD: Pearl GEMMCD 9388

London
March 1937
	LPO
	Heifetz
		78: HMV DB 3159-3162/
		     DB 8282-8285 auto
		78: Victor M 536
		LP: Angel 60221
		LP: EMI 143 3511/EX 749 3751
		CD: EMI CDH 764 0302
		CD: Biddulph LAB 026
		CD: RCA/BMG 09026 617782/
		     09026 617492
		CD: Pearl GEMMCDS 9157

New York Date to be confirmed	NYPO Piastro	CD: Dutton/Barbirolli Society awaiting publication

Andante cantabile

Manchester August 1957	Hallé	LP: Mercury MG 50161/SR 90161 LP: Pye GGC 4076/GSGC 14076 LP: Pye GGCD 303/GH 515/GH 522 LP: Reader's Digest RDS 8015 CD: EMI CDM 763 9602

Francesca da Rimini

New York February 1938	NYPO	78: HMV DB 3658-3660/ DB 8597-8599 auto 78: Victor M 598 <u>May have been issued on LP by RCA</u>
London October 1969	New Philharmonia	LP: EMI ASD 2738 CD: EMI CDZ 762 6032/CDE 767 7892 CD: EMI CDU 565 0532

Marche slave

Manchester April 1959	Hallé	LP: Nixa CCL 30154 LP: Pye GGC 4029/GSGC 14029 LP: Pye GSGC 2021/GGCD 303 LP: Vanguard SRV 139/SRV 139SD CD: EMI CDM 763 9602

Romeo and Juliet

Manchester June 1957	Hallé	LP: Nixa CCL 30128 LP: Pye GGL 0301/GSGL 10301 CD: EMI CDM 763 7762
London July 1969	New Philharmonia	LP: Barbirolli Society SJB 103 Incomplete EMI recording

Serenade for strings

London September 1964	LSO	LP: HMV ALP 2099/ASD 646 LP: Angel 36269 LP: EMI ASD 2738/SXLP 30239 CD: EMI CDM 763 9622/CZS 767 7702 CD: EMI CDM 764 8432 Waltz only 45: HMV 7P 383 LP: Angel 3750 LP: EMI SEOM 10/YKM 5004

Swan Lake, Ballet suite

London July 1933	LPO	78: HMV C 2619-2620/DB 4238-4239 78: Victor 11666-11667 CD: Koch 3-7077-2 Selection only 45: HMV 7P 222
London October 1950	Hallé	78: HMV DB 21185-21186/ DB 9549-9550 auto LP: HMV BLP 1004 Selection only 45: HMV 7ER 5106/7EB 6038 DB 21185-21186 not published

Theme and Variations (Suite No 3)

New York April 1942	NYPO	78: Columbia (USA) X 226 LP: Columbia (USA) ML 4121

THOME

Simple aveu, arranged for cello and piano

London October 1911	Barbirolli, cello R.Barbirolli, piano	Edison Bell VF 1132 78: Winner 2274 LP: Pearl GEMM 105 VF 1132 coupled with Pergolesi Tre giorni

TOSTI

Addio

London June 1931	Orchestra Gigli Sung in English	78: HMV DB 1526 78: Victor 8767 LP: EMI HLM 7019 CD: Pearl GEMMCD 9033 78 versions coupled with Sullivan The Lost chord

TURINA

Danzas fantasticas

Manchester December 1951	Hallé	78: HMV DB 21433-21434/ DB 9738-9739 auto Orgia only LP: EMI SLS 796 First commercial recording made in the re-built Free Trade Hall

Unspecified song

Manchester May 1957	Hallé de Gabarain	Nixa unpublished

VAN BIENE

Broken Melody, arranged for cello and piano

London October 1911	Barbirolli, cello R.Barbirolli, piano	Edison Bell VF 1131 78: Winner 2148 CD: Pearl GEMMCDS 9984-9986 78 versions coupled with Wagner O Star of Eve

VAUGHAN WILLIAMS

Symphony No 2 "A London Symphony"

Manchester December 1957	Hallé	LP: Nixa CCL 30134 LP: Pye GGC 4012/GSGC 14012 LP: Pye GSGC 15035/GSGC 2035 LP: Vanguard SRV 134/SRV 134SD CD: Precision PVCD 8375 CD: Nixa NIXCD 6001 CD: EMI CDM 764 1972
London July 1967	Hallé	LP: EMI ASD 2360/SXLP 30180 LP: Angel 36478 LP: EMI EMX 41 20871 CD: EMI CDM 565 1092

Symphony No 5

Manchester February 1944	Hallé	78: HMV C 3388-3392/7599-7603 auto LP: EMI EH 769 1681 CD: Dutton CDAX 8011
London May 1962	Philharmonia	LP: HMV ALP 1957/ASD 508/ASD 2698 LP: Angel 35952 CD: EMI CDM 565 1102

Symphony No 6

Boston October 1964	Boston SO	CD: Music and Arts CD 251
Manchester December 1969	Hallé	Unpublished private recording Recorded at Barbirolli's 70th birthday concert
Munich April 1970	Bavarian RO	CD: Orfeo C265 921B

Symphony No 7 "Sinfonia antartica"

Manchester June and September 1953	Hallé Hallé Choir Ritchie	LP: HMV ALP 1102 LP: Barbirolli Society SJB 100

Symphony No 8

Manchester June 1956	Hallé	LP: Nixa NCT 17000 LP: Mercury MG 50115/SR 90115 LP: Pye GGC 4061/GSGC 14061 LP: Pye GSGC 15017/GSGC 2059 LP: Vanguard SRV 184/SRV 184SD CD: Precision PVCD 8380 CD: Nixa NIXCD 6001 CD: EMI CDM 764 1972

Greensleeves Fantasia

Manchester February 1948	Hallé	78: HMV C 3819 45: HMV 7ER 5082 <u>78 version coupled with Grainger Londonderry Air</u>
Manchester May 1957	Hallé	Nixa unpublished
London May 1962	Sinfonia of London	45: HMV 7P 383 LP: HMV ALP 1970/ASD 521 LP: Angel 36101 LP: EMI SLS 796/ESD 154 5844 LP: EMI EMTVD 45/EMX 41 20874 CD: EMI CDC 747 5372/CDS 790 3532 CD: EMI CDZ 762 5022/767 5932 CD: EMI CDZ 762 5272

Oboe Concerto

London July 1955	LSO Rothwell	LP: HMV BLP 1078/HQM 1016 LP: Barbirolli Society SJB 102

Phantasy Quintet for strings

London December 1925	Pougnet, viola Music Society String Quartet, of which Barbirolli was a member	78: National Gramophonic Society NGS 54-55 LP: Barbirolli Society BS 03

Thomas Tallis Fantasia

Manchester June 1946	Hallé	78: HMV C 3507-3508
London May 1962	Sinfonia of London	LP: HMV ALP 1970/ASD 521 LP: Angel 36101/3750 LP: EMI ASD 2698/EMTVD 72 CD: EMI CDC 747 5372/781 4212

Tuba Concerto

London June 1954	LSO Catelinet	LP: HMV BLP 1078/HQM 1016 LP: Barbirolli Society SJB 102

5 Variants of Dives and Lazarus

Manchester December 1953	Hallé	LP: HMV BLP 1049/HQM 1016 LP: Barbirolli Society SJB 102

The Wasps, Overture

Manchester June 1953	Hallé	78: HMV DB 21623 45: HMV 7ER 5082/7P 250 LP: Barbirolli Society SJB 102

VERDI

Requiem

Watford August 1969 and January 1970	New Philharmonia Orchestra & Chorus Caballé, Cossotto, Vickers, Raimondi	LP: EMI SLS 950 LP: Angel 3757 LP: EMI CFP 41 44283 CD: EMI CZS 762 8922 Excerpts LP: EMI SLS 796/CFP 4532/CFP 4590 CD: EMI 568 4124

Aida

London June 1953	Covent Garden Orchestra & Chorus Callas, Simionato, Baum, Neri, Walters	CD: Legato LCD 187 Act 3 excerpts LP: FWR 646/RHR 500 CD: Eklipse EKRCD 14 CD: Melodram MEL 36513

Un Ballo in maschera: Excerpt (Eri tu)

London June 1929	Covent Garden Orchestra Inghilleri	78: HMV D 1823

Don Carlo: Excerpt (O don fatale)

London March 1928	Orchestra Offers	78: HMV DB 1158 Coupled with Condotta ell'era (Il Trovatore)

Falstaff: Excerpt (L'onore)

London	Orchestra	78: HMV C 1822
December 1929	Fear	Coupling not conducted by
	Sung in English	Barbirolli

La Forza del destino, Overture

Manchester	Hallé	LP: Nixa CCL 30147/CSCL 70005
June 1957		LP: Pye GGC 4016/GSGC 14016/GH 508
		LP: Pye GGC 4095/GSGC 14095
		LP: Reader's Digest RDS 8011
		CD: EMI CDM 764 1952

London	Hallé	LP: Barbirolli Society SJB 103
July 1967		CD: EMI CDM 764 1384/CZS 568 1162

La Forza del destino: Excerpt (Madre pietosa vergine)

London	Orchestra	78: HMV DB 1217
December 1928	Chorus	LP: EMI EX 29 10753
	Giannini	CD: Preiser 89044

La Forza del destino: Excerpt (Pace, pace, mio Dio)

London	Orchestra	78: HMV DB 1228
December 1928	Giannini	CD: Preiser 89044

Otello

Walthamstow	New Philharmonia	LP: EMI SLS 940/EX 29 01373
August and	Ambrosian Chorus	LP: Angel 3742
October 1968	Jones, Di Stasio,	CD: EMI CMS 565 2962
	McCracken, Andreolli,	Excerpts
	Fischer-Dieskau,	LP: EMI ASD 2690/SEOM 2/EMX 2114
	Monreale, Giacometti	CD: EMI CDEMX 2114

Otello: Excerpt (Inaffia l'ugola!)

London June 1929	Covent Garden Orchestra & Chorus Inghilleri, Dua, Cilla	78: HMV D 1698 CD: Pearl GEMMCDS 9926 <u>78 version coupled with Rossini</u> <u>Largo al factotum (Barbiere)</u>

Otello: Excerpt (Dio! mio potevi scagliar)

London May 1928	Orchestra Zanelli	78: HMV DB 1173 LP: EMI EX 29 01693 CD: Pearl GEMMCD 9028/GEMMCDS 9926 <u>78 version coupled with Niun mi</u> <u>tema; same 78 catalogue number</u> <u>also used for Zanelli's later</u> <u>recording of the same extracts</u> <u>conducted by Sabajno</u>
London December 1929	New SO Melchior <u>Sung in German</u>	78: HMV D 2037 LP: EMI 1C 147 01259-01260 LP: EMI EX 29 10753 LP: Pearl GEMM 228-229 CD: Pearl GEMMCD 9500 CD: Danacord DACOD 315-316 CD: Nimbus NI 7816 CD: Preiser 89086 <u>78 version coupled with</u> <u>Niun mi tema</u> <u>Also issued on LP by Danacord</u> <u>and Preiser</u>

Otello: Excerpt (Niun mi tema)

London May 1928	Orchestra Zanelli	78: HMV DB 1173 LP: EMI 1C 049 03005/EX 29 01693 CD: Pearl GEMMCD 9028/GEMMCDS 9926 <u>78 version coupled with Dio! mio</u> <u>potevi; same 78 catalogue number</u> <u>also used for Zanelli's later</u> <u>recording of the same extracts</u> <u>conducted by Sabajno</u>
London December 1929	New SO Melchior <u>Sung in German</u>	78: HMV D 2037 LP: EMI 1C 147 01259-01260 LP: EMI EX 29 10753 LP: Pearl GEMM 228-229 CD: Pearl GEMMCD 9500 CD: Danacord DACOD 315-316 CD: Nimbus NI 7816 CD: Preiser 89086 <u>78 version coupled with Dio!</u> <u>mio potevi</u> <u>Also issued on LP by Danacord</u> <u>and Preiser</u>

La Traviata, Preludes to Acts 1 and 3

Manchester	Hallé	45: HMV 7ER 5034
January 1954		LP: EMI HQM 1122
		CD: EMI CDM 764 1952

Il Trovatore: Excerpt (Stride la vampa)

| London | Orchestra | 78: HMV DA 825 |
| February 1928 | Offers | |

Il Trovatore: Excerpt (Condotta ell' era)

| London | Orchestra | 78: HMV DB 1158 |
| March 1928 | Offers | Coupled with O don fatale (Don Carlo) |

VIEUXTEMPS

Violin Concerto No 4

London	LPO	78: HMV DB 2447-2446/
March 1935	Heifetz	DB 7857-7859 auto
		78: Victor M 297
		LP: RCA ARM4-0944
		LP: EMI EX 749 3751
		CD: Biddulph LAB 025
		CD: EMI CDH 764 2512
		CD: RCA/BMG 09026 617782/ 09026 617342

VILLA-LOBOS

Bachianas Brasileiras No 4

| Manchester | Hallé | LP: HMV ALP 1335 |
| January 1955 | | |

VIVES

Unspecified song

| Manchester | Hallé | Nixa unpublished |
| May 1957 | da Gabarain | |

WAGNER

Der fliegende Holländer, Overture

London December 1927	Orchestra	78: Edison Bell X 521-522 <u>Coupled with Meistersinger Act 3 Prelude</u>
Manchester September 1960	Hallé	LP: Pye GGD 0094/GSGD 10094 LP: Pye GGC 4053/GSGC 14053 LP: Vanguard SRV 149/SRV 149SD LP: Reader's Digest RDS 8013 CD: EMI CDM 764 1412

Der fliegende Holländer: Excerpt (Summ und brumm)

London August 1928	Covent Garden Orchestra & Chorus Walker <u>Sung in English</u>	78: HMV D 1517 78: Victor 7117 <u>Coupled with Traft ihr das Schiff</u>

Der fliegende Holländer: Excerpt (Traft ihr das Schiff im Meere an)

London August 1928	Covent Garden Orchestra & Chorus Austral <u>Sung in English</u>	78: HMV D 1517 78: Victor 7117 LP: Victor LCT 6701 LP: HMV CSLP 502 <u>78 versions coupled with Summ und brumm</u>

Lohengrin, Prelude

Manchester June 1946	Hallé	78: HMV C 3545/DB 4251
Manchester September 1960	Hallé	LP: Pye GGD 0094/GSGD 10094 LP: Pye GGC 4053/GSGC 14053 LP: Vanguard SRV 149/SRV 149SD LP: Reader's Digest RDS 8013 CD: EMI CDM 764 1412

Lohengrin, Act 3 Prelude

Manchester June 1946	Hallé	78: HMV C 3558/DB 4242

Lohengrin: Excerpt (In fernem Land)

London July 1929	Orchestra Hislop Sung in English	78: HMV DB 1351 CD: Pearl GEMMCD 9956 78 version coupled with Morgendlich leuchtend (Meistersinger)

Die Meistersinger von Nürnberg, Overture

London September 1969	LSO	LP: EMI SLS 796/YKM 5016

Die Meistersinger von Nürnberg, Act 3 Prelude

London December 1927	Orchestra	78: Edison Bell X 522 Coupled with Holländer Overture

Die Meistersinger von Nürnberg, Act 3 Suite arranged by Barbirolli (Prelude; Dance of the Apprentices; Procession of the Masters; Homage to Sachs; Finale)

New York November 1938	NYPO	CD: Dutton/Barbirolli Society CDSJB 1001
Manchester September 1944	Hallé	78: HMV C 3416-3417
Manchester September 1960	Hallé	LP: Pye GGD 0094/GSGD 10094 LP: Pye GGC 4053/GSGC 14053 LP: Pye GSGC 14095 LP: Vanguard SRV 149/SRV 149SD CD: EMI CDM 764 1412

Die Meistersinger von Nürnberg: Excerpt (Was duftet doch der Flieder)

London December 1929	Orchestra Fear Sung in English	78: HMV C 2072 Coupling not conducted by Barbirolli

Die Meistersinger von Nürnberg: Excerpt (Selig wie die Sonne)

London May 1931	LSO Schumann, Parr, Melchior, Williams, Schorr	78: HMV D 2002 78: Victor 7682 45: Victor WCT 4 LP: Victor LCT 1003 LP: HMV COLH 137/SLS 796 LP: Angel 60189 LP: EMI RLS 7711/EX 29 02123 CD: Danacord DACOD 315-316 CD: EMI CMS 764 0082 CD: Pearl GEMMCD 9944/Preiser 89214 Also issued on LP by Danacord; 78 coupling not conducted by Barbirolli

Die Meistersinger von Nürnberg: Excerpt (Morgendlich leuchtend)

London July 1929	Orchestra Hislop Sung in English	78: HMV DB 1351 CD: Pearl GEMMCD 9956 78 version coupled with In fernem Land (Lohengrin)
London May 1931	LSO Melchior	78: HMV DB 1858 45: HMV 7P 350 LP: Preiser LV 124 CD: Danacord DACOD 315-316 CD: Beulah 2PD 4 CD: Pearl GEMMCD 9040

Parsifal: Excerpt (Ich sah das Kind)

London May 1931	LSO Leider	78: HMV DB 1545 78: Victor 7523 45: Victor WCT 2 LP: Victor LCT 1001 LP: HMV COLH 132 LP: Preiser LV 30 LP: EMI 1C 147 30785-30786M LP: EMI 1C 181 30669-30678M LP: EMI RLS 7711/EX 29 02123 CD: Preiser 89004 CD: EMI CMS 764 0082 CD: Pearl GEMMCD 9331 CD: Memoir CDMOIR 408 78 versions coupled with Liebestod

Rienzi, Overture

New York November 1938	NYPO	CD: Dutton/Barbirolli Society CDSJB 1001
Manchester September 1944	Hallé	78: HMV C 3425-3426 Coupled with Mendelssohn Scherzo (A Midsummer Night's Dream)

Rienzi: Excerpt (Allmächt'ger Vater)

London	LSO	78: HMV D 2057
May 1930	Melchior	78: Victor 7656
		LP: EMI 1C 147 01259-01260
		CD: Danacord DACOD 315-316
		CD: EMI CDH 769 7892
		CD: Nimbus NI 7812
		CD: Preiser 89086
		Also issued on LP by Danacord; 78 versions coupled with Dir töne Lob (Tannhäuser)

Siegfried Idyll

New York	NYPO	CD: Dutton/Barbirolli Society
November 1938		CDSJB 1001

Tannhäuser, Overture

Manchester	Hallé	LP: Nixa CCL 30156
April 1959		LP: Pye GGL 0302/GGC 4089/GSGC 14089
		LP: Pye GSGC 2038/GH 508
		CD: EMI CDM 764 1382

Tannhäuser, Venusberg Music

New York	NYPO	CD: Dutton/Barbirolli Society
November 1938		CDSJB 1001

Tannhäuser, orchestral selection arranged by Gibilaro

London	LSO	78: HMV C 2293
September 1931		

Tannhäuser: Excerpt (Dir töne Lob)

London	LSO	78: HMV D 2057
May 1930	Melchior	78: Victor 7656
		LP: Pearl GEMM 228-229
		LP: EMI EX 29 01693
		CD: Danacord DACOD 315-316
		CD: Nimbus NI 7816
		CD: Pearl GEMMCD 9500
		CD: Preiser 89086
		Also issued on LP by Danacord; 78 versions coupled with Allmächt'ger Vater (Rienzi)

Tannhäuser: Excerpt (O star of Eve), arranged for cello and piano

London October 1911	Barbirolli, cello R.Barbirolli, piano	Edison Bell VF 1131 LP: Pearl GEMM 105 <u>78 version coupled with Van Biene Broken Melody</u>

Tristan und Isolde, Prelude and Liebestod

New York November 1938	NYPO	CD: Dutton/Barbirolli Society CDSJB 1001
Manchester September 1960	Hallé	LP: Pye GGD 0094/GSGD 10094 LP: Pye GGC 4053/GSGC 14053 LP: Vanguard SRV 149/SRV 149SD LP: Reader's Digest RDS 8013 CD: EMI CDM 764 1412

Tristan und Isolde: Excerpt (Mild und leise)

London May 1931	LSO Leider	78: HMV DB 1545 78: Victor 7523 45: Victor WCT 2 LP: Victor LCT 1001 LP: HMV COLH 132 LP: Preiser LV 30 LP: EMI 1C 147 30785-30786 CD: Legato LCD 146 CD: Preiser 89004 CD: Pearl GEMMCD 9331 CD: Nimbus NI 7818 <u>78 versions coupled with Ich sah das Kind (Parsifal)</u>

Die Walküre: Excerpt (Winterstürme wichen dem Wonnemond)

London May 1931	LSO Melchior	78: HMV DA 1227 CD: Danacord DACOD 315-316 CD: EMI CDH 769 7892 CD: Nimbus NI 7856 CD: Preiser 89086 <u>Also issued on LP by Preiser and Danacord</u>

Die Walküre: Excerpt (Der alte Sturm, die alte Müh'!)

London April 1932	LSO Schorr, Leisner	78: HMV DB 1720-1721 78: Victor 7742-7743 LP: Preiser LV 125 CD: Pearl GEMMCD 9357/GEMMCDS 9137

Träume (Wesendonk-Lieder)

London May 1928	Orchestra Leider	78: HMV DB 1553 78: Victor 7708 LP: Preiser LV 1370 LP: EMI 1C 147 30785-30786 CD: Preiser 89004 Coupled with Schmerzen

Schmerzen (Wesendonk-Lieder)

London May 1931	LSO Leider	78: HMV DB 1553 78: Victor 7708 LP: Preiser LV 1370 LP: EMI 1C 147 30785-30786 LP: EMI EX 29 01693 CD: Preiser 89004 Coupled with Träume

WALDTEUFEL

Les patineurs, Waltz

Manchester May 1957	Hallé	45: Nixa CEC 32005

WALLACE

Maritana, Overture

London December 1929	Covent Garden Orchestra	78: HMV C 1927 LP: Pearl GEMM 814

WARLOCK

Serenade for the 60th Birthday of Frederick Delius

London December 1927	NGS Chamber Orchestra	78: National Gramophonic Society NGS 75

WEBER

Euryanthe, Overture

Manchester June 1946	Hallé	78: HMV C 3560/DB 4269

Der Freischütz, Overture

Manchester May 1951	Hallé	78: HMV DB 21504 LP: EMI HQM 1122

Oberon, Overture

New York October 1938	NYPO	Unpublished radio broadcast
Manchester April 1959	Hallé	LP: Nixa CCL 30156 LP: Pye GGL 0302/GGC 4089 LP: Pye GSGC 14089/GSGC 2038 CD: EMI CDM 764 1382

Oberon: Excerpt (Ozean, du Ungeheuer!)

London August 1928	Covent Garden Orchestra Austral	78: HMV D 1504 LP: HMV COLH 147 LP: Rubini RDA 005

WEINBERGER

Christmas

New York December 1939	NYPO	Unpublished radio broadcast

WIENIAWSKI

Violin Concerto No 2

London
March 1935
	LPO
	Heifetz
		78: HMV DB 2447-2449/
		    DB 7866-7868 auto
		78: Victor M 275
		LP: RCA ARM4-0944
		LP: EMI EX 749 3751
		CD: Biddulph LAB 026
		CD: EMI CDH 764 2512
		CD: RCA/BMG 09026 617782/
		    09026 617342

WOLF-FERRARI

Il segreto di Susanna, Overture

Manchester February 1945	Hallé	HMV unpublished

MISCELLANEOUS

Auld Lang Syne

Eindhoven December 1944	Hallé	Unpublished radio broadcast

Elizabethan Suite, arranged by Barbirolli

New York April 1942	NYPO	Columbia (USA) unpublished
Manchester January 1954	Hallé	LP: HMV BLP 1065
London May 1967	BBCSO	LP: EMI ASD 2496

God Save the King

London April 1928	Barbirolli Chamber Orchestra	HMV unpublished

3 Irish Melodies: Golden Slumbers; Ancient Lullaby; My love's an Arbutus

London July 1929	Barbirolli, cello Bartlett, piano	78: National Gramophonic Society NGS 132 Golden Slumbers only LP: EMI SLS 796 78 coupling not conducted by Barbirolli

Turn ye to me, arranged by Gibilaro; O' a' the airts the wind can blow, arranged by Moffat

London May 1929	Orchestra Hislop	78: HMV B 3155 LP: Rubini RS 308 CD: Moidart MIDCD 003

BARBIROLLI SPEAKS

JB: a portrait of Sir John Barbirolli

BBC TV
1965

Unpublished video recording
"Monitor" production by Melvyn Bragg, scripted by Charles Reid and narrated by Huw Wheldon; includes interview material and rehearsal extracts from Bruckner 7, Elgar 2, Berlioz Hungarian March (Hallé Orchestra) and Tchaikovsky 4 (Manchester Royal College of Music Students' Orchestra)

Memories of Cheltenham

BBC 1951

Unpublished radio broadcast

Barbirolli introduces recordings by Yvonne Arnaud

London
December 1951

LP: HMV Special pressing RLP 10

Interview with C.B. Rees

BBC
June 1960

LP: Barbirolli Society BS 03

Speech at Golden Jubilee dinner

Manchester   LP: Barbirolli Society BS 02
December 1961

Interview with Michael Kennedy

BBC   LP: Barbirolli Society BS 01
December 1963

Interview with Kinloch Anderson

London   LP: EMI SLS 796
April 1964

Barbirolli announces the death of Winston Churchill to his concert audience in Boston

Boston   LP: Barbirolli Society BS 01
January 1965

Interview with Eamonn Andrews

ITV   LP: EMI SLS 796
May 1966

Speech at 70th birthday concert

Manchester   Unpublished private recording
December 1969

Radio talk

BBC   Unpublished radio broadcast
December 1969

Sir Reginald Goodall
1901-1990

Discography compiled by John Hunt

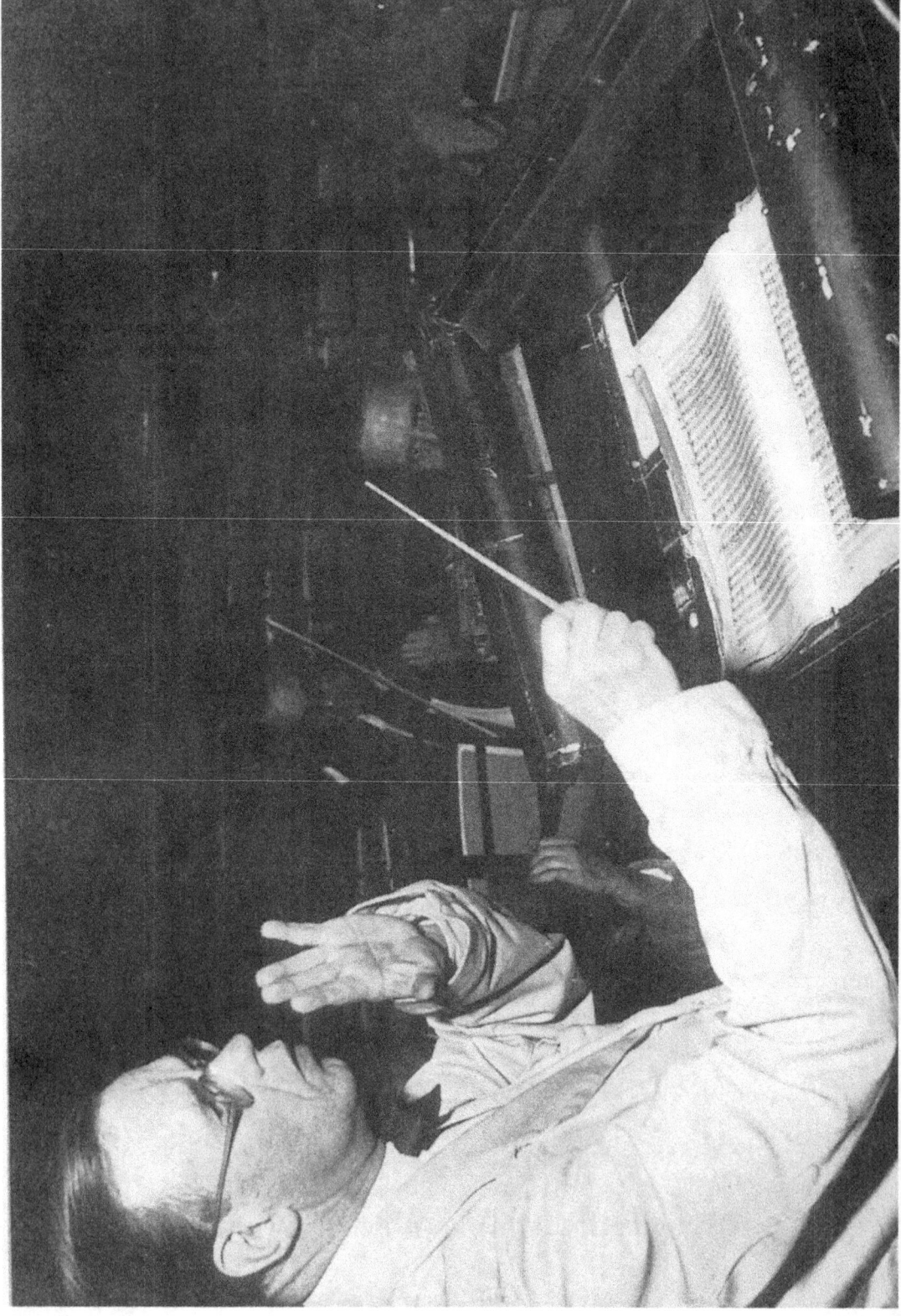

BEETHOVEN

Coriolan, Overture

London
November 1945

National SO

78: Decca K 1355
Not published

Leonore No 1, Overture

London
January 1946

National SO

78: Decca K 1471
Not published

BRITTEN

Peter Grimes, Excerpts (1. Whatever you say; 2. Now the Great Bear; 3. Church Scene; 4. In dreams I've built myself some kindlier home; 5. Embroidery in childhood; 6. Interlude VI; 7. Grimes!..Steady, there you are)

London July 1948	Covent Garden Orchestra BBC Theatre Chorus Cross, Pears, Culbert	LP: EMI RLS 707 (3,5,6,7) CD: EMI CMS 764 7272

The Rape of Lucretia, original version

London October 1946	Glyndebourne Chamber Orchestra Cross, Ritchie, Ferrier, Pollak, Pears, Brannigan, O.Kraus, Sharp	Unpublished radio broadcast; recording preserved incomplete Never again must we two dare to part LP: BBC Records REGL 368 LP: Arabesque 8070

The Rape of Lucretia, abridged revised version

London July and October 1947	English Opera Group Orchestra Cross, Ritchie, N.Evans, Nielsen, Pears, Dowling, Lumsden, Sharp	78: HMV C 3699-3706/ C 7706-7713 auto 78: Victor DM 1288 LP: EMI MFP 2119 CD: EMI CMS 764 7272 Excerpts LP: EMI EX 29 00233 Section beginning Here the thirsty evening not originally published but included in the CD edition

BRUCKNER

Symphony No 7

London November 1971	BBCSO	Unpublished radio broadcast

Symphony No 8

London September 1969	BBCSO	Unpublished radio broadcast

FLOTOW

Martha: Excerpt (M'appari)

London	Covent Garden	HMV unpublished
June 1951	Orchestra	
	Midgley	

MEYERBEER

L'Africaine: Excerpt (O paradiso!)

London	Covent Garden	HMV unpublished
June 1951	Orchestra	
	Midgley	

MOZART

The aria Dalla sua pace (Don Giovanni), recorded by Midgley with the Philharmonia Orchestra under Walter Süsskind on an unpublished 78, was issued by EMI (LP EX 769 7411 and CD CMS 769 7412) and incorrectly described as being accompanied by the Covent Garden Orchestra under Reginald Goodall

TCHAIKOVSKY

1812, Overture

| London | National SO | 78: Decca K 1349-1350 |
| November 1945 | | |

WAGNER

Götterdämmerung

London August 1977	ENO Orchestra and Chorus Hunter, Curphey, Pring, Remedios, Haugland, Welsby, Hammond-Stroud Sung in English	LP: EMI SLS 5118/SLS 5146 CD: EMI CMS 764 2442 Also published on LP in USA by Musical Heritage Society

Götterdämmerung, Act 3 scenes 2 and 3 (Der uns das Wild verscheuchte...to end)

London December 1972	Sadlers Wells Orchestra & Chorus Hunter, Curphey, Remedios, Bailey, Grant Sung in English	LP: Unicorn UNS 245-246 CD: Chandos CHAN 8534

Götterdämmerung, Siegfried's Funeral March

Snape October 1974	ENO Orchestra	Unpublished radio broadcast

Die Meistersinger von Nürnberg

London September 1968	Sadlers Wells Orchestra & Chorus Curphey, Robson, Byrne, Dempsey, Bailey, Grant, Hammond-Stroud Sung in English	Unpublished radio broadcast

Die Meistersinger von Nürnberg, Overture

Snape October 1974	ENO Orchestra	Unpublished radio broadcast

Die Meistersinger von Nürnberg: Excerpt (Wahn! Wahn! Ueberall Wahn!)

London April 1985	ENO Orchestra Howell Sung in English	Unpublished video recording

Parsifal

London May 1971	Covent Garden Orchestra & Chorus Shuard, Vickers, Hendriks, Bailey, McIntyre, Langdon	Unpublished radio broadcast
Swansea June 1984	WNO Orchestra and Chorus Meier, Ellsworth, McIntyre, Folwell, Joll, Gwynne	LP: EMI EX 27 01783 CD: EMI CDS 749 1828

TRISTAN UND ISOLDE

Cardiff New Theatre
8, 15 & 22 September 1979
Birmingham Hippodrome Theatre
29 September 1979
Bristol Hippodrome Theatre
6 October 1979

Opera in three acts by Richard Wagner
Text by the composer performed in the original German

First performance at the Munich Hoftheater on 10 June 1865
First performance of this production at the Cardiff New Theatre on 8 September 1979

Cast

Isolde	**Linda Esther Gray**
Brangäne	**Anne Wilkens**
Tristan	**John Mitchinson**
Kurwenal	**Bent Norup** *(except Bristol)*
	Phillip Joll *(Bristol)*
King Marke	**Gwynne Howell**
Melot	**Nicholas Folwell**
Shepherd	**Arthur Davies**
Helmsman	**Geoffrey Moses**
Sailor	**Mark Hamilton**
Conductor	**Reginald Goodall**
Producer	**Peter Brenner**
Designer	**Klaus Teepe**
Staff Producer	**Timothy Tyrrel**

Scenery, properties and costumes made in the Company's workshops.
Tárogató supplied by Mrs. Szili, Külkereskedelmi Vállalat, Budapest.

There is an interval of half an hour after Act I and a long interval of one hour after Act II.

The performance lasts approximately 5 hours 40 minutes.

WESSEX
PHILHARMONIC ORCHESTRA
BOURNEMOUTH

Leader: JOHN GREENSTONE

Conductor: REGINALD GOODALL

Soloist: MARK HAMBOURG

CARNEGIE TRUST CONCERT

Programme

Overture, "Oberon"	Weber
"Eine Kleine Nachtmusik"	Mozart
Piano Concerto in E flat ("The Emperor")	Beethoven
Symphony No. 4 in G	Dvorak

Members of the audience who desire to enter or leave the hall during the concert are requested to do so between and not during the items.

DE MONTFORD HALL, LEICESTER
TUESDAY, SEPTEMBER 8th, at 6.45 p.m.
Doors open 6.15 p.m.

8 December 1942

Das Rheingold

| London
March 1975 | ENO Orchestra
McDonall, Pring,
Collins, Belcourt,
Dempsey, Welsby,
Bailey, Lloyd,
Hammond-Stroud,
Grant
Sung in English | LP: EMI SLS 5032/SLS 5146
LP: Angel 3825
CD: EMI CMS 764 1102
Also published on LP in USA by
Musical Heritage Society |

Das Rheingold: Excerpt (Abendlich strahlt der Sonne Auge)

| London
February 1968 | Covent Garden
Orchestra
Ward | LP: Decca MET 392-393/
SET 392-393 |

Siegfried

| London
August 1973 | ENO Orchestra
Hunter, M.London,
Collins, Remedios,
Dempsey, Bailey,
Hammond-Stroud,
Grant
Sung in English | LP: EMI SLS 875/SLS 5146
CD: EMI CMS 763 5952
Also published on LP in USA by
Musical Heritage Society |

Tristan und Isolde

Cardiff September 1979	WNO Orchestra and Chorus Gray, Wilkens, Mitchinson, Norup, Howell	Unpublished radio broadcast
London December 1979	WNO Orchestra and Chorus Gray, Wilkens, Mitchinson, Norup, Howell	Unpublished radio broadcast
Swansea November 1980 and January 1981	WNO Orchestra and Chorus Gray, Wilkens, Mitchinson, Joll, Howell	LP: Decca D250 D5 LP: London (USA) LDR 575001 CD: Decca 443 6822

Tristan und Isolde, Prelude

London November 1971	BBCSO	Unpublished radio broadcast

Tristan und Isolde, Prelude and Liebestod

London March 1969	LSO	Unpublished radio broadcast

Die Walküre

London December 1975	ENO Orchestra Hunter, Curphey, Howard, Remedios, Bailey, Grant Sung in English	LP: EMI SLS 5063/SLS 5146 LP: Angel 3826 CD: EMI CMS 763 9182 Also published on LP in USA by Musical Heritage Society
Cardiff February 1984	WNO Orchestra Evans, Harries, Payne, Ellsworth, Joll, Earle Sung in English	Unpublished radio broadcast

Die Walküre, Act 1

Snape October 1974	ENO Orchestra Curphey, Remedios, Howell Sung in English	Unpublished radio broadcast

Wesendonk-Lieder

London November 1971	BBCSO Baker	Unpublished radio broadcast

MISCELLANEOUS

The Quest for Reginald Goodall: TV documentary with interviews and musical extracts

1984	WNO Orchestra Evans, Howell, McIntyre, H.Burton & others	Unpiblished video recording

Interview with John Amis

August 1969	BBC	Unpublished radio broadcast

Interview with Alan Blyth

June 1973	BBC	Unpublished radio broadcast

Characters in order of appearance

Siegmund	Alberto Remedios
Sieglinde	Margaret Curphey
Hunding	Clifford Grant
Wotan	Norman Bailey
Brünnhilde	Rita Hunter
Fricka	Ann Howard
Gerhilde	Katie Clarke
Ortlinde	Anne Conoley
Waltraute	Elizabeth Connell
Schwertleite	Helen Attfield
Helmwige	Anne Evans
Siegrune	Sarah Walker
Grimgerde	Shelagh Squires
Rossweisse	Anne Collins

Conductor Reginald Goodall
Producers Glen Byam Shaw John Blatchley
Designer Ralph Koltai
Lighting Robert Ornbo
Staff Producer David Ritch

Reginald Goodall appears by permission of the General Administrator, Royal Opera House, Covent Garden

---

Sadler's Wells Opera at the London Coliseum

The Mastersingers of Nuremberg

An Opera in Three Acts by Richard Wagner

English Translation by Frederick Jameson
Revised by Norman Feasey and Gordon Kember

Conductor: Reginald Goodall
Producers: Glen Byam Shaw and John Blatchley
Scenery: Motley
Costumes: David Walker
Lighting: Charles Bristow
Choreographer: Harry Haythorne
Staff Producer: William Royston

Saturday, September 14, 1968
37th performance by Sadler's Wells Opera in London
Sixth performance at the London Coliseum

'Die Meistersinger von Nürnberg' was first produced at the Royal Court Theatre, Munich on June 21, 1868. Its first performance in England was at the Theatre Royal, Drury Lane in 1882. This production was first performed at Sadler's Wells Theatre on January 31, 1968.

Characters

Hans Sachs	Norman Bailey
Veit Pogner	Noel Mangin
Kunz Vogelgesang	Robin Donald
Konrad Nachtigal	Julian Moyle
Sixtus Beckmesser	Derek Hammond Stroud
Fritz Kothner	David Bowman
Balthasar Zorn	John Brecknock
Ulrich Eisslinger	Francis Egerton
Augustin Moser	Louis Browne
Hermann Ortel	James Singleton
Hans Schwartz	Gerwyn Morgan
Hans Foltz	Eric Stannard
Walther von Stolzing	Connell Byrne
David	Gregory Dempsey
Eva	Margaret Curphey
Magdalene	Ann Robson
Night Watchman	Ian Comboy

Reginald Goodall appears by permission of The General Administrator, Royal Opera House, Covent Garden.

Connell Byrne appears by permission of the Nationaltheater, Mannheim.

There will be two intervals, the first of fifteen minutes, the second of forty-five.

Sir Malcolm Sargent
1895-1967

with valuable assistance
from Malcolm Walker

Discography compiled by John Hunt

ALFVEN

Midsummer Vigil (Swedish Rhapsody No 1)

London March 1963	RPO	LP: Readers Digest RDM 2022/RDS 6022

ANDERSON

The Syncopated Clock

London March 1963	RPO	LP: Readers Digest RDM 2022/RDS 6022

ARNE

Rule Britannia, arranged Sargent

London April 1952	Philharmonia Royal Choral Society	78: HMV C 4213 45: HMV 7P 229 Coupled with Parry Jerusalem
London September 1966	BBCSO Sinclair	LP: BBC Radio Enterprises RE 10 With audience participation and encored; Sargent's last Prom conducting appearance

Shakespeare's Carol, arranged Sargent

London 1960	Royal Choral Society	LP: HMV ALP 1792/ASD 383

BACH

Air (Suite No 3), arranged Sargent

London November 1928	New SO	78: HMV B 2913 Coupled with Londonderry Air
Liverpool October 1946	Liverpool PO	78: Columbia DX 1479 Coupled with Sibelius Valse triste

Concerto for 2 violins BWV 1060

London May 1961	New SO Heifetz Friedman	LP: Victor LSC 2577/3266/5015 LP: RCA RB 16277/SB 2146/RL 00720 LP: RCA/BMG 09026 617782

Saint Matthew Passion: Excerpt (Erbarme dich)

London February 1946	National SO Ferrier Sung in English	78: Decca K 1465 45: Decca 45-71037 LP: Decca LXT 6934/417 4661 CD: Decca 430 0962/433 4702/433 8022

Sinfonia (Easter Oratorio), arranged Whittaker

Liverpool October 1943	Liverpool PO	78: Columbia DX 1138 Coupled with Cimarosa Oboe Concerto

Sanctus (Mass in B minor)

London 1928-1929	Orchestra Royal Choral Society	HMV unpublished According to Sargent's biographer Charles Reid, this was a live recording made in the Royal Albert Hall

BARTOK

Piano Concerto No 3

London October 1965	Philharmonia Ogdon	LP: HMV ASD 2347 LP: EMI SXLP 30514

Violin Concerto No 2

London October 1950	LSO Rostal	LP: Decca LXT 2574

BAX

Coronation March (1953)

London April 1953	LSO	LP: Decca LXT 2793/LW 5057 LP: Decca ACL 137/ECS 649 CD: Decca 425 6622 CD: Beulah 1PD 13

Morning Song

London February 1947	Orchestra Cohen	78: Columbia DX 1838

BEETHOVEN

Symphony No 3 "Eroica"

London May 1961	RPO	LP: HMV XLP 20040/SXLP 20040

Symphony No 4

London November 1945	National SO	78: Decca 1384-1387

Symphony No 5

London January 1945	National SO	78: Decca K 1126-1129

Piano Concerto No 1

London
March 1932

LSO
Schnabel

78: HMV DB 1690-1694/7514-7518 auto
78: Victor M 158
LP: Victor LCT 6700
LP: HMV COLH 1
LP: World Records SHB 63
LP: EMI 2C 153 03881-03884M
LP: Arabesque AR 8103
CD: Arabesque Z 6549
CD: World Classics WC 44006
CD: Pearl GEMMCD 9063

Piano Concerto No 2

London
April 1935

LPO
Schnabel

78: HMV DB 2573-2576/7945-7948 auto
78: Victor M 295
LP: Victor LCT 6700
LP: World Records SHB 63
LP: EMI 2C 153 03881-03884M
LP: Arabesque AR 8103
CD: Arabesque Z 6549
CD: World Classics WC 44007
CD: Pearl GEMMCD 9063

Piano Concerto No 3

London November 1929	Symphony Orchestra Hambourg	78: HMV C 1865-1868 CD: Pearl GEMMCD 9147
London February 1933	LPO Schnabel	78: HMV DB 1940-1944/7377-7381 auto 78: Victor M 194 LP: Victor LCT 6700 LP: World Records SHB 63 LP: EMI 2C 153 03881-03884M LP: Arabesque AR 8103 CD: Arabesque Z 6550 CD: World Classics WC 44008 CD: Pearl GEMMCD 9063
London December 1950	Philharmonia Moiseiwitsch	78: HMV C 4160-4163/7904-7907 auto 45: Victor WBC 1012 LP: Victor LBC 1012 CD: International Piano Archives IPAM 1109

Piano Concerto No 4

London February 1933	LPO Schnabel	78: HMV DB 1886-1889/7340-7443 auto 78: Victor M 156 LP: Victor LCT 6700 LP: World Records SHB 63 LP: EMI 2C 153 03881-03884M LP: Arabesque AR 8103 CD: Arabesque Z 6550 CD: World Classics WC 44007 CD: Pearl GEMMCD 9063
London February 1946	National SO Lympany	78: Decca K 1467-1470

Piano Concerto No 5 "Emperor"

London March 1932	LSO Schnabel	78: HMV DB 1685-1689/7509-7513 auto 78: Victor M 155 LP: Victor LCT 6700 LP: World Records SHB 63 LP: EMI 2C 153 03881-03884M LP: Arabesque AR 8103 CD: Arabesque Z 6551 CD: World Classics WC 44008 CD: Pearl GEMMCD 9063

Violin Concerto

London December 1959	RPO Ferras	LP: World Records T 971/ST 971

Triple Concerto

London May 1958	Philharmonia Oborin, Oistrakh, Knushevitsky	LP: Columbia 33C 1062/S80 2753 LP: Angel 35697 LP: EMI SXLP 20081/EMX 2035 CD: EMI CDZ 767 2542

Die Ehre Gottes (Gellert-Lieder)

London 1963	Royal Choral Society	LP: HMV ALP 2018/ASD 568 LP: EMI XLP 50009/SXLP 50009

Moonlight Sonata, arranged Weninger

London October 1930	New Light SO	78: HMV C 2234 Coupled with Pathétique Sonata

Pathétique Sonata, arranged Weninger

London October 1930	New Light SO	78: HMV C 2234 Coupled with Moonlight Sonata

Egmont Overture

London 1965	BBCSO	Unpublished radio broadcast

BERLIOZ

Adieu des bergers (L'enfance du Christ)

London 1963	Royal Choral Society	LP: HMV ALP 2018/ASD 568 LP: EMI XLP 50009/SXLP 50009

Béatrice et Bénédict, Overture

London February 1946	National SO	78: Decca K 1416

Le carnaval romain, Overture

London May 1952	BBCSO	HMV unpublished
London October 1960	RPO	LP: HMV XLP 20034/SXLP 20034

Marche troyenne (Les Troyens)

Liverpool April 1944	Liverpool PO	Columbia unpublished

BIZET

L'Arlésienne, Suite No 1

Manchester July 1942	Hallé	78: Columbia DX 1085-1087 LP: Columbia (USA) RL 3051

L'Arlésienne, Suite No 2

London December 1948	Philharmonia	78: Columbia DX 1605-1606 LP: Columbia (USA) RL 3051

Carmen: Excerpt (La fleur que tu m'avais jetée)

Liverpool August 1944	Liverpool PO Nash Sung in English	78: HMV C 3405 Coupled with Salut demeure (Faust)

Jeux d'enfants, Suite

London September 1966	RPO	Unpublished radio broadcast

Patrie, Overture

London February 1928	New SO	78: HMV C 2348-2349

Les pêcheurs de perles: Excerpt (Je crois entendre encore)

Liverpool August 1944	Liverpool PO Nash Sung in English	78: HMV C 3409 LP: EMI HQM 1089 Coupled with Spirto gentil (La Favorita)

BLISS

Piano Concerto

London May 1962	Philharmonia Barnard	LP: HMV ALP 1948/ASD 499 LP: EMI SLS 5080

BOCCHERINI

Minuet

London February 1929	New SO	78: HMV B 3036 <u>Coupled with German</u> <u>Merrymaker's Dance</u>

BORODIN

Nocturne (String Quartet No 2), arranged Sargent

London December 1948	Philharmonia	78: Columbia DX 1618 45: Columbia SCD 2099 LP: Columbia (USA) RL 3042

Andantino (Polovtsian Dances)

London 1960	LSO	CD: Bescol CD 528

BOITO

Mefistofele: Excerpt (L'altra notte)

London October 1959	RPO Callas	LP: BJR Records BJR 143 LP: Foyer FO 1007 LP: Legendary LR 148 CD: Legato LR 162
London May 1961	Sargent, piano Callas	LP: Penzance PR 15 LP: HRE Records HRE 219 CD: Legato LR 162

BRAHMS

Academic Festival Overture

Liverpool March 1947	Liverpool PO	78: Columbia DX 1447-1448 Coupled with Hungarian Dance No 5

Haydn Variations

Manchester July 1942	Hallé	78: Columbia DX 1105-1106

Hungarian Dance No 5

London October 1927	Covent Garden Orchestra	78: HMV C 1415 Coupled with Tchaikovsky Sleeping Beauty Waltz
Liverpool March 1947	Liverpool PO	78: Columbia DX 1448 LP: Columbia (USA) RL 3050 Coupled with Academic Festival Overture

Hungarian Dance No 6

London October 1927	Covent Garden Orchestra	78: HMV C 1874 Coupled with Schubert Rosamunde Overture

4 ernste Gesänge, orchestrated by Sargent

London January 1949	BBCSO Ferrier Sung in English	LP: Decca LXT 6934/414 0951 CD: Decca 433 4722/433 8022

FIFTY-FOURTH SEASON OF

HENRY WOOD

PROMENADE CONCERTS

Conductors
SIR MALCOLM SARGENT   BASIL CAMERON

Associate Conductor
STANFORD ROBINSON

Saturday 31 July at 7.30

Conductor: SIR MALCOLM SARGENT

OVERTURE, The Barber of Seville	*Rossini*
RECIT. AND ARIA, Non mi dir (Don Giovanni)	*Mozart*
THE WALK TO THE PARADISE GARDEN (A Village Romeo and Juliet)	*Delius*
PIANOFORTE CONCERTO No. 3, in D minor	*Rachmaninoff*
SYMPHONIC POEM, Don Juan	*Strauss*

INTERVAL

ORGAN CONCERTO in G minor (Op. 4, No. 1)	*Handel*
CAPRICCIO ESPAGNOLE	*Rimsky-Korsakov*

ELENA DANIELI

Solo Pianoforte IRENE KOHLER

Solo Organ JEANNE DEMESSIEUX

THE BBC SYMPHONY ORCHESTRA
Leader: Paul Beard

DE MONTFORT HALL, LEICESTER

Tuesday, August 25th, 1942, at 7 p.m.

MUSICAL CULTURE LIMITED

presents

"The Dream of Gerontius"

(EDWARD ELGAR)

THE
London Philharmonic Orchestra

THE
Leicester Philharmonic Society

Conductor:
DR. MALCOLM SARGENT

Soloists:
MARY JARRED   HEDDLE NASH
HENRY CUMMINGS

BRITTEN

Peter Grimes, 4 Sea Interludes

| London
November 1947 | LSO | 78: Columbia DX 1441-1442
78: Columbia (USA) MX 303
LP: Columbia (USA) ML 2145/ML 4197 |

Simple Symphony

| London
January 1961 | RPO | LP: HMV ALP 1873/ASD 443
LP: EMI SXLP 30114 |

Young Person's Guide to the Orchestra

| London
1946 | LSO
Sargent also
narrates | CD: Beulah 1PD 13
VHS Video: Beulah RT 152
Premiere performance as
composed for this film |

| Liverpool
October 1946 | Liverpool PO | 78: Columbia DX 1307-1309
78: Columbia (USA) MM 703
LP: Columbia (USA) ML 4197
Fugue only
CD: EMI CDM 763 3702 |

| London
August 1956 | BBCSO | LP: HMV BLP 1101/BSD 754
LP: EMI SXLP 30114 |

BROADHURST

A Cowboy Carol, arranged Sargent

| London
March 1953 | Royal Choral
Society | LP: HMV ALP 1159/SRS 5094 |

| London
1960 | Royal Choral
Society | LP: HMV ALP 1792/ASD 383 |

BRUCH

Violin Concerto No 1

| London
May 1951 | LSO
Heifetz | LP: Victor LM 9007/ARM4 0947
LP: HMV ALP 1124
CD: RCA/BMG 09026 617782 |

| London
May 1962 | New SO
Heifetz | LP: Victor LSC 2652/4011/LSB 4061
LP: RCA RB 6527/SB 6527
CD: RCA/BMG 09026 617782 |

Scottish Fantasy

London May 1962	New SO Heifetz	LP: Victor LSC 2603/3205/LSB 4105 LP: RCA RB 6503/SB 6503 CD: RCA/BMG 09026 617782

CHABRIER

Fête polonaise (Le roi malgré lui)

London May 1958	BBCSO	LP: HMV ALP 1658/ASD 536

CHAUSSON

Poème for violin and orchestra

London May 1963	LSO Friedman	LP: Victor LM 2689/LSC 2689 CD: RCA/BMG 09026 612102

CHOPIN

Piano Concerto No 1

London October 1962	RPO Wild	LP: Readers Digest CD: Chesky CD 93

Polonaise No 4 and Prélude No 15 "Raindrop", arranged Sargent

London February 1965	Fairey, Foden's and Morris Brass Bands	LP: Columbia 33SX 1752/TWO 101

Les Sylphides, Ballet music

London July 1935	LPO	78: HMV C 2781-2783/7465-7467 auto Arranged White
London December 1962	Covent Garden Orchestra	LP: HMV XLP 20049/SXLP 20049 Arranged Sargent

CIMAROSA

Oboe Concerto, arranged Benjamin

Liverpool October 1943	Liverpool PO L.Goossens	78: Columbia DX 1137-1138 LP: Columbia (USA) ML 4782 LP: EMI CLP 1698/HQM 1087 78 version coupled with Bach Sinfonia (Easter Oratorio)

COLERIDGE TAYLOR

The Death of Minnehaha (The Songs of Hiawatha)

London 1929-1930	Orchestra Royal Choral Society Suddaby, Fry, Baker	78: HMV C 2210-2213 According to Sargent's biographer Charles Reid, some sides for this and the following item were recorded live at the Royal Albert Hall and others in the Kingsway Hall recording studio

Hiawatha's Wedding Feast (The Songs of Hiawatha)

London May 1929	Orchestra Royal Choral Society Glynne	78: HMV C 1931-1934
London May 1961	Philharmonia Royal Choral Society R.Lewis	LP: HMV ALP 1899/ASD 467 LP: EMI ESD 7161 CD: EMI CDM 769 6892 Excerpt LP: EMI HQM 1115

Hiawatha's Wedding Feast: Excerpt (On away! Awake beloved!)

Liverpool July 1944	Liverpool PO Booth	78: HMV C 3407 LP: EMI HLM 7109 LP: Rococo 5272 CD: EMI CDM 763 3702 CD: Dutton CDAX 8012 78 version coupled with Goring Thomas O vision entrancing (Esmeralda)

A Christmas Overture

London September 1932	Orchestra	78: HMV C 2485 CD: Pearl GEMMCD 9065

Intermezzo

London February 1934	New Light SO	78: HMV B 8113 CD: Pearl GEMMCD 9065

Othello, Suite

London June 1932	New SO	78: HMV B 4273-4274 CD: Beulah 1PD 13

Petite Suite de concert

London September 1931	LSO	78: HMV C 2372-2373

DELIBES

Sylvia, excerpts

| London | Covent Garden | 78: HMV C 1417-1418 |
| October 1927 | Orchestra | |

DELIUS

Brigg Fair, extract

London	BBCSO	Unpublished radio broadcast
January 1965		Excerpt
		LP: BBC Radio Enterprises RE 10

Cello Concerto

| London | RPO | LP: HMV ALP 2097/ASD 644 |
| January 1965 | Du Pré | CD: EMI CZS 568 1322 |

Piano Concerto

| London | BBCSO | Unpublished radio broadcast |
| August 1955 | Moiseiwitsch | |

On hearing the first cuckoo in spring

| Liverpool | Liverpool PO | 78: Columbia DX 1643 |
| March 1947 | | CD: Testament SBT 1014 |

A Song before sunrise

| London | RPO | LP: HMV ALP 2097/ASD 644 |
| March 1965 | | CD: EMI CDEMX 2198 |

Songs of Farewell

London	RPO	LP: HMV ALP 2097/ASD 644
April 1964	Royal Choral	CD: EMI CDEMX 2198
	Society	

Violin Concerto

Liverpool	Liverpool PO	78: Columbia DX 1160-1162/
July 1944	Sammons	DX 8197-8199 auto
		78: Columbia (USA) M 672
		LP: World Records SH 224
		CD: Testament SBT 1014

DOHNANYI

Suite in F sharp minor

London December 1948	LSO	78: Columbia DX 1742-1745/ DX 8377-8380 auto LP: Columbia 33S 1001
London October 1961	RPO	LP: HMV ALP 1926/ASD 437 CD: EMI CDM 763 1832

Variations on a Nursery Song

Liverpool February 1944	Liverpool PO C.Smith	78: Columbia DX 1148-1150/ DX 8194-8196 auto 78: Columbia (USA) M 779 LP: Columbia (USA) ML 4146
London January 1953	Philharmonia C.Smith	LP: Columbia 33SX 1018/33SX 1579

DONIZETTI

La Favorita: Excerpt (Spirto gentil)

Liverpool August 1944	Liverpool PO Nash Sung in English	78: HMV C 3409 <u>Coupled with Bizet Je crois entendre</u> <u>encore (Les pêcheurs de perles)</u>

DUKAS

L'apprenti sorcier

London 1960	LSO	CD: Bescol CD 528
London September 1966	RPO	Unpublished radio broadcast

DVORAK

Cello Concerto

London June 1955	Philharmonia Tortelier	LP: HMV ALP 1306 LP: EMI XLP 30018/SXLP 30018 CD: EMI CMS 764 0692

Violin Concerto

London January 1961	LSO Ricci	LP: Decca LXT 5641/SXL 2279

Serenade for strings

London January and March 1965	RPO	LP: HMV CLP 3539/CSD 3539

The Spectre's Bride: Excerpt (Where art thou?)

London August 1947	Philharmonia Baillie	78: Columbia DX 1471 LP: EMI HQM 1118

Slavonic Dance No 1 in C

Date not confirmed	Covent Garden Orchestra	78: HMV C 2149
London March 1963	RPO	LP: Readers Digest RDM 2022/RDS 6022

Slavonic Dance No 6 in D

Date not confirmed	Covent Garden Orchestra	78: HMV C 2149

Slavonic Dance No 10 in E minor

London May 1958	BBCSO	LP: HMV ALP 1658/ASD 536
London October 1963	RPO	LP: Readers Digest RDM 2022/RDS 6022

Symphonic Variations

London February 1956	Philharmonia	LP: HMV ALP 1372 LP: EMI XLP 20065/SXLP 20065

DYSON

The Canterbury Pilgrims: Excerpt (Wyf of Bathe)

London August 1947	Philharmonia Baillie	LP: EMI HQM 1015

ELGAR

Symphony No 1, conclusion of final movement

Date not confirmed	BBCSO	LP: BBC Radio Enterprises RE 10

Symphony No 2

Bristol January 1964	BBCSO	Unpublished radio broadcast
London January 1965	BBCSO	Unpublished radio broadcast

Cello Concerto

London May 1953	BBCSO Tortelier	LP: HMV BLP 1043 CD: Testament SBT 2025
London 1963	BBCSO Du Pré	CD: Intaglio INCD 7351

Violin Concerto

London June 1949	LSO Heifetz	78: HMV DB 21056-21060 LP: HMV ALP 1014 LP: Victor LM 2919/ARM4 0946/LSB 4022 CD: RCA/BMG GD 87966/09026 617782/617382

The Dream of Gerontius

Huddersfield April 1945	Liverpool PO Huddersfield Choral Society Ripley, Nash, Noble, Walker	78: HMV C 3435-3446/7611-7622 auto LP: EMI RLS 709 LP: Turnabout THS 65102-65103 CD: Testament SBT 2025 Excerpt CD: EMI CDM 763 3702
Huddersfield November 1954	Liverpool PO Huddersfield Choral Society M.Thomas, Lewis, Cameron	LP: Columbia 33CX 1247-1248 CD: EMI CHS 763 3762 Excerpt LP: EMI HQM 1115

Enigma Variations

London November 1945	National SO	78: Decca AK 1351-1354
London January 1953	LSO	LP: Decca LXT 2786 LP: Decca ACL 55/ECS 588
London March and June 1959	Philharmonia	LP: HMV XLP 20007/SXLP 20007 Nimrod LP: EMI HQM 1115
London August 1966	BBCSO	CD: Radio Classics BBCRD 9104

Imperial March

London March 1953	LSO	LP: Decca ECS 649 CD: Decca 425 6622

I sing the birth

London December 1928	Royal Choral Society	78: HMV C 1740 LP: Elgar Society CD: Pearl GEMMCD 9380 CD: Beulah 1PD 13

The Kingdom: Excerpt (The sun goeth down)

London August 1947	Philharmonia Baillie	78: Columbia DX 1443 LP: EMI HQM 1015

The Music Makers

London April 1965	LSO Various choirs M.Thomas	CD: Intaglio INCD 7351 We are the music makers LP: BBC Radio Enterprises RE 10

Pomp and Circumstance, March No 1

London December 1948	Philharmonia	78: Columbia DX 1561 45: Columbia SCD 2026 LP: Columbia (USA) RL 3042 Coupled with March No 4
London May 1953	LSO	LP: Decca LXT 2793/LW 5058 LP: Decca ACL 137/ECS 649 CD: Beulah 1PD 13
London March 1958	BBCSO	LP: HMV ALP 1658/ASD 536 LP: EMI HQM 1115

Pomp and Circumstance, March No 4

London December 1948	Philharmonia	78: Columbia DX 1561 45: Columbia SCD 2026 LP: Columbia (USA) RL 3042 Coupled with March No 1
London May 1953	LSO	LP: Decca LXT 2793/LW 5058 LP: Decca ACL 137/ECS 649 CD: Beulah 1PD 13

Pomp and Circumstance, March No 5

London   National SO   78: Decca AK 1351
November 1945   LP: Decca LK 4020
                                                          78 version coupled with
                                                          Enigma Variations

Serenade for strings

London   Philharmonia   LP: EMI SXLP 30126
June 1959   CD: EMI CDEMX 2141

The Serious Doll (Nursery Suite)

Liverpool   Liverpool PO   78: Columbia DX 1120
May 1943   Coupled with John Field Suite

The Wand of Youth, Suite No 1

Liverpool   Liverpool PO   78: Columbia DX 1582-1584/
June 1949   DX 8331-8333 auto
                                                          Coupled with Londonderry Air

The Wand of Youth, Suite No 2

London   BBCSO   78: HMV DB 9783-9784
October 1952   LP: HMV BLP 1019
                                                          78 version coupled with Vaughan
                                                          Williams Tallis Fantasia

FALLA

The 3-Cornered Hat, Suite

London   New Light SO   78: HMV B 2721-2722
February 1928   Sargent's first electrical
                                                          studio recording

FAURÉ

Pavane

London May 1947	Philharmonia and Chorus	78: Columbia DX 1369
London August 1956	BBCSO	HMV unpublished

FIELD

A John Field Suite, arranged Harty

Liverpool   Liverpool PO   78: Columbia DX 1118-1120
March and   LP: Columbia (USA) RL 3043
May 1943   CD: EMI CDM 763 3702
                                                                  CD: Dutton CDAX 8012
                                                                   <u>78 version coupled with</u>
                                                                   <u>Elgar The Serious Doll</u>

GAY

The Beggars' Opera

London   Pro Arte   LP: HMV CLP 1052-1053/CSD 1516-1517
May 1955   Orchestra & Chorus LP: EMI ESDW 704
                       Morison, Sinclair,
                       Shacklock, Young,
                       Brannigan

GARDINER

Shepherd's Fennel's Dance

Liverpool   Liverpool PO   78: Columbia DX 1393
April 1947   LP: Columbia (USA) RL 3050
                                                    CD: Dutton CDAX 8012

GERMAN

Country Dance (Nell Gwynn Dances)

London   New SO
February 1929

78: HMV B 2987
Coupled with Pastoral Dance

London   Pro Arte
November 1960   Orchestra

LP: HMV XLP 20032/SXLP 20032
CD: EMI CDCFP 4611

Merrie England, selection

London   New SO
February 1929

78: HMV C 2196

Merrymakers' Dance (Nell Gwynn Dances)

London   New SO
February 1929

78: HMV B 3036
Coupled with Boccherini Minuet

London   Pro Arte
November 1960   Orchestra

LP: HMV XLP 20032/SXLP 20032
CD: EMI CDCFP 4611

Morris Dance (Henry VIII Dances)

London   New SO
February 1929

78: HMV B 2981
Coupled with Shepherd's
and Torch Dances

London   Pro Arte
November 1960   Orchestra

LP: HMV XLP 20032/SXLP 20032

Pastoral Dance (Nell Gwynn Dances)

London   New SO
February 1929

78: HMV D 2987
Coupled with Country Dance

London   Pro Arte
November 1960   Orchestra

LP: HMV XLP 20032/SXLP 20032
CD: EMI CDCFP 4611

Shepherd's Dance (Henry VIII Dances)

London   New SO
February 1929

78: HMV B 2981
Coupled with Morris & Torch Dances

London   Pro Arte
November 1960   Orchestra

LP: HMV XLP 20032/SXLP 20032

Tom Jones, selection

London   New SO
November 1931

78: HMV C 2442

Torch Dance (Henry VIII Dances)

London February 1929	New SO	78: HMV B 2981 Coupled with Morris and Shepherd's Dances
London November 1960	Pro Arte Orchestra	LP: HMV XLP 20032/SXLP 20032

GIBBONS

Hosanna to the Son of God

London December 1928	Royal Choral Society	78: HMV C 1740

GLUCK

Alceste, Overture

Liverpool December 1947	Liverpool PO	78: Columbia DX 1508

Orfeo ed Euridice, Dance of the blessed spirits)

London May 1958	BBCSO	HMV unpublished

Orfeo ed Euridice: Excerpt (Che farò)

London February 1946	LSO Ferrier Sung in English	78: Decca K 1466 45: Decca 45-71034/CEP 724 LP: Decca LW 5072/ACL 308 LP: Decca PA 172/SPA 355 LP: Decca AKF 1-7 CD: Decca 430 0962/433 4702/433 8022

GORING THOMAS

Esmeralda: Excerpt (O vision entrancing)

Liverpool July 1944	Liverpool PO Booth	78: HMV C 3407 LP: EMI HQM 1228 LP: Rococo 5272 78 version coupled with Coleridge Taylor On away! Awake beloved! (Hiawatha's Wedding Feast)

GOUNOD

Faust: Excerpt (Salut demeure)

Liverpool August 1944	Liverpool PO Nash Sung in English	78: HMV C 3405 LP: EMI HQM 1228 78 version coupled with Bizet Flower Song (Carmen)

TO CELEBRATE
THE BICENTENARY OF THE FIRST PERFORMANCE
(April, 1742)

OF

HANDEL'S

"MESSIAH"

THE

LEICESTER PHILHARMONIC SOCIETY
(CHORUS MASTER—W. STANLEY VANN, F.R.C.O.)

Present the work

IN ITS ENTIRETY

with

ISOBEL BAILLIE	*Soprano*
GLADYS RIPLEY	*Contralto*
DINO BORGIOLI	*Tenor*
HENRY CUMMINGS	*Bass*

and

DR. MALCOLM SARGENT

CONDUCTING THE

LEICESTER SYMPHONY ORCHESTRA
(Leader—Grace Burrows)

SUNDAY, 12th APRIL, 1942, at 2.45 p.m.

at the

DE MONTFORT HALL, LEICESTER

FIFTY-FIFTH SEASON OF

HENRY WOOD
PROMENADE CONCERTS

Saturday 3 September at 7.30

OVERTURE, The Barber of Seville	*Rossini*
RECIT. AND ARIA, O mio Fernando (La Favorita)	*Donizetti*
LYRIC SUITE	*Grieg*
SYMPHONIE ESPAGNOLE	*Lalo*
FINALE, ACT II (Aïda)	*Verdi*

INTERVAL

WALTZ, The Blue Danube	*Johann Strauss*
THE WALK TO THE PARADISE GARDEN (A Village Romeo and Juliet)	*Delius*
THE YOUNG PERSON'S GUIDE TO THE ORCHESTRA	*Benjamin Britten*

VICTORIA SLADEN   GLADYS RIPLEY
JAMES JOHNSTON   RODERICK JONES
GEORGE JAMES   TREVOR ANTHONY

Solo Violin
IDA HAENDEL

THE ROYAL CHORAL SOCIETY

THE BBC SYMPHONY ORCHESTRA
Leader: Paul Beard

CONDUCTOR   **SIR MALCOLM SARGENT**

GRAINGER

Handel in the Strand; Mock Morris

| London June 1930 | New Light SO | 78: HMV C 2002 |

GRIEG

Lyric Suite

| London January 1946 | National SO | 78: Decca AK 1412-1413 |
| London February 1959 | Philharmonia | 45: HMV 7ER 5161/RES 4264 |

Songs with orchestra: Det foerste moete; Et haab; Fyremaal; Jeg elsker dig

| London September 1957 | BBCSO Flagstad | LP: Ed Smith UORC 264 LP: Rococo 5380 CD: AS-Disc AS 360 CD: Memories HR 4456-4457 CD: Hunt CDHP 576 |

Songs with orchestra: En svane; Eros; Fra Monte Pincio; Guten; Til en I; Til en II; Ved Rundarne

| London September 1957 | BBCSO Flagstad | LP: Ed Smith UORC 264 CD: AS-Disc AS 360 CD: Memories HR 4456-4457 CD: Hunt CDHP 576 |

GRUBER

Silent night, arranged Sargent

| London January 1953 | Royal Choral Society | 45: HMV 7EG 8403 LP: HMV ALP 1159/SRS 5094 |
| London January 1961 | Royal Choral Society | LP: HMV ALP 1792/ASD 383 |

HANDEL

Messiah

Huddersfield September 1946	Liverpool PO Huddersfield Choral Society Baillie, Ripley, Johnston, Walker	78: Columbia DX 1283-1301/ DX 8223-8241 auto 78: Columbia (USA) M 666 LP: Columbia (USA) SL 151 Excerpts 78: Columbia (USA) 72733D
Huddersfield January 1954	Liverpool PO Huddersfield Choral Society Morison, M.Thomas, Lewis, Walker	LP: Columbia 33CX 1146-1148 LP: EMI XLP 30050-30052 Excerpts 45: Columbia SCB 115/SCD 2017 45: Columbia SEL 1512/1513/1517 1518/1519/1520 LP: EMI XLP 30096/HQM 1115
Huddersfield June and August 1959	Liverpool PO Huddersfield Choral Society Morison, M.Thomas, Lewis, Milligan	LP: Columbia 33CX 1668-1670/ SAX 2308-2310 CD: EMI CFPD 4718 Excerpts LP: EMI CFP 40020
London June 1965	RPO Royal Choral Society Harwood, Procter, Young, Shirley-Quirk	LP: Readers Digest 90321-90322 LP: Quintessence P3C 2701 Also issued on Vanguard label

Messiah, Overture (Sinfonia) and Pastoral Symphony

London October 1930	LSO	78: HMV C 2071
London February 1946	LSO	78: Decca K 1499

Messiah: Excerpt (All we like sheep)

London	Royal Albert	78: Victor 9019
April 1926	Hall Orchestra	CD: Koch 3-7703-2 /Pearl GEMMCD 9380
	Royal Choral	78 version coupled with
	Society	Surely he has borne our grief

Messiah: Excerpt (Amen)

London	Royal Albert	78: HMV D 1135
April 1926	Hall Orchestra	78: Victor 9125
	Royal Choral	CD: Koch 3-7703-2 /Pearl GEMMCD 9380
	Society	78 versions coupled with
		And the Glory of the Lord

Messiah: Excerpt (And the Glory of the Lord)

London	Royal Albert	78: HMV D 1135
April 1926	Hall Orchestra	78: Victor 9125
	Royal Choral	CD: Koch 3-7703-2 /Pearl GEMMCD 9380
	Society	78 versions coupled with
		Amen Chorus

London	LSO	78: HMV C 2489
September 1932	Royal Choral	Coupled with Hallelujah Chorus
	Society	

Messiah: Excerpt (Behold the Lamb of God)

London	Royal Albert	78: HMV D 1108
April 1926	Hall Orchestra	CD: Koch 3-7703-2 /Pearl GEMMCD 9380
	Royal Choral	78 version coupled with
	Society	Hallelujah Chorus

London	LSO	78: HMV C 2548
September 1932	Royal Choral	Coupled with Glory to God
	Society	

Messiah: Excerpt (Glory to God)

London	Royal Albert	78: Victor 9018
April 1926	Hall Orchestra	CD: Pearl GEMMCD 9380
	Royal Choral	
	Society	

London	LSO	78: HMV C 2548
September 1932	Royal Choral	Coupled with Behold the Lamb of God
	Society	

According to Sargent's biographer Charles Reid, many of the earliest Messiah chorus recordings with the Royal Choral Society were taken live in performances at the Royal Albert Hall

Messiah: Excerpt (Hallelujah)

London April 1926	Royal Albert Hall Orchestra Royal Choral Society	78: HMV D 1108 CD: Koch 3-7703-2/Pearl GEMMCD 9380 <u>78 version coupled with</u> <u>Behold the Lamb of God</u>
London September 1932	LSO Royal Choral Society	78: HMV C 2489 <u>Coupled with And the Glory</u> <u>of the Lord</u>
London May and October 1948	LSO Royal Choral Society	78: Decca K 2132 <u>Coupled with They loathed</u> <u>to drink (Israel in Egypt)</u>
London May 1951	Festival Orchestra and Chorus	78: HMV DB 21274 <u>Recorded at opening concert</u> <u>in Royal Festival Hall</u>

Messiah: Excerpt (Surely he has borne our grief)

London April 1926	Royal Albert Hall Orchestra Royal Choral Society	78: Victor 9019 CD: Koch 3-7703-2/Pearl GEMMCD 9380 <u>78 version coupled with</u> <u>All we like sheep</u>

Messiah: Excerpt (I know that my redeemer liveth)

London May 1948	LSO Alsop	78: Decca K 2137

Messiah: Excerpt (If God be with us)

Liverpool March 1944	Liverpool PO Baillie	78: Columbia DX 1154 LP: EMI RLS 714/RLS 7703 CD: Dutton CDLX 7013 <u>78 version coupled with</u> <u>Rejoice greatly</u>

Messiah: Excerpt (Rejoice greatly)

Liverpool March 1944	Liverpool PO Baillie	78: Columbia DX 1154 LP: EMI RLS 714/RLS 7703 <u>78 version coupled with</u> <u>If God be with us</u>

Acis and Galatea: Excerpt (O didst thou know?/As when the dove)

Liverpool March 1944	Liverpool PO Baillie	78: Columbia DX 1158 LP: EMI HQM 1118/RLS 7703

Acis and Galatea: Excerpt (Would you gain the tender creature)

London September 1957	LSO R.Lewis	LP: HMV ALP 1575 LP: EMI CFP 111 <u>Stereo version also published</u>

Alexander's Feast: Excerpt (Revenge, Timotheus cries)

London May 1948	LSO Anthony	78: Decca K 2138

Alexander's Feast: Excerpt (War, he sang, is toil and trouble)

London September 1957	LSO R.Lewis	LP: HMV ALP 1575 LP: EMI CFP 111 <u>Stereo version also published</u>

Israel in Egypt

Huddersfield June 1955	Liverpool PO Huddersfield Choral Society Morison, Sinclair, R.Lewis	LP: Columbia 33CX 1347-1348

Israel in Egypt: Excerpt (They loathed to drink)

London May 1948	LSO Royal Choral Society	78: Decca K 2132 <u>Coupled with Hallelujah Chorus</u>

Israel in Egypt: Excerpt (He spake the word)

London May 1948	LSO Royal Choral Society	78: Decca K 2133

Israel in Egypt: Excerpts (He gave them hailstones; He sent a thick darkness)

London May 1948	LSO Royal Choral Society	78: Decca K 2134

Jephtha: Excerpts (Waft her angels / Deeper and deeper still)

Liverpool July 1944	Liverpool PO Booth	78: HMV C 3414 LP: EMI HLM 7109
London September 1957	LSO R.Lewis	LP: HMV ALP 1575 LP: EMI CFP 111 <u>Stereo version also published</u>

Joshua: Excerpt (While Kedron's brook)

London September 1957	LSO R.Lewis	LP: HMV ALP 1575 LP: EMI CFP 111 <u>Stereo version also published</u>

Judas Maccabaeus: Excerpt (From mighty kings)

London	LSO	45: Columbia SED 5557
February 1949	Baillie	LP: EMI HQM 1015

Judas Maccabaeus: Excerpts (How vain is man; Sound an alarm)

London LSO LP: HMV ALP 1575
September 1957 R.Lewis LP: EMI CFP 111
　　　　　　　　　　　Stereo version also published

Rodelinda: Excerpt (Art thou troubled?)

London LSO 78: Decca K 1466
February 1946 Ferrier 45: Decca 45-71034
　　　　　　　　　　LP: Decca LW 5072/ACL 308
　　　　　　　　　　LP: Decca PA 172/AKF 1-7
　　　　　　　　　　CD: Decca 430 0962/433 4702/433 8022

Samson, Overture arranged Sargent

London RPO 45: HMV 7ER 5165/RES 4266
February 1959 　　　LP: HMV ALP 1710/ASD 286

Samson: Excerpt (Total eclipse)

London LSO LP: HMV ALP 1575
September 1957 R.Lewis LP: EMI CFP 111
　　　　　　　　　　Stereo version also published

Semele: Excerpt (Where'er you walk)

London LSO 78: Decca K 2135
January 1948 R.Lewis

London LSO LP: HMV ALP 1575
September 1957 R.Lewis LP: EMI CFP 111
　　　　　　　　　　Stereo version also published

Serse: Excerpt (Ombra mai fù)

London LSO Decca unpublished
May 1948 Ferrier

London LSO 78: Decca K 2135
October 1948 Ferrier 45: Decca 45-71039/CEP 724
　　　　　　　　　　LP: Decca LW 5072/ACL 308/AKF 1-7
　　　　　　　　　　CD: Decca 430 0962/433 4702/433 8022
　　　　　　　　　　Includes recitative Frondi tenere

Solomon: Excerpt (From the censer curling rise)

Huddersfield March 1958	Liverpool PO Huddersfield Choral Society	45: HMV 7ER 5134 LP: HMV ALP 1628 CD: EMI CDM 763 3702

Solomon: Excerpt (Arrival of the Queen of Sheba)

London February 1946	LSO	78: Decca AK 1503 Coupled with Haydn Symphony No 98

Zadok the Priest, Coronation Anthem

London May 1948	LSO Royal Choral Society	78: Decca
Huddersfield March 1958	Liverpool PO Huddersfield Choral Society	45: HMV 7ER 5134 LP: HMV ALP 1628

Overture in D minor, arranged Elgar

London February 1959	RPO	45: HMV 7ER 5165/RES 4266 LP: HMV ALP 1710/ASD 286

Overture to an Occasional Oratorio, arranged by Sargent

London February 1959	RPO	HMV unpublished

Music for the Royal Fireworks, Suite

Liverpool December 1947	Liverpool PO	78: Columbia DX 1494-1495 78: Columbia (USA) MX 319 LP: Columbia (USA) ML 4197
London January 1953	BBCSO	LP: HMV BLP 1059
London February 1959	RPO	45: HMV 7ER 5167/RES 4268 LP: HMV ALP 1710/ASD 286

Water Music Suite, arranged Harty

Manchester August 1942	Hallé	78: HMV C 3306-3307 78: HMV DB 4233-4234
London February 1946	National SO	78: Decca AK 1414-1415
London January 1953	BBCSO	LP: HMV BLP 1059
London February 1959	RPO	LP: HMV ALP 1710/ASD 286

HAYDN

Symphony No 94 "Surprise"

Liverpool October 1947	Liverpool PO	78: Columbia DX 1490-1492/ DX 8313-8315 auto 78: Columbia (USA) MM 781 LP: Columbia (USA) ML 4276

Symphony No 98

London February 1946	LSO	78: Decca AK 1500-1503

Cello Concerto in D

London November 1936	LPO Feuermann	78: Columbia L 472-475/ LX 8227-8230 auto 78: Columbia (USA) M 262 CD: Pearl GEMMCD 9442

Die Jahreszeiten: Excerpt (Schon eilet froh der Ackersmann)

London August 1947	Philharmonia Walker Sung in English	78: Columbia DX 1407 LP: EMI HLM 7007 Includes opening recitative

Die Schöpfung: Excerpts (Die Himmel erzählen; Vollendet ist das edle Werk)

London September 1932	LSO Royal Choral Society Sung in English	78: HMV C 2513 78: Victor 11960 CD: Pearl GEMMCD 9380

HÉROLD

Zampa, Overture

Liverpool June 1947	Liverpool PO	78: Columbia DX 1467

HOLST

Beni Mora, Oriental Suite

London August 1956	BBCSO	LP: HMV BLP 1101 LP: EMI SXLP 30126 CD: EMI CDEMX 2141

The Hymn of Jesus

Liverpool May 1944	Liverpool PO Huddersfield Choral Society	78: HMV C 3399-3401 CD: Dutton CDAX 8012

The Perfect Fool, Ballet music

London March 1946	LPO	78: Decca AK 1561-1562 CD: Beulah 1PD 13 Coupled with Wagner Ride of the Valkyries conducted by De Sabata
London January 1961	RPO	LP: HMV ALP 1873/ASD 443 CD: EMI CDU 565 0412

The Planets

London May 1954	LSO Chorus	LP: Decca LXT 2871/ACL 26 Mars and Jupiter 45: Decca CEP 544
London August and September 1957	BBCSO BBC Womens' Chorus	LP: HMV ALP 1600/ASD 269/EMX 2003 Mars and Jupiter 45: HMV 7ER 5112/RES 4254 Uranus and Neptune 45: HMV 7ER 5123/RES 4260 Mercury LP: EMI HQM 1115
London February 1965	BBCSO BBC Womens' Chorus	CD: Radio Classics BBCRD 9104

The Planets, Venus and Mercury

Melbourne May 1966	Melbourne SO	CD: ABC Classics 434 8962

Choral Symphony

London January 1964	BBCSO BBC Choruses Harper	CD: Intaglio INCD 7401

Saint Paul's Suite

London January 1965	RPO	LP: HMV CLP 3539/CSD 3539 LP: EMI SXLP 30126 CD: EMI CDEMX 2141

HUMPERDINCK

Hänsel und Gretel, Overture

London December 1952	BBCSO	78: HMV DB 21591 45: EMV 7ER 5029

IBERT

Elizabethan Suite

London September 1955	Philharmonia Mandikian Chorus	HMV unpublished

IRELAND

A London Overture

Liverpool April 1944	Liverpool PO	78: Columbia DX 1155-1156 CD: Dutton CDAX 8012 78 version coupled with J.Strauss Radetzky March

JAERNEFELT

Berceuse

London October 1927	Covent Garden Orchestra	78: HMV B 2618 Coupled with Praeludium

Praeludium

London February 1927	Covent Garden Orchestra	78: HMV B 2618 Coupled with Berceuse

KHATCHATURIAN

Sabre Dance (Gayaneh)

London 1960	LSO	CD: Bescol CD 528

LISZT

Piano Concerto No 1

London October 1962	RPO Wild	LP: Reader's Digest LP: RCA GL 32526 LP: Quintessence PMC 7031 CD: Chesky CD 93

Piano Concerto No 2

London October 1962	RPO Lympany	LP: Reader's Digest LP: RCA GL 32526

LITOLFF

Scherzo (Concerto symphonique)

London August 1958	BBCSO Cherkassky	LP: HMV ALP 1658/ASD 536

MAHLER

Ich atmet' einen linden Duft (Rückert-Lieder)

London June 1938	Orchestra Kullmann	78: Columbia DB 1787 CD: Claremont GSE 78 50 56 Coupled with Schoenberg songs not conducted by Sargent; issued as part of Columbia History of Music

MARTINU

The Epic of Gilgamesh

London April 1959	BBCSO BBC Chorus Cantelo, Herbert, Cameron, Anthony, Lidell	Unpublished radio broadcast British premiere performance

MASSENET

Le Cid: Excerpt (Pleurez mes yeux)

London May 1961	Sargent, piano Callas	LP: Penzance PR 15 CD: Legato LR 162

MENDELSSOHN

Elijah

Huddersfield May and June 1947	Liverpool PO Huddersfield Choral Society Baillie, Ripley, Johnston, Williams	78: Columbia DX 1408-1423/ DX 8280-8295 auto 78: Columbia (USA) MM 715 LP: Columbia (USA) SL 53/SL 155 LP: EMI RLS Is not his word CD: EMI CDM 763 3702
Huddersfield April- June 1956	Liverpool PO Huddersfield Choral Society Morison, M.Thomas, Lewis, Cameron	LP: Columbia 33CX 1431-1433 Excerpts LP: EMI HQM 1115

Elijah, Excerpts

Liverpool May and November 1964	RPO Royal Choral Society Harwood, M.Thomas, Lewis, Shirley-Quirk	LP: HMV ALP 2077/ASD 625

Elijah: Excerpts (Help, Lord; Yet doth the Lord see it not)

London October 1928	Orchestra Royal Choral Society	78: HMV C 1668 CD: Pearl GEMMCD 9380

Elijah: Excerpts (Thanks be to God; Be not afraid)

London October 1928	Orchestra Royal Choral Society Falkner	78: HMV C 1670

According to Sargent's biographer Charles Reid, the 1928 Elijah chorus recordings were taken from live performances in February of that year, including a considerable number of rejected and unpublished sides

Symphony No 3 "Scotch"

Liverpool October 1947	Liverpool PO	78: Columbia DX 1451-1454

Violin Concerto

Liverpool May and October 1943 and January 1945	Liverpool PO Holst	Columbia unpublished
London November 1951	LSO De Vito	LP: HMV BLP 1008 Issued on LP by Toshiba

Piano Concerto No 1

London October 1962	RPO Lympany	LP: Reader's Digest LP: RCA GL 32534

A Midsummer Night's Dream, incidental music

London July and August 1954	BBCSO & Chorus Brockless, P.Howard	LP: HMV ALP 1262-1264 Performed within framework of recorded performance of the play

A Midsummer Night's Dream, Nocturne and Wedding March

London August 1965	BBCSO	CD: Radio Classics BBCRD 9105

The Hebrides, Overture

Manchester July 1941	Hallé	78: Columbia DX 1053 LP: Columbia (USA) RL 3072
London November 1960	RPO	LP: HMV XLP 20034/SXLP 20034

Ruy Blas, Overture

London December 1929	Symphony Orchestra	78: HMV C 1813
London May 1952	BBCSO	78: HMV DB 21601

Hark the herald angels

Date not confirmed	Royal Choral Society Organ	78: Decca F 8935
London January 1953	Royal Choral Society Grier	LP: HMV ALP 1159/SRS 5094

MIASKOVSKY

Cello Concerto

London March 1956	Philharmonia Rostropovich	LP: HMV ALP 1427 CD: EMI CDC 749 5482/CDM 565 4192

LEOPOLD MOZART

Toy Symphony (Cassation in G)

London September 1929	Orchestra	78: HMV C 1776

MOZART

Symphony No 40

London March and April 1927	Covent Garden Orchestra	78: HMV C 1347-1349

Clarinet Concerto

London March 1940	LPO Kell	78: HMV C 3167-3170/7543-7546 auto 78: Victor M 708 CD: Testament SBT 1007
London September 1964	BBCSO Brymer	CD: Radio Classics BBCRD 9105

Horn Concerto No 3

London July 1953	BBCSO Brain	Unpublished radio broadcast

Horn Concerto No 4

Manchester June 1943	Hallé Brain	78: Columbia DX 1123-1124 78: Columbia (USA) X 285 LP: Columbia (USA) ML 2088 LP: EMI RLS 7701 <u>Second and third movements conducted by Laurance Turner</u>

Piano Concerto No 19

London January 1937	LSO Schnabel	78: HMV DB 3095-3098/ 　　DB 8298-8300 auto 78: Victor M 389 LP: HMV COLH 90 LP: World Records SH 142 CD: Arabesque Z 6590 CD: EMI CHS 763 7032

Piano Concerto No 21

London January 1937	LSO Schnabel	78: HMV DB 3099-3102/ 　　DB 8355-8358 auto 78: Victor M 486 LP: HMV COLH 67 LP: World Records SH 142 LP: EMI 1C 053 01341M CD: Arabesque Z 6591 CD: EMI CHS 763 7032 CD: Grammofono AB 78531

Violin Concerto No 4

| London | LPO | 78: HMV DB 3734-3736 |
| February 1938 | Kreisler | 78: Victor M 623 |

| Liverpool | Liverpool PO | 78: HMV DB 6146-6148/ |
| March 1943 | Menuhin | DB 8950-8952 auto |

London	New SO	LP: Victor LSC 2652/LSC 3265
May 1962	Heifetz	LP: RCA RB 6527/SB 6527/LSB 4063
		CD: RCA/BMG 09026 617782

Violin Concerto No 5

London	LSO	78: HMV DB 21472-21475
May 1951	Heifetz	LP: HMV ALP 1124
		LP: Victor LM 9014/CRM6 2264
		CD: RCA/BMG 09026 617782

Violin Concerto No 6

| Hayes | Orchestra | 78: HMV DB 1018-1020 |
| February 1927 | Thibaud | CD: Biddulph LAB 016 |

Andantino (Divertimento No 11)

Manchester	Hallé	78: Columbia DX 1128/DX 8190
June 1943		Coupled with Borodin Symphony No 2
		conducted by Constant Lambert

Minuet (Divertimento No 11)

| Manchester | Hallé | Columbia unpublished |
| June 1943 | | |

Fantasia K608, arranged Sargent

| London | Fairey, Foden's & | LP: Columbia 33SX 1752/TWO 101 |
| February 1965 | Morris Brass Bands | |

Ave verum corpus, arranged Sargent

| London | Royal Choral | LP: HMV ALP 1159 |
| March 1953 | Society | |

| London | Royal Choral | LP: HMV ALP 1792/ASD 383 |
| 1960 | Society | |

Die Entführung aus dem Serail, Overture arranged by Sargent

| London | BBCSO | CD: Radio Classics BBCRD 9105 |
| August 1965 | | |

Don Giovanni: Excerpts (Dalla sua pace; Il mio tesoro)

Liverpool	Liverpool PO	78: HMV C 3372
October 1943	Booth	LP: EMI HLM 7109
	Sung in English	

Die Zauberflöte: Excerpt (Ach, ich fühl's)

Liverpool	Liverpool PO	HMV unpublished
October 1943	Hammond	
	Sung in English	

Die Zauberflöte: Excerpt (Dies Bildnis ist bezaubernd schön)

Liverpool	Liverpool PO	78: HMV C 3402
October 1943	Booth	
	Sung in English	

MUSSORGSKY

Pictures from an exhibition

London	LSO	LP: Vox GBYE 15020
1960		LP: Saga 5383
		CD: Bescol CD 528

Night on a bare mountain

London	LSO	LP: Vox GBYE 15020
1960		LP: Saga 5383
		CD: Bescol CD 528

Gopak (Sorochinsky Fair)

London	LSO	CD: Bescol CD 528
1960		

NETTLEFORD

Il pensiero

London	LPO	78: Private recording for the composer
September 1937	Suddaby	

Edward

London	LPO	78: Private recording for the composer
September 1937	Sale	

The Midnight Hour; Olivia

London	LPO	78: Private recording for the composer
September 1937		

PARRY

Jerusalem

London December 1928	Royal Choral Society Organ	78: HMV B 3125/CD: Pearl GEMMCD 9380 Coupled with Webber Now once again our hearts we raise
	Royal Choral Society Organ	78: Decca F 9242 Coupled with God rest ye merry gentlemen
London April 1952	Philharmonia Royal Choral Society	78: HMV C 4213 45: HMV 7P 229 LP: EMI HQM 1115 78 version coupled with Arne Rule Britannia
London September 1966	BBCSO Sinclair	LP: BBC Radio Enterprises RE 10 With audience participation; Sargent's last Prom conducting appearance

Welcome Yule

London 1960	Orchestra Royal Choral Society	LP: HMV ALP 2018/ASD 568 LP: EMI XLP 50009/SXLP 50009/SRS 5094

PEARSALL

In dulci jubilo

London 1931	Royal Choral Society	78: HMV C 2070/CD: Pearl GEMMCD 9380 Coupled with Christ in his garden
London 1960	Royal Choral Society	LP: HMV ALP 2018/ASD 568 LP: EMI XLP 50009/SXLP 50009/SRS 5094

PFITZNER

Adoramus te

London 1963	Royal Choral Society	LP: HMV ALP 2018/ASD 568 LP: EMI XLP 50009/SXLP 50009

PONCHIELLI

Dance of the Hours (La Gioconda)

Manchester July 1941	Hallé	78: Columbia DX 1029 45: Columbia SCD 2011

PROKOFIEV

Symphony No 1 "Classical"

London April 1959	LSO	LP: Decca SPA 90 CD: Decca 433 6122

Symphony No 5

London 1960	LSO	LP: Vanguard/Hallmark HM 537

Peter and the Wolf

London April 1959	LSO Richardson	LP: Decca SPA 90/VIV 40 CD: Decca 433 6122

Sinfonia Concertante for cello and orchestra

London 1958	RPO Rostropovich	LP: HMV ALP 1640 CD: EMI CDC 749 5482

Lieutenant Kije, Suite

London 1960	LSO	LP: World Records T 130/ST 130 CD: Everest EVC 9019 Also issued on LP by Everest

PUCCINI

La Bohème: Excerpt (Si mi chiamano Mimì)

London October 1959	RPO Callas	LP: BJR Records BJR 143 LP: Foyer FO 1007 CD: Legato LR 162

Madama Butterfly: Excerpt (Vieni la sera/Bimba degli occhi)

Liverpool October 1943	Liverpool PO Hammond, Booth Sung in English	78: HMV C 3378 LP: EMI RLS 29 00143

Turandot, orchestral selection

London 1929-1930	Covent Garden Orchestra	78: HMV B 8073

PURCELL

Suite from the dramatic music, arranged Coates

London January 1953	LSO	LP: Decca LXT 2786/ACL 55

QUILTER

Childrens' Overture

London September and October 1928	New Light SO	78: HMV B 2860-2861

RACHMANINOV

Symphony No 3

London May 1953	BBCSO	LP: HMV ALP 1118 LP: EMI MFP 2078

Piano Concerto No 1

London December 1948	Philharmonia Moiseiwitsch	78: HMV C 3932-3934/7769-7771 auto LP: APR LPAPR 7004

Piano Concerto No 2

London June 1947	Liverpool PO C.Smith	78: Columbia DX 1424-1428/ DX 8296-8300 auto
London October 1960	RPO Lympany	LP: HMV CLP 1478/CSD 1388 LP: EMI CFP 167

Rhapsody on a theme of Paganini

London October 1948	Philharmonia C.Smith	78: Columbia DX 1608-1610/ DX 8334-8336 auto LP: Columbia 33SX 1579

Prelude in C sharp minor, arranged Sargent

London September 1931	LSO	78: HMV C 2292 Coupled with Cavalleria rusticana Intermezzo conducted by Barbirolli

RAFF

Cavatina

London October 1930	New Light SO	78: HMV C 2176 Coupled with Walford Davies Solemn March

RAVEL

Tzigane for violin and orchestra

London	LSO	LP: RCA LM 2689/LSC 2689
May 1963	Friedman	CD: RCA/BMG 09026 612102

Pavane pour une infante défunte

London	RPO	LP: Readers Digest RDM 2022/RDS 6022
March 1963		

RAWSTHORNE

Piano Concerto No 2

London	LSO	LP: Decca LX 3066
October 1951	Curzon	
London	BBCSO	LP: HMV CLP 1164
October 1956	Matthews	LP: EMI HQM 1025/SLS 5080

RESPIGHI

Fontane di Roma

London	LSO	LP: Vanguard/Hallmark HM 502
1960		CD: Priceless D 24770/Everest EVC 9018

Pini di Roma

London	LSO	LP: Vanguard/Hallmark HM 502
1960		CD: Priceless D 24770/Everest EVC 9018

RIMSKY-KORSAKOV

Capriccio espagnol

Liverpool January 1945	Liverpool PO	78: Columbia DX 1180-1181

ROSSINI

Il Barbiere di Siviglia, Overture

Manchester July 1941	Hallé	78: Columbia DX 1033
Vienna November 1961	VPO	LP: HMV ALP 1865/ASD 435 CD: EMI CDZ 767 2552 Also on LP by Classics for Pleasure

Guglielmo Tell, Overture

London February 1927	Covent Garden Orchestra	78: HMV B 2437-2438
Vienna November 1961	VPO	LP: HMV ALP 1865/ASD 435 CD: EMI CDZ 767 2552 Also on LP by Classics for Pleasure

Guglielmo Tell, Passo a tre e coro tirolese

London December 1962	Covent Garden Orchestra	LP: HMV XLP 20049/SXLP 20049

La scala di seta, Overture

London November 1960	RPO	LP: HMV XLP 20034/SXLP 20034

Semiramide, Overture

London December 1945	National SO	78: Decca K 1475-1476
Vienna November 1961	VPO	LP: HMV ALP 1865/ASD 435 Also issued on Classics for Pleasure

Il Signor Bruschino, Overture

London March 1963	RPO	LP: Reader's Digest RDM 2022/RDS 6022

Il Viaggio a Reims, Overture

Vienna November 1961	VPO	LP: HMV ALP 1865/ASD 423 Also issued on Classics for Pleasure

RUBBRA

Piano Concerto

London August 1956	BBCSO Matthews	LP: HMV CLP 1194/SLS 5080

SAINT-SAENS

Cello Concerto No 1

London March 1956	Philharmonia Rostropovich	LP: HMV ALP 1427

Havanaise for violin and orchestra

London May 1963	LSO Friedman	LP: RCA LM 2689/LSC 2689 CD: RCA/BMG 09026 612102

Le rouet d'Omphale

Liverpool March 1944	Liverpool PO	78: Columbia DX 1151 LP: Columbia (USA) RL 3050

Samson et Dalila: Excerpt (Printemps qui commence)

Liverpool July 1944	Liverpool PO Ripley Sung in English	78: HMV C 3404 Coupled with Verdi O don fatale (Don Carlo)

SARASATE

Zigeunerweisen

London May 1963	LSO Friedman	LP: RCA LM 2689/LSC 2689 CD: RCA/BMG 09026 612102

SCHUBERT

Symphony No 8 "Unfinished"

Liverpool July 1946	Liverpool PO	78: Columbia DX 1266-1268/ DX 8220-8222 auto
London October 1960	RPO	LP: HMV XLP 20029/SXLP 20029
London September 1964	BBCSO	CD: Radio Classics BBCRD 9105

Symphony No 9 "Great"

London February 1946	LSO	78: Decca K 1459-1464

Overture in the Italian style D591

Liverpool March 1944	Liverpool PO	78: Columbia DX 1157 78: Columbia (USA) 72764D

Rosamunde, Overture

London December 1929	Symphony Orchestra	78: HMV C 1873-1874 <u>Coupled with Brahms Hungarian Dance No 6/Rosamunde is a live recording from the Royal Albert Hall</u>
London October 1960	RPO	LP: HMV XLP 20029/SXLP 20029

Rosamunde, Entr'acte No 3

Liverpool April 1947	Liverpool PO	78: Columbia DX 1520 LP: Columbia (USA) RL 3050 <u>Coupled with Marche militaire</u>
London October 1960	RPO	LP: HMV XLP 20029/SXLP 20029

Rosamunde, Ballet Music No 2

London October 1960	RPO	LP: HMV XLP 20029/SXLP 20029

Marche militaire No 1 in D, arranged Sargent

Liverpool April 1947	Liverpool PO	78: Columbia DX 1520 <u>Coupled with Rosamunde Entr'acte</u>
London February 1965	Fairey, Foden's & Morris Brass Bands	LP: Columbia 33SX 1752/TWO 101

SCHUMANN

Cello Concerto

London   Philharmonia   LP: Columbia 33CX 1407/SAX 2282
March 1956   Fournier

SHOSTAKOVICH

Symphony No 9

London   LSO   LP: World Records T 130/ST 130
1959   LP: Everest SDBR 3054
                                          CD: Everest EVC 9005

SIBELIUS

Symphony No 1

London August 1956	BBCSO	LP: HMV ALP 1542/ASD 260 LP: EMI MFP 2018 CD: EMI CDM 763 0942

Symphony No 2

London August 1957	BBCSO	LP: HMV ALP 1639 LP: EMI MFP 2052

Symphony No 5

London August 1958	BBCSO	LP: HMV ALP 1732/ASD 303 CD: EMI CDM 763 0942

En saga

Vienna November 1961	VPO	LP: HMV ALP 1990/ASD 541 CD: EMI CDM 763 3672

Finlandia

London December 1929	Symphony Orchestra	78: HMV C 1827
London May 1952	BBCSO	78: HMV DB 21522 45: HMV 7ER 5029/7P 319
Vienna November 1961	VPO	LP: HMV ALP 1990/ASD 541 CD: EMI CDM 763 3672

Karelia Suite

Vienna November 1961	VPO	LP: HMV ALP 1990/ASD 541 CD: EMI CDM 763 3672

Pohjola's Daughter

London August 1958	BBCSO	LP: HMV ALP 1732/ASD 303 CD: EMI CDM 763 3672

The Swan of Tuonela

Vienna November 1961	VPO	LP: HMV ALP 1990/ASD 541 CD: EMI CDM 763 3672

Valse triste

Liverpool March 1947	Liverpool PO	78: Columbia DX 1479 LP: Columbia (USA) RL 3050 Coupled with Bach Air

SMETANA

Má Vlast

London February 1964	RPO	LP: EMI XLP 20064-20065/ SXLP 20064-20065 CD: EMI CDU 565 0232 Vltava only CD: EMI WHS 568 4102

The Bartered Bride, Overture

London October 1960	RPO	LP: HMV XLP 20034/SXLP 20034
London September 1966	RPO	Unpublished radio broadcast

EDUARD STRAUSS

Bahn frei, Polka

Liverpool April 1944	Liverpool PO	78: Columbia DB 2156 Coupled with J.Strauss Annen Polka

JOHANN STRAUSS FATHER

Radetzky March, arranged by Gordon Jacob

Liverpool   Liverpool PO   78: Columbia DX 1156
April 1944   LP: Columbia (USA) RL 3050
                                                 Coupled with Ireland
                                                 London Overture

JOHANN STRAUSS

An der schönen blauen Donau, Waltz

London   RPO   LP: HMV XLP 20041/SXLP 20041
May 1961

Annen Polka

Liverpool   Liverpool PO   78: Columbia DB 2156
April 1944   Coupled with Eduard Strauss
                                                 Bahn frei Polka

G'schichten aus dem Wienerwald, Waltz

London   RPO   LP: HMV XLP 20041/SXLP 20041
May 1961

Kaiserwalzer

London   RPO   LP: HMV XLP 20041/SXLP 20041
May 1961

Künstlerleben, Waltz

London   RPO   LP: HMV XLP 20041/SXLP 20041
May 1961

Perpetuum mobile

London   RPO   LP: Reader's Digest RDM 2022/RDS 6022
March 1963

Wein, Weib und Gesang, Waltz

London   RPO   LP: HMV XLP 20041/SXLP 20041
May 1961

JOHANN & JOSEF STRAUSS

Pizzicato Polka

London March 1963	RPO	LP: Reader's Digest RDM 2022/RDS 6022

RICHARD STRAUSS

Le bourgeois gentilhomme, Intermezzo

London June 1938	Symphony Orchestra	78: Columbia DB 1784 Coupled with Elgar Sospiri conducted by Goehr; issued as part of Columbia History of Music

SULLIVAN

Di Ballo, Overture

| London
September 1931 | LSO | 78: HMV C 2308 |

| London
May 1958 | BBCSO | LP: HMV ALP 1658/ASD 536
CD: EMI CDS 747 8318/CMS 764 4002 |

In Memoriam, Concert Overture

| London
1930 | New SO | 78: HMV C 1992
CD: Pearl GEMMCD 9380 |

Cox and Box, Overture

| London
November 1960 | Pro Arte
Orchestra | LP: HMV XLP 20032/SXLP 20032
LP: EMI CFP 4529
CD: EMI CDCFP 4529/CDS 747 7858/
CMS 764 4092 |

The Gondoliers

| London
March and
May 1931 | Orchestra
Chorus
Oldham, Rands,
Ackland, Moxon,
Baker, Booth,
Grenville, Walker | 78: HMV B 3866-3871/7012-7017 auto
Abridged version |

| London
March 1957 | Pro Arte
Orchestra
Glyndebourne
Chorus
Morison, M.Thomas,
Sinclair, Lewis,
Young, Milligan,
Evans, Brannigan | LP: HMV ALP 1504-1505/ASD 265-266
LP: Angel 3570/6103
LP: EMI SXDW 3027
CD: EMI CDS 747 7758/CMS 764 3942
Overture
LP: HMV XLP 20003/SXLP 20003
LP: Angel 35929
LP: EMI SXLP 30172/CFP 4529
CD: EMI CDCFP 4529
Excerpts CD: EMI WHS 568 3982 |

HMS Pinafore

London February, March and June 1930	Orchestra Chorus Griffin, Briercliffe, Lewis, Lytton, Fancourt, Baker	78: HMV D 1844-1852/7511-7519 auto 78: Victor C 13 LP: HMV ALP 1293-1294
London April 1958	Pro Arte Orchestra Glyndebourne Chorus Morison, M.Thomas, Sinclair, Lewis, Cameron, Milligan, Brannigan, Baker	LP: HMV ALP 1650-1651/ASD 415-416 LP: Angel 3589 LP: EMI SXLP 30088-30089 LP: EMI SXDW 3034/EX 749 5941 CD: EMI CDS 747 7798/CMS 764 3972 Overture LP: HMV XLP 20003/SXLP 20003 LP: Angel 35929 LP: EMI SXLP 30172/CFP 4529 CD: EMI CDCFP 4529 Excerpts CD: EMI WHS 568 3982

HMS Pinafore, Overture

London 1965	RPO	LP: Decca LK 4768/PFS 4097 CD: Belart 461 0062

HMS Pinafore: Excerpt (We sail the ocean blue)

London 1965	RPO Chorus	LP: Decca LK 4768/PFS 4097 CD: Belart 461 0062

HMS Pinafore: Excerpt (My gallant crew, good morning!)

London 1965	RPO Chorus Styler	LP: Decca LK 4768/PFS 4097 CD: Belart 461 0062

HMS Pinafore: Excerpt (Now give three cheers)

London 1965	RPO Chorus Styler, Reed, Wales	LP: Decca LK 4768/PFS 4097 CD: Belart 461 0062

HMS Pinafore: Excerpt (When I was a lad)

London 1965	RPO Chorus Reed	LP: Decca LK 4768/PFS 4097 CD: Belart 461 0062

HMS Pinafore: Excerpt (For he's the Captain of the Pinafore)

London 1965	RPO Chorus Styler, Palmer, Reed, Wales	LP: Decca LK 4768/PFS 4097 CD: Belart 461 0062

Iolanthe

London October and December 1929	Orchestra Chorus Moxon, Elvin, Briercliffe, Lawson, Lewis, Oldham, Baker, Fancourt	78: HMV D 1785-1795 78: Victor C 10 LP: World Records SHB 64
London April and October 1958	Pro Arte Orchestra Glyndebourne Chorus Cantelo, Sinclair, M.Thomas, Young, Wallace, Cameron, Brannigan, Baker	LP: HMV ALP 1757-1758/ASD 323-324 LP: Angel 3597 LP: EMI SXLP 30112-30113 LP: EMI SXDW 3047/EX 749 5971 CD: EMI CDS 747 8318/CMS 764 4002 Overture LP: HMV XLP 20003/SXLP 20003 LP: Angel 35929 LP: EMI SXLP 30172/CFP 4529 CD: EMI CDCFP 4529 Excerpts CD: EMI WHS 568 3982

Iolanthe, Overture

Liverpool October 1946	Liverpool PO	78: Columbia DX 1378
London February 1965	Fairey, Foden's & Morris Brass Bands	LP: Columbia 33SX 1752/TWO 101

The Mikado

London May, June and August 1956	Pro Arte Orchestra Glyndebourne Chorus Morison, M.Thomas, Lewis, Wallace, Evans, Brannigan	LP: HMV ALP 1485-1486/ASD 256-257 LP: Angel 3573 LP: EMI SXDW 3019 CD: EMI CDS 747 7738/CMS 764 4032 <u>Overture</u> LP: HMV XLP 20003/SXLP 20003 LP: Angel 35929 LP: EMI SXLP 30172/CFP 4529 CD: EMI CDCFP 4529 <u>Excerpts</u> CD: EMI WHS 568 3982

The Mikado: Excerpt (The flowers that bloom in the spring)

London 1965	RPO Hood, Reed, Masterson, Wales, Sandford	LP: Decca LK 4768/PFS 4097 CD: Belart 461 0062

The Mikado: Excerpt (A more humane Mikado)

London 1965	RPO Chorus Adams	LP: Decca LK 4768/PFS 4097 CD: Belart 461 0062

The Mikado: Excerpt (On a tree by a river)

London 1965	RPO Reed	LP: Decca LK 4768/PFS 4097 CD: Belart 461 0062

The Mikado: Excerpt (3 little maids)

London 1965	RPO Masterson, Wales, P.Jones	LP: Decca LK 4768/PFS 4097 CD: Belart 461 0062
London ca. 1960	BBC Concert Orchestra Members of BBC & Royal Choral Societies	LP: BBC Radio Enterprises RE 10

The Mikado: Excerpt (A wandering minstrel)

London 1965	RPO Chorus Potter	LP: Decca LK 4768/PFS 4097 CD: Belart 461 0062

Patience

London February and September 1930	Orchestra Chorus Briercliffe, Mackay, Lawson, Eyre, Oldham, Baker, Green, Fancourt	78: HMV D 1909-1918/7844-7853 auto 78: Victor C 14
London February 1959 and October 1961	Pro Arte Orchestra Glyndebourne Chorus Harwood, Harper, Morison, M.Thomas, Sinclair, Young, Cameron, Baker,	LP: HMV ALP 1918-1919/ASD 484-485 LP: Angel 3635 LP: EMI SXDW 3031/EX 749 5971 CD: EMI CDS 747 7838/CMS 764 4062 Overture LP: HMV XLP 20032/SXLP 20032 LP: EMI CFP 4529 CD: EMI CDCFP 4529

Patience, Overture

Liverpool October 1946	Liverpool PO	78: Columbia DX 1339 45: Columbia SCD 2003 LP: Columbia (USA) RL 3050

The Pirates of Penzance

London February and March 1929	Orchestra Chorus Robertson, Gill, Dawson, Oldham, Briercliffe, Walker, Griffin, Baker, Sheffield	78: HMV D 1678-1688/7730-7740 auto 78: Victor C 6 CD: Arabesque Z 8068
London February and December 1959 and January 1960	Pro Arte Orchestra Glyndebourne Chorus Morison, Harper, M.Thomas, Sinclair, Lewis, Brannigan, Milligan, Cameron, Baker	LP: HMV ALP 1801-1802/ASD 381-382 LP: Angel 3609/6102 LP: EMI SXLP 30131-30132 LP: EMI SXDW 3041/EX 749 6931 CD: EMI CDS 747 7858/CMS 764 4092 Overture LP: HMV XLP 20003/SXLP 20003 LP: Angel 35929 LP: EMI SXLP 30172/CFP 4529 CD: EMI CDCFP 4529 Excerpts CD: EMI WHS 568 3982

The Pirates of Penzance, abridged version

London March and May 1931	Orchestra Chorus Soloists presumably as in 1929 version	78: HMV B 3846-3851

The Pirates of Penzance: Excerpt (Hold, monsters!)

London 1965	RPO Chorus Masterson, Reed, Raffell	LP: Decca LK 4768/PFS 4097 CD: Belart 461 0062

The Pirates of Penzance: Excerpt (I am the very model of a modern Major General)

London 1965	RPO Chorus Reed	LP: Decca LK 4768/PFS 4097 CD: Belart 461 0062

The Pirates of Penzance: Excerpt (When the foreman bares his steel)

London 1965	RPO Chorus Masterson, Hood, Adams	LP: Decca LK 4768/PFS 4097 CD: Belart 461 0062

The Pirates of Penzance: Excerpt (With cat-like tread)

London 1965	RPO Chorus Raffell	LP: Decca LK 4768/PFS 4097 CD: Belart 461 0062

Princess Ida

London September and October 1932	Orchestra Chorus Baker, Watson, Lytton, Moxon, Briercliffe, Evens, Oldham, Goulding	78: HMV DB 4016-4025/ DB 7271-7280 auto 78: Victor C 20
London 1965	RPO Chorus Harwood, Hood, Masterson, Palmer, Sandford, Reed, Potter, Adams	LP: Decca LK 4708-4709/ SKL 4708-4709 CD: Decca 425 1962 Excerpts LP: Decca LK 4845/SKL 4845

Princess Ida, Overture

London November 1960	Pro Arte Orchestra	LP: HMV XLP 20032/SXLP 20032 LP: EMI CFP 4529 CD: EMI CDCFP 4529/CDS 747 7858/ CMS 764 4092

Ruddigore

London September 1931	Orchestra Chorus Gill, Dickson, Baker, Oldham, Briercliffe, Grenville, Fancourt, Robertson	78: HMV DB 4005-4013/ DB 7522-7530 auto 78: Victor C 19
London November 1960 and December 1962	Pro Arte Orchestra Glyndebourne Chorus Morison, Harwood, Sinclair, Lewis, Brannigan, Baker, Rouleau, Blackburn	LP: HMV ALP 3013-2014/ASD 563-564 LP: EMI SXDW 3029/EX 749 6931 CD: EMI CDS 747 7878/CMS 764 4122 Overture LP: HMV XLP 20032/SXLP 20032 LP: EMI CFP 4529 CD: EMI CDCFP 5429

Ruddigore: Excerpt (There grew a little flower)

London 1965	RPO Palmer, Adams	LP: Decca LK 4768/PFS 4097 CD: Belart 461 0062

The Sorcerer, Overture

London November 1960	Pro Arte Orchestra	LP: HMV XLP 20032/SXLP 20032 LP: Angel 35929 LP: EMI CFP 4529 CD: EMI CDCFP 4529/CDS 747 7858/ CMS 764 4092

Trial by Jury

London December 1960	Pro Arte Orchestra Glyndebourne Chorus Morison, Lewis, Cameron, Baker, Brannigan	LP: HMV ALP 1851/ASD 419 LP: Angel 35966 LP: HMV SXLP 30089 LP: ENI SXDW 3034/EX 749 6961 CD: EMI CDS 747 7798/CMS 764 3972

The Yeomen of the Guard

London September and October 1928	Orchestra Chorus Briercliffe, Gill, Millidge, Lawson, Oldham, Baker	78: HMV D 1549-1559/7719-7729 auto 78: Victor C 17
London December 1957	Pro Arte Orchestra Glyndebourne Chorus Morison, M.Thomas, Sinclair, Lewis, Young, Brannigan, Evans, Cameron	LP: HMV ALP 1601-1602/ASD 364-365 LP: Angel 3596 LP: HMV SXLP 30120-30121 LP: EMI SXDW 3033/EX 749 5941 CD: EMI CDS 747 7818/CMS 764 4152 Overture LP: HMV XLP 20003/SXLP 20003 LP: Angel 35929 LP: EMI SXLP 30172/CFP 4529 CD: EMI CDCFP 4529

London
1964
	RPO
	Chorus
	Harwood, Hood,
	Sandford, Adams,
	Raffell, Potter
		LP: Decca LK 4624-4625/
		    SKL 4624-4625
		CD: Decca 417 3582
		Excerpts
		45: Decca DFE 8630
		LP: Decca LK 4069/LK 4809/
		    SKL 4809

The Yeomen of the Guard, Overture

Liverpool 1946	Liverpool PO	78: Columbia DX 1339 45: Columbia SCD 2003 LP: Columbia (USA) RL 3050
London February 1965	Fairey, Foden's & Morris Brass Bands	LP: Columbia 33SX 1752/TWO 101 Arranged Sargent

Excerpts from the HMV LP series of Gilbert and Sullivan under Sargent also issued on compilation LPs and EPs, principally on HMV ALP 1904/ASD 472, ALP 1922/ASD 487 and ALP 1932/ASD 495

Sargent also conducted the music for Sidney Gilliatt's 1953 film The Story of Gilbert and Sullivan

SUPPÉ

Poet and Peasant, Overture

London January 1946	National SO	78: Decca K 1411

TCHAIKOVSKY

Symphony No 4

London 1945-1946	National SO	78: Decca K 1226-1230

Symphony No 5

London January 1955	BBCSO	LP: HMV ALP 1236 Third movement only 45: HMV 7ER 5067
London 1960	LSO	LP: Vanguard/Hallmark HM 511

Violin Concerto

London January 1950	New SO Ricci	78: Decca AX 336-339 LP: Decca LXT 2509
London January 1961	LSO Ricci	LP: Decca LXT 5641/SXL 2279 CD: Decca 417 6762
London September 1966	RPO Ughi	Unpublished radio broadcast

Rococo Variations

London March 1956	Philharmonia Fournier	LP: Columbia 33CX 1407/SAX 2282

Theme and Variations (Suite No 3)

Liverpool December 1942 and March 1943	Liverpool PO	78: HMV C 3338-3340/7577-7579 auto Coupled with Cossack Dance (Mazeppa)
London March and June 1955	Philharmonia	LP: HMV ALP 1372 Variation 12 only 45: HMV 7ER 5067

Andante cantabile (String Quartet No 1)

London   BBCSO   LP: HMV ALP 1658/ASD 536
May 1958

Eugene Onegin: Excerpts (Waltz and Polonaise)

Manchester   Hallé   78: Columbia DX 1044
July 1941

Eugene Onegin: Excerpt (Tatiana's Letter Scene)

London   BBCSO   LP: HMV ALP 1658/ASD 536
March 1958   Hammond
                Sung in English

Humoresque, arranged by Sargent

London   RPO   LP: Reader's Digest RDM 2022/RDS 6022
March 1963

Legend (Christ in his garden)

London   Royal Choral   78: HMV C 2070/B 3977
1931   Society   C 2070 coupled with Pearsall
                                     In dulci jubilo; B 3977
                                     coupled with The First Nowell

Marche slave

London December 1948	Philharmonia	78: Columbia DX 1574 LP: Columbia (USA) RL 3091
London October 1952	BBCSO	78: HMV DB 21569 45: HMV P 259
London January 1960	RPO	LP: HMV XLP 20023/SXLP 20023

Mazeppa: Excerpt (Cossack Dance)

Liverpool March 1943	Liverpool PO	78: HMV C 3340/C 7577 Coupled with Theme and Variations (Suite No 3)

1812 Overture

London January 1960	RPO	LP: HMV XLP 20023/SXLP 20023

Romeo and Juliet

London January 1960	RPO	LP: HMV XLP 20023/SXLP 20023

Sleeping Beauty Waltz

London October 1927	Covent Garden Orchestra	78: HMV C 1415 Coupled with Brahms Hungarian Dance No 5
Manchester July 1941	Hallé	78: Columbia DX 1079 45: Columbia SCD 2088 CD: Dutton CDAX 8010 78 version coupled with Borodin Prince Igor Overture conducted by Leslie Heward; 45 version coupled with Vaughan Williams Greensleeves Fantasia
London January 1960	RPO	LP: HMV XLP 20023/SXLP 20023

VAUGHAN WILLIAMS

Fantasia on Greensleeves

Manchester July 1942	Hallé	78: Columbia DX 1087 45: Columbia SCD 2088 <u>78 version coupled with Bizet L'Arlésienne Suite no 1; 45 version coupled with Tchaikovsky Sleeping Beauty Waltz</u>
London May 1957	LSO	LP: HMV ALP 1499 LP: EMI MFP 2060 CD: EMI CDM 763 3822

Hugh the Drover, abridged version

London September and October 1924	Orchestra Chorus Lewis, Willis, Davies, Collier, Anderson, Michael, Dawson	78: HMV D 922-926 LP: Pearl GEMM 218 CD: Pearl GEMMCD 9468 Excerpt CD: Beulah 1PD 13 <u>Sargent's first recording</u>

The Lark Ascending

London March 1928	Orchestra Menges	78: HMV C 1622-1623
Liverpool April 1947	Liverpool PO Wise	78: Columbia DX 1386-1387 CD: Dutton CDAX 8012

Romance for harmonica and orchestra

London October 1952	String Orchestra Adler	78: Columbia DX 1861 LP: Columbia 33S 1023 CD: EMI CDM 565 4662

Serenade to Music

London May 1957	LSO Morison, M.Thomas, Robertson, Anthony	LP: HMV ALP 1499 LP: EMI MFP 2060 CD: EMI CDM 763 3822

Thomas Tallis Fantasia

London November 1952	BBCSO	78: HMV DB 9783-9784 LP: HMV BLP 1019 <u>78 version coupled with Elgar Wand of Youth Suite No 2</u>
London June 1959	Philharmonia	LP: HMV XLP 20007/SXLP 20007

Towards the Unknown Region

London May 1957	LSO Chorus	LP: HMV ALP 1499 LP: EMI MFP 2060 CD: EMI CDM 763 3822
London 1962	BBCSO BBC Chorus	Unpublished radio broadcast

The Wasps, Overture

Manchester July 1942	Hallé	78: Columbia DX 1088
London May 1957	LSO	LP: HMV ALP 1499 LP: EMI MFP 2060/HQM 1115 CD: EMI CDM 763 3822

VERDI

Aida: Excerpt (Celeste Aida)

Liverpool October 1943	Liverpool PO Booth Sung in English	78: HMV C 3379 LP: EMI HLM 7109 78 version coupled with Leoncavallo Vesti la giubba (I Pagliacci) not conducted by Sargent

Don Carlo: Excerpt (O don fatale)

Liverpool July 1944	Liverpool PO Ripley Sung in English	78: HMV C 3404 Coupled with Saint-Saens Printemps qui commence (Samson et Dalila)

Don Carlo: Excerpt (Tu che la vanità)

London May 1961	Sargent, piano Callas	LP: Penzance PR 15 CD: Legato LR 162

VIEUXTEMPS

Violin Concerto No 5

London May 1947	LSO Heifetz	78: HMV DB 6547-6548 LP: HMV ALP 1124 LP: Victor LM 1121/ARM4-0946 CD: RCA/BMG 09026 617782
London May 1961	New SO Heifetz	LP: Victor LSC 2603 LP: RCA RB 6503/SB 6503 CD: RCA/BMG 09026 617782

WAGNER

Die Meistersinger von Nürnberg, Overture

London October 1960	RPO	LP: HMV XLP 20034/SXLP 20034

Die Meistersinger von Nürnberg: Excerpt (Wach auf, es nahet gen den Tag)

London February 1929	Orchestra Royal Choral Society Sung in English	78: HMV B 3122 Coupled with Treulich geführt

Lohengrin: Excerpt (Treulich geführt)

London February 1929	Orchestra Royal Choral Society Sung in English	78: HMV B 3122 Coupled with Wach auf

Das Rheingold, Prelude

London December 1948	Philharmonia	78: Columbia DX 1607 Coupled with Ride of the Valkyries

Tannhäuser: Excerpt (Freudig begrüssen wir die edle Halle)

London February 1929	Orchestra Royal Choral Society Sung in English	HMV unpublished

Tristan und Isolde: Excerpt (Mild und leise)

London October 1953	BBCSO Flagstad	CD: Notes PGG 11019 CD: AS-Disc AS 360 CD: Memories HR 4456-4457

Die Walküre, Ride of the Valkyries

London December 1948	Philharmonia	78: Columbia DX 1607 LP: Columbia (USA) RL 3091 Coupled with Rheingold Prelude

Wesendonk-Lieder

London October 1953	BBCSO Flagstad	CD: AS-Disc AS 360 CD: Memories HR 4456-4457

According to Sargent's biographer Charles Reid, the 3 Wagner choruses recorded in February 1929 were taken from live performances in the Royal Albert Hall

WALFORD DAVIES

Solemn Melody

| London 1929-1930 | New Light SO | 78: HMV C 2176 Coupled with Raff Cavatina; according to Sargent's biographer Charles Reid, the Davies item was a live recording made in the Royal Albert Hall |

WALTON

Symphony No 1

London
October 1966

New Philharmonia

LP: HMV ALP 2299/ASD 2299
LP: EMI SXLP 30138
CD: EMI CDM 763 2692

Viola Concerto

London
1953

RPO
Primrose

LP: Philips ABL 3045

Belshazzar's Feast

Huddersfield
February and
March 1958

Liverpool PO
Huddersfield
Choral Society
Milligan

LP: HMV ALP 1628
CD: EMI CHS 763 3762
Excerpt
LP: EMI HQM 1115

Belshazzar's Feast, concluding section

London
Date uncertain

BBCSO
Various Choirs

LP: BBC Radio Enterprises RE 10

Facade, Orchestral Suite

London
January 1961

RPO

LP: HMV ALP 1873/ASD 443
LP: EMI SXLP 30114

Orb and Sceptre, Coronation March

London
April 1954

LSO

LP: Decca LXT 2793/LW 5057
LP: Decca ACL 137/ECS 649
CD: Decca 425 6622

Johannesburg Festival Overture

London
1957

BBCSO

Unpublished radio broadcast

WARLOCK

Capriol Suite

London January 1965	RPO	LP: HMC CLP 3539/CSD 3539 LP: EMI SXLP 30126 CD: EMI CDEMX 2141

WEBBER

Now once again our hearts we raise

London December 1928	Royal Choral Society Organ	78: HMV B 3125 Coupled with Parry Jerusalem
London March 1953	Royal Choral Society	45: HMV 7EG 8403 LP: HMV ALP 1159

WEBER

Bassoon Concerto

Liverpool December 1947	Liverpool PO Brooke	78: Columbia DX 1656-1657 CD: Testament SBT 1009

Konzertstück for piano and orchestra

London October 1962	RPO Lympany	LP: Reader's Digest RDM 1113/RDS 6113 LP: RCA GL 32534

Aufforderung zum Tanz, arranged Johnstone

Liverpool 1947	Liverpool PO	78: Columbia DX 1549 LP: Columbia (USA) RL 3091

TRADITIONAL CHRISTMAS CAROLS

All God's chillun, arranged Sargent

London 1960	Royal Choral Society	LP: HMV ALP 1792/ASD 383

Bethlehem

London 1963	Orchestra Royal Choral Society	LP: HMV ALP 2018/ASD 568 LP: EMI XLP 50009/SXLP 50009

The Boar's Head, arranged Sargent

London January 1953	Royal Choral Society	LP: HMV ALP 1159/SRS 5094
London 1960	Royal Choral Society	LP: HMV ALP 1792/ASD 383

Carol of Beauty, arranged Sargent

London January 1953	Royal Choral Society	LP: HMV ALP 1159
London 1960	Royal Choral Society	LP: HMV ALP 1792/ASD 383

Cherry Tree Carol, arranged Sargent

London 1960	Royal Choral Society	LP: HMV ALP 1792/ASD 383/SRS 5094

Christmas is coming, arranged Walford Davies

London March 1953	Royal Choral Society	LP: HMV ALP 1159

Coventry Carol, arranged Stainer

London January 1953	Royal Choral Society	45: HMV 7EG 8612 LP: HMV ALP 1159

Dark the night

London 1963	Orchestra Royal Choral Society	LP: HMV ALP 2018/ASD 568 LP: EMI XLP 50009/SXLP 50009 LP: EMI SRS 5094

Ding-dong merrily on high, arranged Wood-Woodward

London March 1953	Royal Choral Society	45: HMV 7EG 8403 LP: HMV ALP 1159/SRS 5094

The First Nowell

Date not confirmed	Royal Choral Society Organ	78: HMV B 3977 Coupled with Tchaikovsky Christ in his garden
London March 1953	Royal Choral Society Grier	LP: HMV ALP 1159/SRS 5094

God rest you, merry gentlemen

London November 1933	Royal Choral Society	78: HMV B 8073 Coupled with I saw 3 ships; Holly and the ivy; See amid the winter's snow
Date not confirmed	Royal Choral Society Organ	78: Decca F 9242

Good King Wenceslas

Date not confirmed	Royal Choral Society Organ	78: Decca F 8935

Greensleeves, arranged Sargent

London March 1953	Royal Choral Society	45: HMV 7EG 8612 LP: HMV ALP 1159/SRS 5094
London 1960	Royal Choral Society	LP: HMV ALP 1792/ASD 383

Hawaiian Lullaby

London 1963	Orchestra Royal Choral Society	LP: HMV ALP 2018/ASD 568 LP: EMI XLP 50009/SXLP 50009 LP: EMI SRS 5094

The holly and the ivy, arranged Stainer

London November 1933	Royal Choral Society	78: HMV B 8073 Coupled with God rest you merry gentlemen; I saw three ships; See amid the winter's snow

I saw three ships, arranged Stainer

London November 1933	Royal Choral Society	78: HMV B 8073 Coupled with God rest you merry gentlemen; Holly and the ivy; See amid the winter's snow

Little David, play on yo' harp, arranged Sargent

London 1960	Royal Choral Society	LP: HMV ALP 1792/ASD 383/SRS 5094

Lullaby

London 1963	Orchestra Royal Choral Society	LP: HMV ALP 2018/ASD 568 LP: EMI XLP 50009/SXLP 50009 LP: EMI SRS 5094

Nature Carol

London 1963	Orchestra Royal Choral Society	LP: HMV ALP 2018/ASD 568 LP: EMI XLP 50009/SXLP 50009

O come all ye faithful (Adeste fideles)

London September 1932	Royal Choral Society Organ	78: HMV B 4304 Coupled with While shepherds watched
London January 1953	Royal Choral Society Grier	45: HMV 7EG 8612 LP: HMV ALP 1159/SRS 5094

On Christmas Day

London 1960	Royal Choral Society	LP: HMV ALP 1792/ASD 383

Praise ye the Lord

London 1963	Orchestra Royal Choral Society	LP: HMV ALP 2018/ASD 568 LP: EMI XLP 50009/SXLP 50009

See amid the winter's snow, arranged Goss

London November 1933	Royal Choral Society Organ	78: HMV B 8073 Coupled with God rest ye merry gentlemen; I saw three ships; The holly and the ivy

Star in the South

London 1960	Royal Choral Society	LP: HMV ALP 1792/ASD 383

To a baby, arranged Sargent

London 1960	Royal Choral Society	LP: HMV ALP 1792/ASD 383

While shepherds watched, arranged Shaw

London September 1932	Royal Choral Society Organ	78: HMV B 4304 Coupled with O come all ye faithful
London March 1953	Royal Choral Society Grier	45: HMV 7EG 8612 LP: HMV ALP 1159/SRS 5094

Winter, arranged Sargent

London March 1953	Royal Choral Society	45: HMV 7EG 8403 LP: HMV ALP 1159

Zither Carol, arranged Sargent

London 1960	Royal Choral Society	LP: HMV ALP 1792/ASD 383/SRS 5094

MISCELLANEOUS

Fantasia on British Sea Songs, arranged Wood

London December 1931	LSO	78: HMV C 2452
London September 1966	BBCSO	LP: BBC Radio Enterprises RE 10 With audience participation; Sargent's final Prom conducting appearance

God Save the Queen, Full verse and half verse

London February 1928	Royal Albert Hall Orchestra	According to Sargent's biographer Charles Reid, this published 78 was taken from a live performance in the Royal Albert Hall
London April 1952	Philharmonia	45: HMV 7P 248

God Save the Queen, arranged Elgar

London April 1952	Philharmonia Royal Choral Society	78: HMV B 10484 45: HMV 7P 248

The Instruments of the Orchestra/spoken commentary by the conductor

London May 1947	Instrumentalists	78: HMV C 3619-3622 Horn (Siegfried's horn call) LP: EMI RLS 7701
London April and December 1959		LP: Decca LXT 5573/SXL 2199

Londonderry Air, arranged Grainger

London   New SO   78: HMV B 2913
November 1927   Coupled with Bach Air
                                          (Suite No 3)

Liverpool   Liverpool PO   78: Columbia DX 1584/DX 8220
June 1947   Coupled with Elgar Wand
                                          of Youth Suite No 1

Ye watchers and ye holy ones

London   Allen   78: HMV B 2424
February 1927   Massed choirs   CD: Pearl GEMMCD 9380

Marching through Georgia; Fire down below

London   Allen, Goss   78: HMV B 2423
February 1927   Massed choirs   CD: Pearl GEMMCD 9380

Sir Malcolm Sargent: Music Maker

Recorded interview excerpts and   LP: BBC Radio Enterprises RE 10
musical examples, including
Last Night of the Proms 1966
and Sargent's farewell speech at
end of season (see under
Delius, Elgar, Sullivan, Walton);
Sargent speaks of Elgar, Gilbert
and Sullivan, early experiences
as organist and pianist, the
conductor as showman and choral
trainer; the LP also includes
recorded extracts from Sargent's
funeral and memorial services,
with BBC Symphony Orchestra
playing his own arrangement of the
Dead March from Handel's Saul

Another BBC Radio Enterprises LP contained a selection of Sargent's speeches
from Last Nights of the Proms

· MUSIC FROM THE OPERA ·

PETER GRIMES

Four Sea Interludes — *Britten*

Dawn
Sunday Morning } - - - - DX 1441

Moonlight
Storm } - - - - - - DX 1442

The London Symphony Orchestra
conducted by
SIR MALCOLM SARGENT

COLUMBIA GRAPHOPHONE COMPANY LIMITED, HAYES, MIDDLESEX

CREDITS

Valuable help with information for
the preparation of these discographies
came from :

Mike Ashman, Ware
Mimi Basson, Berlin
Paul Brooks, Oxford
Richard Chlupaty, London
Clifford Elkin, Glasgow
Mathias Erhard, Berlin
Michael Gray, Alexandria VA
Syd Gray, Hove
Ken Jagger, EMI Classics London
Lyndon Jenkins, Birmingham
Roderick Krüsemann, Amsterdam
Paul Lawley, Exmouth
Alan Newcombe, DG Hamburg
Brian Pinder, Halifax
Vivienne Rendall, Great Ayton
Alan Sanders, Richmond
Robin Scott, Bradford
Ulrich Seibert, Munich
Neville Sumpter, Northolt
Giovanna Visconti, Jackson Heights
Malcolm Walker, Harrow

Music and Books published by Travis & Emery Music Bookshop:

Anon.: Hymnarium Sarisburense, cum Rubris et Notis Musicus
Agricola, Johann Friedrich from Tosi: Anleitung zur Singkunst. (Faksimile 1757)
Bach, C.P.E.: edited W. Emery: Nekrolog or Obituary Notice of J.S. Bach.
Bateson, Naomi Judith: Alcock of Salisbury
Bathe, William: A Briefe Introduction to the Skill of Song
Bax, Arnold: Symphony #5, Arranged for Piano Four Hands by Walter Emery
Burney, Charles: The Present State of Music in France and Italy
Burney, Charles: The Present State of Music in Germany, The Netherlands …
Burney, Charles: An Account of the Musical Performances … Handel
Burney, Karl: Nachricht von Georg Friedrich Handel's Lebensumstanden.
Burns, Robert (jnr): The Caledonian Musical Museum (1810 volume)
Cobbett, W.W.: Cobbett's Cyclopedic Survey of Chamber Music. (2 vols.)
Corrette, Michel: Le Maitre de Clavecin
Crimp, Bryan: Dear Mr. Rosenthal … Dear Mr. Gaisberg …
Crimp, Bryan: Solo: The Biography of Solomon
d'Indy, Vincent: Beethoven: Biographie Critique
d'Indy, Vincent: Beethoven: A Critical Biography
d'Indy, Vincent: César Franck (in French)
Fischhof, Joseph: Versuch einer Geschichte des Clavierbaues
Frescobaldi, Girolamo: D'Arie Musicali per Cantarsi. Primo Libro & Secondo Libro.
Geminiani, Francesco: The Art of Playing the Violin.
Handel; Purcell; Boyce; Green et al: Calliope or English Harmony: Volume First.
Hawkins, John: A General History of the Science and Practice of Music (5 vols.)
Herbert-Caesari, Edgar: The Science and Sensations of Vocal Tone
Herbert-Caesari, Edgar: Vocal Truth
Hopkins and Rimboult: The Organ. Its History and Construction.
Hunt, John: some 40 discographies – see list of discographies
Isaacs, Lewis: Hänsel and Gretel. A Guide to Humperdinck's Opera.
Isaacs, Lewis: Königskinder (Royal Children) A Guide to Humperdinck's Opera.
Lacassagne, M. l'Abbé Joseph : Traité Général des élémens du Chant.
Lascelles (née Catley), Anne: The Life of Miss Anne Catley.
Mainwaring, John: Memoirs of the Life of the Late George Frederic Handel
Malcolm, Alexander: A Treaty of Music: Speculative, Practical and Historical
Marx, Adolph Bernhard: Die Kunst des Gesanges, Theoretisch-Practisch
May, Florence: The Life of Brahms
Mellers, Wilfrid: Angels of the Night: Popular Female Singers of Our Time
Mellers, Wilfrid: Bach and the Dance of God

Travis & Emery Music Bookshop
17 Cecil Court, London, WC2N 4EZ, United Kingdom.
Tel. (+44) 20 7240 2129

Music and Books published by Travis & Emery Music Bookshop:

Mellers, Wilfrid: Beethoven and the Voice of God
Mellers, Wilfrid: Caliban Reborn - Renewal in Twentieth Century Music
Mellers, Wilfrid: François Couperin and the French Classical Tradition
Mellers, Wilfrid: Harmonious Meeting
Mellers, Wilfrid: Le Jardin Retrouvé, The Music of Frederic Mompou
Mellers, Wilfrid: Music and Society, England and the European Tradition
Mellers, Wilfrid: Music in a New Found Land: ... ... American Music
Mellers, Wilfrid: Romanticism and the Twentieth Century (from 1800)
Mellers, Wilfrid: The Masks of Orpheus: ...... the Story of European Music.
Mellers, Wilfrid: The Sonata Principle (from c. 1750)
Mellers, Wilfrid: Vaughan Williams and the Vision of Albion
Panchianio, Cattuffio: Rutzvanscad Il Giovine.
Pearce, Charles: Sims Reeves, Fifty Years of Music in England.
Pettitt, Stephen: Philharmonia Orchestra: Complete Discography 1945-1987
Playford, John: An Introduction to the Skill of Musick.
Purcell, Henry et al: Harmonia Sacra ... The First Book, (1726)
Purcell, Henry et al: Harmonia Sacra ... Book II (1726)
Quantz, Johann: Versuch einer Anweisung die Flöte traversiere zu spielen.
Rameau, Jean-Philippe: Code de Musique Pratique, ou Methodes.
Rastall, Richard: The Notation of Western Music.
Rimbault, Edward: The Pianoforte, Its Origins, Progress, and Construction.
Rousseau, Jean Jacques: Dictionnaire de Musique
Rubinstein, Anton : Guide to the proper use of the Pianoforte Pedals.
Sainsbury, John S.: Dictionary of Musicians. Vol. 1. (1825). 2 vols.
Simpson, Christopher: A Compendium of Practical Musick in Five Parts
Spohr, Louis: Autobiography
Spohr, Louis: Grand Violin School
Tans'ur, William: A New Musical Grammar; or The Harmonical Spectator
Terry, Charles Sanford: Four-Part Chorals of J.S. Bach. (German & English)
Terry, Charles Sanford: Joh. Seb. Bach, Cantata Texts, Sacred and Secular.
Terry, Charles Sanford: The Origins of the Family of Bach Musicians.
Tosi, Pierfrancesco: Opinioni de' Cantori Antichi, e Moderni
Van der Straeten, Edmund: History of the Violoncello, The Viol da Gamba ...
Van der Straeten, Edmund: History of the Violin, Its Ancestors... (2 vols.)
Walther, J. G.: Musicalisches Lexikon ober Musicalische Bibliothec (1732)

Travis & Emery Music Bookshop
17 Cecil Court, London, WC2N 4EZ, United Kingdom.
Tel. (+44) 20 7240 2129

© Travis & Emery 2009

Discographies by Travis & Emery:

Discographies by John Hunt.

1987: From Adam to Webern: the Recordings of von Karajan.
1991: 3 Italian Conductors and 7 Viennese Sopranos: 10 Discographies: Arturo Toscanini, Guido Cantelli, Carlo Maria Giulini, Elisabeth Schwarzkopf, Irmgard Seefried, Elisabeth Gruemmer, Sena Jurinac, Hilde Gueden, Lisa Della Casa, Rita Streich.
1992: Mid-Century Conductors and More Viennese Singers: 10 Discographies: Karl Boehm, Victor De Sabata, Hans Knappertsbusch, Tullio Serafin, Clemens Krauss, Anton Dermota, Leonie Rysanek, Eberhard Waechter, Maria Reining, Erich Kunz.
1993: More 20th Century Conductors: 7 Discographies: Eugen Jochum, Ferenc Fricsay, Carl Schuricht, Felix Weingartner, Josef Krips, Otto Klemperer, Erich Kleiber.
1994: Giants of the Keyboard: 6 Discographies: Wilhelm Kempff, Walter Gieseking, Edwin Fischer, Clara Haskil, Wilhelm Backhaus, Artur Schnabel.
1994: Six Wagnerian Sopranos: 6 Discographies: Frieda Leider, Kirsten Flagstad, Astrid Varnay, Martha Moedl, Birgit Nilsson, Gwyneth Jones.
1995: Musical Knights: 6 Discographies: Henry Wood, Thomas Beecham, Adrian Boult, John Barbirolli, Reginald Goodall, Malcolm Sargent.
1995: A Notable Quartet: 4 Discographies: Gundula Janowitz, Christa Ludwig, Nicolai Gedda, Dietrich Fischer-Dieskau.
1996: The Post-War German Tradition: 5 Discographies: Rudolf Kempe, Joseph Keilberth, Wolfgang Sawallisch, Rafael Kubelik, Andre Cluytens.
1996: Teachers and Pupils: 7 Discographies: Elisabeth Schwarzkopf, Maria Ivoguen, Maria Cebotari, Meta Seinemeyer, Ljuba Welitsch, Rita Streich, Erna Berger.
1996: Tenors in a Lyric Tradition: 3 Discographies: Peter Anders, Walther Ludwig, Fritz Wunderlich.
1997: The Lyric Baritone: 5 Discographies: Hans Reinmar, Gerhard Hüsch, Josef Metternich, Hermann Uhde, Eberhard Wächter.
1997: Hungarians in Exile: 3 Discographies: Fritz Reiner, Antal Dorati, George Szell.
1997: The Art of the Diva: 3 Discographies: Claudia Muzio, Maria Callas, Magda Olivero.
1997: Metropolitan Sopranos: 4 Discographies: Rosa Ponselle, Eleanor Steber, Zinka Milanov, Leontyne Price.
1997: Back From The Shadows: 4 Discographies: Willem Mengelberg, Dimitri Mitropoulos, Hermann Abendroth, Eduard Van Beinum.
1997: More Musical Knights: 4 Discographies: Hamilton Harty, Charles Mackerras, Simon Rattle, John Pritchard.
1998: Conductors On The Yellow Label: 8 Discographies: Fritz Lehmann, Ferdinand Leitner, Ferenc Fricsay, Eugen Jochum, Leopold Ludwig, Artur Rother, Franz Konwitschny, Igor Markevitch.
1998: More Giants of the Keyboard: 5 Discographies: Claudio Arrau, Gyorgy Cziffra, Vladimir Horowitz, Dinu Lipatti, Artur Rubinstein.

1998: Mezzo and Contraltos: 5 Discographies: Janet Baker, Margarete Klose, Kathleen Ferrier, Giulietta Simionato, Elisabeth Höngen.
1999: The Furtwängler Sound Sixth Edition: Discography and Concert Listing.
1999: The Great Dictators: 3 Discographies: Evgeny Mravinsky, Artur Rodzinski, Sergiu Celibidache.
1999: Sviatoslav Richter: Pianist of the Century: Discography.
2000: Philharmonic Autocrat 1: Discography of: Herbert Von Karajan [Third Edition].
2000: Wiener Philharmoniker 1 - Vienna Philharmonic & Vienna State Opera Orchestras: Disc. Part 1 1905-1954.
2000: Wiener Philharmoniker 2 - Vienna Philharmonic & Vienna State Opera Orchestras: Disc. Part 2 1954-1989.
2001: Gramophone Stalwarts: 3 Separate Discographies: Bruno Walter, Erich Leinsdorf, Georg Solti.
2001: Singers of the Third Reich: 5 Discographies: Helge Roswaenge, Tiana Lemnitz, Franz Völker, Maria Müller, Max Lorenz.
2001: Philharmonic Autocrat 2: Concert Register of Herbert Von Karajan Second Edition.
2002: Sächsische Staatskapelle Dresden: Complete Discography.
2002: Carlo Maria Giulini: Discography and Concert Register.
2002: Pianists For The Connoisseur: 6 Discographies: Arturo Benedetti Michelangeli, Alfred Cortot, Alexis Weissenberg, Clifford Curzon, Solomon, Elly Ney.
2003: Singers on the Yellow Label: 7 Discographies: Maria Stader, Elfriede Trötschel, Annelies Kupper, Wolfgang Windgassen, Ernst Häfliger, Josef Greindl, Kim Borg.
2003: A Gallic Trio: 3 Discographies: Charles Münch, Paul Paray, Pierre Monteux.
2004: Antal Dorati 1906-1988: Discography and Concert Register.
2004: Columbia 33CX Label Discography.
2004: Great Violinists: 3 Discographies: David Oistrakh, Wolfgang Schneiderhan, Arthur Grumiaux.
2006: Leopold Stokowski: Second Edition of the Discography.
2006: Wagner Im Festspielhaus: Discography of the Bayreuth Festival.
2006: Her Master's Voice: Concert Register and Discography of Dame Elisabeth Schwarzkopf [Third Edition].
2007: Hans Knappertsbusch: Kna: Concert Register and Discography of Hans Knappertsbusch, 1888-1965. Second Edition.
2008: Philips Minigroove: Second Extended Version of the European Discography.
2009: American Classics: The Discographies of Leonard Bernstein and Eugene Ormandy.

Discography by Stephen J. Pettitt, edited by John Hunt:
1987: Philharmonia Orchestra: Complete Discography 1945-1987

Available from: Travis & Emery at 17 Cecil Court, London, UK. (+44) 20 7 240 2129. email on sales@travis-and-emery.com .

© Travis & Emery 2009

www.ingramcontent.com/pod-product-compliance
Lightning Source LLC
Chambersburg PA
CBHW071233300426
44116CB00008B/1012